INSIDE
THE
CRIME
LAB

INSIDE THE CRIME LAB

BY
JAY CAMERON HALL

PRENTICE-HALL, INC.
Englewood Cliffs, New Jersey

Inside the Crime Lab, by Jay Cameron Hall
Copyright © 1974 by Jay Cameron Hall
All rights reserved. No part of this book may be
reproduced in any form or by any means, except
for the inclusion of brief quotations in a review,
without permission in writing from the publisher.
Printed in the United States of America
Prentice-Hall International, Inc., London
Prentice-Hall of Australia, Pty. Ltd., North Sydney
Prentice-Hall of Canada, Ltd., Toronto
Prentice-Hall of India Private Ltd., New Delhi
Prentice-Hall of Japan, Inc., Tokyo

10 9 8 7 6 5 4 3 2 1

Library of Congress Cataloging in Publication Data
Hall, Jay Cameron.
   Inside the crime lab.
   1. Criminal investigation.   I. Title.
HV8073.H22   364.12'1   73-13796
ISBN 0-13-467480-4

For Sibyl, with love

Many years ago, fate decreed I should become the Pasadena police chemist. Some of the happiest moments of my varied life were spent in the Pasadena crime lab.

I had been a policeman for almost eighteen years. And for the next twenty I worked intimately with police agencies, consulting, criticizing, advising, and encouraging. I do today. And some of my best friends are those wonderful, dedicated men who choose this thankless role and who do it well.

My continuing affair with criminalistics has never terminated. It was just set aside. I'd been saving carbons of my case notes for many years, against the day when I'd memorialize the subject in print. So when my agent, Jay Garon, struck a responsive chord with Prentice-Hall, I was ready to bring myself up to date on the fascinating discipline of criminalistics.

How the field had changed since I was intimate with it! The romance was in full bloom when I started the research for this book. And what a challenge it was getting on top of it, since criminalistics embraces the whole of science! But I quickly became ambivalent—excited beyond measure at the current potential of criminalistics, but disillusioned with its utilization. This is one of the principal reasons for this book. The potential of the criminalistics field is almost unlimited—if only it were used. I am the severest critic of those who don't perform up to their capability. But like a parent with a backward child, my most fervent hope is for improvement.

The scientists toiling in the scraggly criminalistics vineyard need public support as much as any group I have ever known. They *know* what could be—and why it isn't. I only hope that this work will help bring about an understanding of the tremendous possibilities for both journeymen policemen and their bosses, and that having read this book, an informed public will start asking questions, demonstrating its support, working for needed change. The properly structured crime laboratory has so much to offer.

Its services are desperately needed if we are to have any hope of reversing the ever-rising criminal tide.

There were so many who helped in the writing of this book. Perhaps my greatest debt is to Bill Harper, my mentor in the beginning, and again, now, all these years later.

Then there is Don Harding, who came to the Pasadena crime lab when I sold the boss on getting a truly qualified police chemist to fill the spot I was vacating. Don opened my eyes to the great potential of criminalistics and helped me keep in touch over the intervening years. He rendered yeoman service in supplying illustrative cases, checking my scientific concepts, and reading many portions of the manuscript.

Jack Cadman taught me much of what I know in criminalistics. During the writing of this book, Jack made the many splendid people on his staff available for further illumination, particularly the distinguished toxicologist Bob Cravey. Bob not only led me through the labyrinth of toxicology and provided fascinating cases, but—stout fellow—read every word of the manuscript critically.

Only a few days before the end of his life, I was accorded many courtesies by FBI Director J. Edgar Hoover and numerous members of his staff.

Two others were kind enough to go over the manuscript with a fine-tooth comb, offering invaluable suggestions: Dr. Brian Parker of the Stanford Research Institute and W. Jerry Chisum, who emphasized the vital role of reconstruction services available from the criminalists.

Mr. D. M. Lucas, past president of the American Academy of Forensic Sciences, was generous beyond belief. And my particular thanks are owed an old friend and outstanding public servant, Evelle J. Younger, attorney general of California.

I must also thank the lovely people who first responded to the hundreds of letters my wife, Sibyl, and I wrote to all quarters of the globe. Peter Bucky first proved that there really was someone out there. Tony Longhetti was the first and perhaps most generous of criminalists who supplied illustrative cases.

How can I thank all the other individuals who have contributed ideas, illustrations, and illumination? The only way I can mention them all is to list them alphabetically—scant compensation for the many hours of dedicated interest that they provided. Until they are better rewarded, I hope they know that their zeal, intelligence, and fervor to improve the field of forensics is deeply appreciated!

Ernest Bonelli, the Finnigan Corporation; Dr. A. S. Curry, Director, British Central Research Establishment; David Q. Burd; Wallace Dillon; Herbert Dodd; Brian S. Finkle; James L. Harris, Sr., Scripps Visibility Laboratory, University of California; Cecil L. Hider; Graham H. Humphrey, Jr.; Harry Johnson; Dr. Peter Jones, the Aerospace Corporation; Dr. Alexander Joseph, John Jay College of Criminal Justice, City University, New York; Dr. L. G. Kersta, Voiceprint Laboratories; Superintendent William Kirwan, New York State Police; Martin Klein; Don Lang; Forest R. Litterly; Charles Livingston, Office Alcohol Countermeasures, National Highway Traffic Safety Administration; John E. Murdock; Detective Lieutenant Ernest W. Nash; Robert Ogle; Joseph L. Peterson, National Institute of Law Enforcement and Criminal Justice; Raymond H. Pinker; Peter J. Pitchess, Sheriff, Los Angeles County; Victor D. Riesau; David Schmidt; Richard F. Shaw; John Thornton, School of Criminology and Criminalistics, University of California; Ernie Vogt; Jim White; and Fred Wymbrandt.

And finally my appreciation and affection to my friend of twenty years, the man I joined professionally to start a new and challenging assignment in the safety profession. In recognition of his encouragement, assistance, and warm friendship I want to thank most especially J. Arthur Rude, managing director of the California Traffic Safety Foundation.

Jay Cameron Hall

INSIDE
THE
CRIME
LAB

The razor-thin laser beam concentrates its dazzling power on a light blue paint chip transferred to the victim's suede jacket from the killer car. The microscopic hole bored by the laser beam is so tiny it must be magnified ten times before the naked eye can detect it. Instantaneously, a handful of molecules explode, emitting a characteristic light pattern. This pattern, read by the spectrograph, will prove the paint exactly similar in chemical makeup to paint remaining on the suspect's car. This scientific evidence, coupled with additional proof the New York State crime lab will produce, might identify the hit-and-run car.

In San Diego, California, scientists at the University of California's Scripps Visibility Laboratory strain their eyes as they concentrate on the TV console which holds the answer to their puzzle. Visibility enhancement, a space-age spinoff, may hold the answer to the identification of a vicious rapist-burglar, who for weeks has been terrorizing women in the Long Beach area. Finally, the criminal slipped up by leaving the impression of a cotton glove he wore to protect himself against leaving fingerprint evidence. Development of the latent glove-print at the scene of the crime represents the first major break in the criminalist's efforts to place the criminal at the scene of his dastardly crimes.

Crime labs as such are a comparatively recent development, particularly those capable of dispensing a broad spectrum of services. The venerable and distinguished FBI laboratory was established only in 1932. Police departments themselves didn't come about until the early nineteenth century. Before this establishment, the protection of hearth, home, and happiness was entirely the personal responsibility of the average citizen. Carrying of arms was commonplace, and violence was rampant. One of the reasons that life expectancy was so short was that large portions of the population existed by murderous crime. There were virtually no safeguards to protect the individual citizen from acts of violence, and those without the money to hire guards took their lives in their hands every time they left the scant protection of their homes.

Then, in 1810, a French ex-convict named Eugène François Vidocq offered the Paris authorities a deal which was to form the cornerstone of future law enforcement. Vidocq had been convicted of several minor crimes. Each time he was locked up, Vidocq exhibited his distaste for jail by promptly escaping confinement. He'd been a fugitive for almost ten years when repeated threats of exposure by criminal elements drove him to the authorities. Once granted amnesty, Vidocq promised he would reveal the tricks of the underworld, turning their own methods against them.

His offer was accepted, and the first efficient police organization, the famed French Sûreté, began to make some headway. Vidocq's axiom—set a thief to catch a thief—was the order of the day for many years. Men were chosen for service in the Sûreté because of their wide knowledge of individual criminals and their practices. A standard drill was the regular review of all arrested criminals, so that they might be recognized and charged with future crimes.

This state of affairs continued for over half a century until the father of police identification, Alphonse Bertillon, created a system of anthropomorphic measurements that enabled police to differentiate one individual from another. Bertillonage, as this practice of exact physical measurement was known, was far from perfect, but it was better than relying on the often subjective and distorted impressions of witnesses. Bertillonage depended on careful attention to detail and exacting accuracy. Since prisoners were often measured by other prisoners, and since precise classification of the measurements was critical, there were relatively few identifications of those who chose to change their appearance in order to avoid being labeled as a known criminal.

The enthusiastic adoption of Bertillonage throughout much of Europe in the late 1800s soon bogged down as its imperfections surfaced. The precision of measurement achieved under the exacting eye of Bertillon himself was seldom duplicated in other agencies. Increasingly, effort was exerted to discover a better identification method than one based on precise measurements of general bodily features.

The next giant stride for forensics—the application of science to the solution of criminal matters—came with the development of fingerprinting, or dactyloscopy. Many ancient civilizations seemed to realize the individuality of ridge patterns on the tips of fingers. Surviving clay tablets from the early Mediterranean cultures bear such impressions sufficiently often to seem deliberate. Certainly, fingerprinting was in common use in Japan as a form of signature when Western people were still inventing written language. Even prehistoric pottery occasionally discloses signature fingerprints of the artists—pressed into the clay by accident or design. It remained for modern man, however, to realize the potential of fingerprints to establish identity in both civil and criminal matters.

The uniqueness of each fingerprint is capable of rediscovery in any age. During the 1800s several men dabbled with the concept, but it remained for Juan Vucetich of Buenos Aires to attempt the first ambitious use of the technique. In 1891 he undertook to fingerprint the entire population of Argentina. Soon tens of thousands of sets of prints stacked up on classification desks. In short order a major problem reared into view. The classification system Vucetich developed failed to allow for uneven distribution by fingerprint type. Some file sections held only a few cards, while others overflowed. In the larger files, an identification match involved tortuous searching, consuming many hours or even days before prints could be matched. Early in its development, the system started to strangle on its own vastness.

Meanwhile, the police in many European countries continued their search for a better way to identify wanted criminals. Most authorities shared the conviction that no two fingerprints were alike. Nature's random distribution of ridges, dots, whorls, and loops provides a nearly infinite variety to the multitudinous shapes assumed by the prints. Two exactly similar fingerprints had never been located, yet no one could conquer the enormously complex task of classifying prints so that simple matching was possible.

That is, not until Inspector General Henry of the police of Nepal, India, developed his inspired classification method. Each of the ten rolled fingerprint impressions was given a numerical value according to the type of pattern it presented. This provided basic classification. Subclassification came from actual ridge counts between significant detail. Alternate classifications were listed in the case of questionable patterns, which occur occasionally. Sufficient subclassification was provided in this system to subdivide even the most voluminous files. Now the dream was accomplished. Sets of fingerprints could be classified—and rapidly matched—with comparative ease.

Henry's stupendous achievement can best be appreciated with a visit to the fingerprint files of the FBI. Even though they number almost two hundred million, it is possible, using the modified Henry method, to make a fingerprint identification of an unknown subject within minutes.

Popular acceptance of the idea of fingerprinting as a sure identification lagged, however. As with most pioneering efforts in forensic science, a blockbuster of a case was needed to stir up public imagination.

In 1896, in London, a portly but suave gentleman was enjoying a certain way with the ladies. So much so that on short acquaintance he managed to sweet-talk any number of them out of their jewelry and other valuables. Unfortunately, the love light scarcely reached full glow before the suitor—and their goodies—disappeared. Soon there was much hue and cry, half a hundred wronged damsels screaming for revenge against the light-fingered Romeo.

In short order, one Adolph Beck was fingered and seized. After first one, then dozens of the victims identified him, he was thrown in the bucket. Convicted, he was placed in cold storage to meditate on his evil ways. His protestations of innocence got the usual reception. After all, ladies who, by their own damaging admission, knew him all too well had identified him beyond question. As far as the law was concerned, Mr. Beck was free to rot.

This particular brand of justice was not only blind; it was dead wrong. Mr. Beck didn't happen to be the culprit. A look-alike scoundrel named William Thomas was the real lady-bilker.

The case of William Thomas alerted the world sufficiently to bring fingerprinting into proper perspective. William Thomas had as many aliases as there were days in the week—for the most part strangely unimaginative ones such as John Smith. His earliest known experiment in dazzling damsels for profit occurred in 1877. A born loser, he pursued the sequence of charm, steal, shriek, and arrest for several years, scarcely peddling the stolen baubles from each seduction before the bobbies bagged him. It was getting so he was whisked to the cooler before he could enjoy his spoils. By 1881 he was just too hot to tarry in England, so he decided to depart.

After assorted trips abroad, he reappeared with his old modus operandi in 1896. His luck improved, however. His look-alike pigeon, Adolph Beck, was lurking in the wings ready to make his unwilling debut with justice just as soon as a Thomas victim accidentally met him and lowered the boom.

Eyewitness testimony enjoys a huge credibility gap with today's scientists. Innumerable studies prove the fallibility of eyewitness identification. Thomas Spencer Jerome states, "Entirely faithful testimony is not the rule but rather a rare exception." Mistaken identification ranks high among the sins of law enforcement in convicting the innocent. In Beck's case, the line-up technique was used in the best modern tradition. This dandy procedure stashes the suspect among half a dozen others who share no common physical characteristics save, perhaps, being male. Victims usually make the predictable choice and select the suspect. The look-alike and near-look-alike haven't got a chance. Trial and false conviction often follow.

While jailed, Beck spent most of his substantial fortune trying to establish his innocence, but to no avail. Not only was he branded with the Thomas-Smith identity; he automatically inherited the Thomas-Smith description—scars and all—as previously recorded in earlier jailings of the real lady-killer. One simple check would have disproved any consideration that Beck and Thomas-Smith were the same person. Smith had a large scar under one ear, and was circumcised. He had been measured for these attributes at a time when Beck could prove he had been mining in South America. A quick look at Beck's ear would have raised doubts; a check with South American associates, which Beck pleaded for, would have established his alibi. But no one listened. They wouldn't even allow Beck the courtesy of dropping his pants to prove his lack of circumcision.

In 1901 a broken Beck was released from prison. The small remainder of his original fortune was thrown to the winds trying to prove his innocence, without success. As a convicted felon, he was severely restricted, condemned by the community, forced to report regularly to his probation officer.

Then in 1904, massive further insult was added to existing injury. Once again Beck was hauled off the street and hustled to trial for defrauding women of their valuables, and convicted—with precisely the same sort of proof which had previously sent him to jail.

This time, however, the real Thomas-Smith was still unshirting his victims when Beck's case came to trial. In the face of continuing complaints, an alert inspector recognized the similarities in the modus operandi.

When all this was revealed—and the real Thomas-Smith apprehended—there was an enormous public outrage. Adolph Beck was awarded five thousand pounds in cash to mollify his injured feelings. The case aroused sufficient attention and strong feelings to create a demand for better identification methods.

The clamor increased when a senseless and brutal double murder further aroused public opinion. An elderly shopkeeper was slain in his place of business and his wife bludgeoned in her bed. The police found a perfect thumb-print on the broken money box. Shortly thereafter, two wicked and savage brothers, Alfred and Albert Stratton, were connected to the crime with a most tenuous thread of evidence. Ordinarily, they never would have been tried, let alone convicted, except that Alfred Stratton's thumb-print proved a match for that inside the bashed money box. Every convolution, every ridge ending, every dot and bifurcation was duplicated in the latent evidence print. For the first time, fingerprint identification held up in court. The fingerprinting of criminals soon became routine business in Britain, and subsequently in the United States.

One after another, the various fields of science have contributed to the magnificent arsenal of the criminalist. Some of these developments were contemporary with Vidocq's deal with the Paris police. One such was the ability to detect arsenic, a food seasoning favored by murderers of the day. Even though the evidence of purchase, possession, motive, and opportunity might be clearly demonstrable, it was exceptionally difficult to convict even the most incompetent poisoner, because the symptoms of arsenic poisoning closely matched those of natural causes, and arsenic itself could not be detected in the body. Those who operated with an even slightly greater degree of subtlety were seldom detected and almost never brought to justice.

The first authoritative work on toxicology was published by Mathieu Joseph Bonaventure Orfelia in 1813. But it was not until 1832 that James Marsh of the Royal British Arsenal developed a technique sensitive enough to detect the presence of arsenic in amounts as small as one-thousandth of one-thousandth of a gram.

The sailing was far from smooth, however. Trials took months, even years. Juries were reluctant to accept evidence of a scientific nature. Who could believe that anyone could detect such tiny amounts of poison? A notorious landmark case, with world-wide publicity, was needed before this and other scientific advancements found a secure place in the practice of justice.

And there were so few working in the field! By 1840 there were only twenty-one men in the entire world who had made forensic medicine their life work. Still, progress was being made, constantly, painfully.

One breakthrough not made until the early 1900s was the ability to distinguish human bloodstains from other reddish materials. Before a biological precipitan test was developed, a Jack the Ripper, caught red-handed, could allege that he had just slaughtered a farm animal, and no existing science could prove otherwise.

Skill in other areas of forensic medicine was growing. In 1912 the famous Dr. Hawley Harvey Crippen case gained world-wide attention. Further, it established the pathologist as a full-fledged member of the forensic team. The pivotal evidence was a small patch of pubic hair which had been discovered with other portions of a mutilated body under the basement of the Crippen home. Mrs. Crippen had borne a scar from a hysterectomy. By cross-section slides of the tissue, pathologist Bernard Spilbury was able to establish clearly that the skin which had been found carried a surgical scar similar to that of the missing Mrs. Crippen. Dr. Crippen was executed for murder.

As startling as it seems today, it was impossible to prove the uniqueness of every gun and its bullets until the development of the comparison microscope. Such an instrument permits separate items—bullets, for example—to be examined at the same time in the search for common scratches. This device grew from the pioneering ballistics work performed by Charles Waite in the 1920s. It also took a case the world was watching—the notorious Sacco-Vanzetti affair—in which the State of Massachusetts alleged that anarchist Sacco's gun had fired the fatal bullets. A blue ribbon commission, headed by Harvard president A. Lawrence Lowell, reviewed the ballistic evidence, which had been developed under the dedicated eye of Calvin Goddard. There was no question as to the conclusions reached with the help of Goddard's comparison microscope. The bullets had, without doubt, been fired by Sacco's gun. Sacco and Vanzetti were executed.

Goddard, with his comparison microscope, had forged another link in the chain of forensic science.

By the 1930s, it became almost impossible for one man to know of all the scientific breakthroughs in forensics, let alone master them. The sciences began to merge. Physics and chemistry increasingly intertwined with man's adventurous exploration of the atom. Now we have such tools as the enormous particle accelerators which thus far have stripped the façade from the "unbreakable" building blocks of matter—the atom—into more than thirty subparticles. The electron microscope magnifies more than half a million times to reveal structures such as bacteria with a width of less than twenty molecules. Biochemists pry loose the secrets of the DNA molecule which contains the basic reproductive arrangement of all living matter. Creation of life itself appears to be only around the corner.

The various pioneers in forensic science contributed immeasurably to the development of the state of the art to the superb level it is occasionally found at today. Yet bits and pieces of forensic science have been used in solving cases in many instances where today's tools were not available.

One such case concerns a murder which occurred in the late forties in Pasadena, California. As murders go, this one was very simple. A recently discharged veteran of World War II decided to travel a bit before settling down. He had a pretty good car and over a thousand dollars in traveler's checks. In Pasadena he found a cheap rooming hotel and was amenable when another tenant suggested that they room together to reduce their housing costs. What he hadn't reckoned on was that his roommate would become envious of his possessions and bludgeon him to death.

The case was prosaic. The roommate borrowed a ball-peen hammer from the landlady with the excuse that he wanted to mend his shoes. The next morning as the veteran was dressing to leave, the roommate beat him over the head with the hammer until he was dead. He then removed his victim's blood-splattered shirt and trousers and shoved the body under the bed near the wall, concealing it from view by draping the blanket to the floor. Next he rinsed off the bloodstained hammer in the room's washbasin and returned it to the landlady, saying he would tidy up the room himself that day.

The murderer then assumed his victim's identity, cashed several of his traveler's checks, and treated himself to some fancy new clothes. Later in the day he journeyed to nearby Los Angeles and sold the victim's car. Now wealthier by a couple of thousand dollars, the murderer celebrated with a champagne evening in Hollywood's best nightclub. He even had his picture taken and autographed it, "To Mom, with love."

Regrettably for the murderer, the body concealed under the bed continued to bleed. By early evening the blood managed to find its way through the floor and emerge on the ceiling of the apartment below, where it dripped on the occupants—a scene right out of a bad melodrama. The police were called, the body was discovered, and the job of collecting evidence began.

When the murderer returned from his jazzy evening, clutching his picture, still redolent with champagne, he was swooped up by the staked-out cops who added the pictures, the remaining checks, the bill of sale for the car and the stolen clothes to the evidence in the case.

It was almost too easy. A perfect example of the open-and-shut case. In nearly every small town in the United States today, little or nothing would be done with the suspected murder weapon and other evidence. The murderer didn't even deny the killing. That was the way the case stood as it went to trial.

However, a nasty surprise was waiting for the detectives who worked on the case. A flamboyant and notoriously effective defense attorney accepted the murderer as her client. Instead of having him plead guilty, she developed a marvelously ingenious justification for the killing. Her client, she freely admitted, was a former homosexual. But, she claimed, he was reformed. Homosexual acts were now abhorrent and repulsive to him.

In her version, the killing occurred when the victim arose, clad only in his shorts. He approached his much slighter roommate with a nasty gleam in his eye, saying he was going to "fuck him in the mouth." The roommate protested and started backing away, trying to escape the evil fate intended for him. It was no use. The larger man advanced ominously. Rape, it appeared, was inevitable. Then the roommate glimpsed the borrowed hammer from the corner of his eye, grabbed it, and threatened resistance. The would-be attacker only sneered and continued his menacing advance. That was when the roommate hit him. Several times. At first just to stop him, then to put him out of his misery, because he cried in such pain.

A ridiculous story? Well, the victim's body *was* found in its shorts, his clothes neatly folded at the foot of his bed. To judge by the expressions on the faces of the members of the jury, they were buying the story. No doubt the lady attorney was in fine form and wonderfully convincing.

She admitted her client had killed—but only in defense of his honor. Could they understand how desperately he wanted to avoid homosexual contact, now that he'd seen the error of his former ways? Could any of them blame him for resisting—yes, even killing—in defense of his new-found integrity?

Stronger cases than this are lost to such tactics. The defendant—epitome of the ninety-pound weakling—could easily be imagined defending himself with the only means possible. He was clearly too small and weak to have resisted physically.

Up to this point the case appeared lost. One could almost make odds that this murderer would never meet the justice he deserved.

In 1948, when this murder occurred, less than a half-dozen cities of 100,000 operated their own crime labs. Pasadena was one of them.

The Pasadena police chemist raced to the sleazy hotel shortly after the landlady had unearthed her gruesome discovery. An I car was waiting for him in front of the entryway, complete with basic camera and evidence-gathered equipment.

Recording the scene exactly as found was the first task, photographing every detail—all four walls, windows, furniture, beds, lavatory, and, naturally, the body. "Show it the way it is" is the ongoing axiom on arrival at any crime setting. Since one major objective is development of investigative leads, good practice calls for scrupulous picture-taking before the search itself changes things. Frequently, investigation brings out possible evidence shown in the original photos whose significance is not understood at the time the photos are taken.

Sketches and measurements routinely followed, to record distance relationships among the room's objects. The careful search for evidence proceeded, with each item photographed with label and scale to establish size, as it was discovered. All evidence was identified—initialed or otherwise individually marked by the gatherer so he can later state without question that this was the particular piece of evidence collected at that specific location and time. Many a case is lost at trial time because the individual who found the evidence is fuzzy about the circumstances or because the chain of possession—the exact whereabouts of the evidence from discovery to trial—is clouded.

Fingerprint search, then and now, is the first order of business after recording the scene. Except for slightly improved dusting products, the technique used in the forties is still in use today. Potential locations are lightly brushed with a miniature feather duster or a camel's hair (now fiberglass) brush until the clinging powder transfers to the latent fingerprint residue. As the print becomes visible, the delicate brushing is continued in the direction of the friction ridge impressions, cleaning out the spaces between ridges. Next, the prints are photographed, either with a standard fingerprint camera if the print is on a flat, contrasting surface, or with special equipment. Finally, the prints are lifted with a good-quality transparent adhesive tape, to which the print clings and is transferred to a clean white card for permanent storage.

The physical evidence search usually operates in tandem with

. 11 .

the human aspects of the case, under the direction of the detectives. Occasionally, the evidence investigator will double in both categories. Too often the detective is relatively ignorant of evidence techniques, but will have sole responsibility for turning up physical evidence.

The detectives in the Pasadena murder case were busy interviewing the landlady, whose story strongly suggested the ball-peen hammer as the likely murder weapon. Ball-peen-type marks on the victim's scalp were also strongly indicative of this possibility. So the hammer was secured from the landlady, marked by the investigator, and stored in a large transparent envelope.

The police chemist was exhausted after hours of squatting, straining into remote corners, and painstakingly searching for clues. At last he gathered his gear, evidence vials, packets, and pouches, and headed back to the crime lab. The room was sealed and a stakeout—cop jargon for concealed policemen lying in wait against the unlikely event that the murderer should return—was arranged. Tomorrow would be soon enough for remaining evidence search for fibers, dusts, and other microscopic material.

The police chemist stowed the evidence in a locked cabinet in the crime lab. Then he checked out the probable murder weapon, just to be sure, even though he longed to call it a day. For this he used the benzidine-hydrogen peroxide procedure with its tremendous sensitivity to peroxidase, an active ingredient in red blood cells.

This test, discovered by Merck about 1900, dramatically identifies bloodstains and is still a popular initial screening test in cases of violence.

Although the possible murder weapon showed no visible traces of blood, the police chemist used a clean surgeon's scalpel to scrape a minute sample from the hammer shaft, where it joined the head. He transferred the tiny speck to a glass microscope slide and carefully slid a drop of saline solution on top. Normal saline is distilled water with enough salt to approximate the concentration of salt in human blood. As soon as the speck disappeared into the clear drop, another drop of saturated benzidine solution was added. Should the material being tested fall into one of several common categories which look like bloodstains, a false indication reaction might follow, which the police chemist could distinguish from the purple precipitation that always occurs later in the presence of genuine blood.

There was an absence of chemical reaction, so it was time to add a drop of hydrogen peroxide, the common household antiseptic.

Precipitating purple appeared in the experimental solution. The police chemist smiled. Further tests were needed for court, but he was certain the hammer was the murder weapon, since it is a rare ball-peen hammer indeed that bears traces of blood on its shaft.

Not that the police chemist could relax. The benzidine-hydrogen peroxide tests offers enormous sensitivity for peroxidase determination. But all blood—other animals' as well as human—contains peroxidase. Outside help was essential for further testing.

The Pasadena crime lab hummed with activity during the next few days. Even where expert assistance is available (as it has been ever since 1932, when the FBI Crime Laboratory was founded), it is one matter to have a modern criminalist on a ten-minute standby for testimony in a courthouse next door, and quite another matter to summon one from across the country. First, Pasadena checked with the Los Angeles crime lab to solicit cooperation. Ray Pinker, whose name was to become a household word from constant use in the *Dragnet* TV series, was happy to help. His reputation was already international, his facilities and competence infinitely greater than those of the Pasadena lab. He agreed to examine the evidence to try to determine if enough blood remained on the hammer to demonstrate human origin.

Since the murderer had obligingly returned to the scene, part of the burden of proof was lifted from the shoulders of the police chemist. Still, it was important to place the attacker at the crime scene with physical evidence, even though the landlady identified him and he freely admitted he was the wanted roommate of the slain victim. Nor did he deny selling the car, forging the documents, or cashing the stolen checks—then. Typically, by trial time the landlady wasn't sure of her own name, let alone the principal characters in the drama. So it was important to examine the evidence further to attempt a reconstruction of the crime.

The police chemist studied the photos he originally took on

arrival at the murder scene. The sparse room contained two cotlike beds, one in the center of the room, the other tight against the outside wall, its blanket not quite concealing the body beneath. A small bench stood at the foot of each bed. Neatly folded on the bench in front of the center bed were a pair of Army pinks, the type of dress trousers worn by officers in World War II. Alongside the folded trousers was a black shirt, also neatly folded. On the floor in front of this bench rested a pair of brown dress shoes.

The police chemist spread the trousers on clean brown wrapping paper on top of a large work table. Previously, the landlady had identified this clothing as belonging to the slain victim. The center bed, she added, was his. The puzzle was the exact location of these clothes during the killing, since the victim was discovered under the bed clad only in his shorts.

First came the overall examination of the garments, using a medium-power broad-field magnifying glass. Each stain or suspected stain was charted, the resultant drawing forming a map of all stains on both garments and on the shoes. After thorough initial examination, the police chemist gathered a supply of scalpels, filter paper, and reagents to undertake the laborious process of testing each and every one of these stains.

Making sure his instruments were scrupulously clean for each test, so there could be no transfer from one stain to another, he scraped a minute sample of each stain from the cloth, and dissolved and tested it with the benzidine-hydrogen peroxide method. Both the negatively and positively reacting stains were faithfully plotted on the map of the clothing, with added details as to the type of reaction. By the time the maps were completed, reconstruction of the position of the clothing during the killing was abundantly clear. *Only if worn could the clothing have accumulated the bloodstains, which splattered every portion.* The negative tests on the shoes indicated they had not been worn. Stains on the inside of the shirt stymied the police chemist in his reconstruction, until a possible explanation occurred to him. These stains could have been made as the murderer dragged the sport shirt over the still bleeding head, in the process of disrobing the body before thrusting it under the bed next to the wall.

As often occurs during trials of this sort, the witnesses were excluded from the courtroom until their turn to testify. This eliminates piggybacking on the testimony of a previous witness.

When it was his turn to testify, the police chemist produced the photos of the scene of the crime, and the shocking color slides of the victim's badly beaten head. His testimony concluded with the presentation of the stained clothing, a description of the testing procedure, and the maps which so clearly demolished the defense's claim that the victim wore only his shorts during the alleged sexual threat.

Ray Pinker followed, with his vast knowledge and impeccable credentials. The defense lawyer had, up to now, failed to attack the weakness of the benzidine-hydrogen peroxide test in being equally sensitive to all blood.

After Pinker's testimony, it was too late. His language, terms, and manner of testimony concerning the residue found under the head of the ball-peen hammer were almost identical with those used by the police chemist. When Pinker concluded by testifying that biological precipitan examination of the hammer shaft proved the stains to be of human origin, it was clear that the jury automatically decided the stains on the victim's clothing were similar.

In spite of an impassioned plea on the part of the defense lawyer, the jury returned a verdict of guilty, with no recommendation for leniency, in less than twenty minutes.

On July 1, 1949, at 10 A.M., Daniel Jerome Zatzke, the murderer, paid for the crime in the gas chamber of San Quentin.

Chapter 2

One of the most valuable contributions the crime lab offers is application of physical evidence to demonstrate what really happened—not what the police think, not what the eyewitnesses said happened. Increasingly, scientific observers suspect eyewitness testimony because of the inescapable fact that we all see a particular event through the filters of our experience, prejudices, and emotions. And, the criminal is hardly inclined to tell the truth of a matter. Thus, the scientific reconstruction of the chain of events related to the crime offers invaluable help in establishing the truth of the matter.

The role of the criminalist is not to slant the case in favor of prosecution or defense, but to present precise facts. Reconstruction considers all the facts, especially the apparently irreconcilable ones, instead of only those comfortable bits of evidence that tend to confirm some preestablished theory.

There is increasing evidence that in many instances the victim is the one who seeks out the criminal. Obvious examples are the man-on-the-town searching out a prostitute, and the pregnant woman going to an illegal abortionist. In still other instances, what appears to be accidental death may turn out to be invited murder. A study in Massachusetts suggested that murder be first considered in all traffic deaths; it might logically be extended to a distrust of all fatal accidents, which may often be suicides.

In one instance, a pedestrian sprang from behind the cover of an overpass abutment directly into the path of a motorist as he drove through the black night. By wild evasive action, the driver managed to miss the man, whereupon the pedestrian fled to a waiting car and sped away. The sweating motorist jotted down the license number and reported the incident to the police. Later that same evening, a man plunged to his death from a tall building. His identification checked with that of the license number taken earlier. Only a rapid reaction prevented the would-be suicide from damaging the life of an innocent motorist.

Similarly, about a quarter of the motorists found to be driving in the wrong direction on limited access highways are found to be doing so purposely. Not all, by any means, are suicide-bent, but clearly many are aimed in that direction.

Numerous cases are authenticated where an individual attacks a police officer under circumstances that virtually demand execution. One recent case involved a prowler call. When the police unit arrived, a man burst from the shadows, pointing a gun and shouting he was "going to kill the pig." After three well-directed police shots, the man collapsed to the ground, his toy cap gun offering mute testimony of his self-destructive intent.

The investigator, then, must maintain a high level of suspiciousness and a deep belief that all is not as it appears. While his search includes the commonplace and expected, he must also be ·alert for the incredible fact. The criminal often blunders in obvious ways which certainly ought to be discovered. It is the clever investigator who seeks to unearth the lesser clues in addition to the self-evident ones.

The first known example of the use of reconstruction techniques in criminal ·investigation comes from ancient China, where a woman had murdered her husband and then set fire to the house so that it burned down, claiming that her husband was burned to death.

The canny magistrate in charge of the investigation experimented with two pigs. One was killed, the other left alive; then both pigs were placed on a heap of burning wood. The previously killed pig had no ashes in its mouth, while the pig which was burned alive was full of ashes. Confronted with this evidence, the wife confessed to the murder.

Sometimes reconstruction frees an individual from criminal charges, and nails the real criminal tighter. In an Ontario case, a suspect in an armed robbery alleged that a confession of guilt had been forcibly obtained by the arresting officer. Counsel for the accused submitted a shirt said to have been worn by his client at the time of the alleged beating. Examination by the lab revealed four stains, a mixture of blood and saliva, which proved to be mirror images of each other. This pattern could have been obtained only from folding the shirt so that the two denser stains were transferred to the folded fabric. When folded on itself in this fashion, the shirt size was decreased so much that the robber could not possibly have been wearing it at the time the stains were made.

In spite of this ploy to gain sympathy, the accused was convicted. And even though it didn't work in the robber's favor, we must note that this was one of the few crime laboratories in North America where evidence which might favor the defendant was processed without question.

Whether it be analyzing molecular contamination by a speck of the explosive used to blow up a safe, the uniquely peculiar voice pattern recorded from a kidnapper's telephone solicitation of ransom, or the photograph of a burglar taken with only the light of a few stars, today's crime lab still has the same basic function—pin the guilty criminal to the scene of his crime, and make it stick in court.

The overall forensic goal of pinning the criminal to the crime scene (and exonerating the innocent) depends, in turn, on a number of subsystems.

First comes the development of investigative leads. This intelligence may include race and coloring of the suspect, deduced from hair evidence telling whether the suspect is of Caucasian, Negroid, or Oriental origin. Analysis of bloodstains may sharpen further investigation by a thousandfold, if rare blood groupings and subtypes are found. Reconstruction of the crime, using intelligent deduction, may completely shift the thrust of an investigation.

Physical evidence often determines whether or not important laws are truly fractured. While the first search evidence may well develop investigative leads, the actual determination as to whether or not a crime has been committed may equally hinge on the discovery of the appropriate items.

Where one or more elements of violation of the law are missing, *no crime has occurred.* A simple example is found in the drunk driving laws. The legal complexity of this concept revolves around that fact that in most states, to be guilty of the crime of drunk driving, the following elements must be present:

1. The defendant must be a *driver*.
2. He must be driving a *motor vehicle*.
3. He must be found *upon a public highway*.
4. He must be *under the influence* of alcohol
   and/or restricted drugs.

The investigator knows that, in a paraphrase of the famous paint slogan, "Lose one element, and you lose all." If any one of the four elements of drunk driving is missing, the crime has evaporated. Most criminal statutes have at least as many elements as the drunk driving laws, all of which must be present before any violation of the law occurs. Often, physical evidence can forge an essential link in establishing one of the necessary elements. First-degree murder, for example, requires premeditation—an exceptionally difficult aspect to prove. In the Judd murder covered later, premeditation was established by a combination of autopsy reports, which proved that Judd couldn't breath at the time of the fatal attack, plus photos of the knife wounds, which demonstrated the victim's immobility prior to the fatal stabbing. The physical evidence completely eliminated any possible plea of self-defense.

Another ancillary effect of physical evidence is corroborating or disproving an alibi. The classic example is the Jack the Ripper, caught red-handed, who claims he's just slain a lamb.

Still another useful function is confrontation of the suspect with provable facts in order to induce an admission or confession. Although court decisions of recent years place many obstacles in the path of securing confessions and admitting them in trials, no decent law enforcement agency objects to observing constitutional protections. It's just tougher, and brains must certainly be substituted for brawn. But when evidence ranging from fingerprints to microscopic traces of paint or glass can conclusively pin a criminal to the scene, he often changes his tune.

Exoneration of the innocent is undoubtedly the most important and least used service of the crime lab. No forensic scientist should allow himself to be put in the position of trying to fit the evidence to the crime. He should not concern himself with guilt or innocence per se. Rather, he should seek only the truth, reversing proposed explanations that fail to fit the physical facts.

If his analyses don't substantiate the preconceived notions of others as to how the crime happened or who did it—tough! The others should readjust their thinking to the facts, and proceed from there.

Even given its relative excellence, in 1948 the vast portion of the Pasadena crime lab's business was photographic. Mug shots of prisoners, "ident" photos for taxi drivers and other regulated employment, and car crash pictures made up the bulk of the work. But in that year, everything changed.

In 1948, even the handful of cities with crime labs were extremely limited in the scope of cases they could process—fingerprint dusting, probably, photography, but little else. Pasadena and a few other bright lights burrowed considerably deeper. There were two reasons: a major survey and reorganization of the police department by O. W. Wilson, who later became famous as the dean of the School of Criminology at the University of California; and the counseling of consulting criminalist William W. Harper, who implemented the scientific aspects of Wilson's plan.

Hoping for assignment to the special field investigation units that came to be known as "I cars," about twenty policemen volunteered for training in their off hours. The intensive course in physical evidence techniques—four hours a day, four times a week, for nine months—produced a group of men capable of intelligent evidence gathering at major crime scenes.

To see the right evidence, the investigator must have good understanding of the scientific possibilities, since the crime lab depends on him to find the material from which biological, chemical, and subvisible evidence can ultimately be teased. Meanwhile, the crime lab will settle for prosaic, run-of-the-mill bloodstains, paint chips, soil samples, toolmarks and finger-, tire-, and footprints.

The average small- to medium-sized city, if their level of training made them even slightly aware of criminalistic potential, relied on large metropolitan centers, state crime labs, and the services of the FBI. Since, even today, there are seventeen states with no agency with a crime laboratory at the state, county, or city level, and an additional thirty-three states in which the crime lab serves primarily the state police, the abysmal state of criminalistics in the 1940s may well be imagined.

The epidemic of public building in the fifties and early sixties scarcely affected the increasing number of crime labs. As agencies decided to go the crime lab route, they followed the noble tradition of Bertillon and tucked the labs into corners and crannies of existing police structures. All too many were crowded and inefficiently arranged, with evidence piled to the roof and spilling out into makeshift storage rooms. Only in the last half-dozen years have we seen a trend to designing proper quarters, with work flow planning and adequate facilities for modern instrumentation.

Crime labs generally tend either to departmentalize, with a high degree of specialization, or to follow the generalist philosophy. Where the entire crime lab operation is the responsibility of only one scientist, he has no choice, of course, but to be a generalist.

In British and Canadian organizations the ratios of staff to workload often permit a high degree of specialization. This is equally true in the government sponsored Swedish crime lab. The Swedes, incidentally, enjoy something that is often the envy of fellow scientists from other countries. There is no adversary proceedings in Swedish court structures. The scientists file a report on their findings, and that is that. A highly desirable by-product of this system is the equal provision of the criminalistic service to persons accused of crime. As Professor Andreas Maehly, director of this fine operation puts it, "There is only one truth. That is the side we are on."

The Centre of Forensic Sciences in Toronto serves the entire province of Ontario, Canada. Universally well-regarded, its philosophy of specialization divides into a number of departments. D. M. Lucas is in charge of administration, with sections on pathology, biology, chemistry, document examination, firearms and toolmarks, and toxicology. The entire lab is served by a special photography unit.

Most of the American crime labs parallel this sort of specialization, except for those in California, which tend toward generalization. While there may be one or two specialists, in these labs the remaining staff work in ballistics one day, wet chemistry the next and chromatography the following day. In addition, most labs in the United States suffer from the common trauma of drug overload, forcing other types of evidence to be set aside—sometimes forever—until the immediate pressures of drug-related crimes are met.

Santa Clara is the second most rapidly growing county in the United States. With the laboratory of criminalistics offering full services to even the smallest cities, the situation there is distinctly better than in the 111 cities with populations over a hundred thousand in this country which have no local crime lab services.

Another top crime lab is found in Orange County, California, which is the Hertz to Santa Clara's Avis, being the fastest growing county in the United States. The chief criminalist of Orange County, W. J. Cadman, pioneered many of the uses of gas chromatography for criminalistics. Since the Orange County operation is representative of generalism, it's worth a close look. This crime lab serves a population area of over two million and the twenty-seven local enforcement agencies at the municipal level, in addition to county-wide groups.

The Orange County crime lab divides into the following main categories: toxicology, chemical and drug analysis, physical and trace analysis, and questioned documents. Each of these subject areas have many subdivisions. Toxicology, for example, includes the processing of narcotics, blood alcohols, metals, bioassay, insecticides, and pesticides.

The philosophy of the Orange County administration tends away from specialization, except for the areas of serology and questioned documents. Any of their scientists can and do double in areas other than those in which each performs the greatest volume of his or her work.

Many of the routine techniques commonly used in the seventies were just as available in the forties. Included are: matching tools to their impressions; jigsaw fits of paint chips into their original location; and the torn button with dangling thread mated to the coat from which it was wrenched. These and many more commonsense matches of footprints, tire tracks, and similar evidence were as inviting then as today.

Even simple drug testing was within the police chemist's

capability in the forties. Marijuana had the same appearance then as it does now. While it scarcely inspired the lifestyle of half the young people of the nation, there were those who cultivated the illegal hemp and whose crop ended up in the crime lab for tentative identification. Maybe the police chemist couldn't testify in court proceedings on the identification of the happy weed; but he could identify it under a low-power glass, as can any layman who is shown the features to look for. With their preliminary judgment confirmed, the detectives could move in on their suspects. Court-quality testimony could be later developed by competent scientists.

Arts which seem almost lost today were occasionally practiced by the police chemist. Perhaps it was easier then. Cloth fibers of the forties numbered only in the dozens, while today they run into the thousands. But at least the Pasadena lab *tried* to mate the tangle of thread caught in the entry window with the tear in the burglar's trousers. With reasonable assurance that they were dealing with the right party, the detectives frequently saved weeks of search and often broke the case, once they were sure of their track.

One of the most useful services of this crime lab was its ability to restore numbers filed from guns, valuable machine parts, and other possessions. With a little knowledge, and a lot of acid and patience, the police chemist was able to restore many an obliterated identification number.

By any standards, though, the abilities of the crime labs of the forties were limited. Most of the modern scientific techniques, to say nothing of the miracle instrumentation, hadn't been invented then. Blood alcohol determination was within the police chemist's grasp—if he had a whole day to spare for exacting processing. Today, in that same day's time, the modern criminalist can precisely evaluate over fifty cases needing measurement of blood alcohol. Then, wet chemical methods were occasionally used to measure unknowns in amounts expressed thus: 0.001 gram = one milligram. Today, using the atomic absorption spectroscope, the criminalist identifies quantities so tiny that no name exists for them. This instrumentation is sensitive to material which only weighs 0.000000001 gram.

Clearly, the technology of criminalistics is changing; nevertheless, much of the work of the forensic scientist still depends on abilities and techniques which are as needed today as in 1948 when George Judd was foully murdered in the shadow of Pasadena's famed Rose Bowl.

A homosexual element insinuates itself into a high percentage of the violent crimes between males, particularly where one of the parties is a male prostitute, known as the *trade*. George Judd, one of Pasadena's most respected bankers, enjoyed a top reputation for placing impossible bank loans. Whether the situation revolved around a structure on a nondedicated road (a private road vs one which has been "dedicated" to public ownership), a questioned title, or some real estate problem equally baffling, Judd was the one man in town renowned for locating tough money.

Divorced for many years and the father of grown children, he lived in a luxurious ranchstyle home nestled near the Rose Bowl. He was particularly close to his married daughter, who regularly checked with him to be sure he was all right, even though he hired regular housekeeping services.

On Thursday morning of January 29, 1948, the daughter tried to call her father. She hadn't heard from him for several days. When he didn't answer his phone, she decided to drive over to his house.

The untidy sink, a silver fork with curiously bent tines, and a long butcher knife lying on the kitchen counter seemed strangely out of place to the daughter. The housekeeper kept things spotless, and her father was a man of fastidious habits.

The woman called into the bedroom, fearing he might be ill. When he didn't respond, she walked to his bedroom door and discovered his dead body, his head lying in a pool of dried blood, a gaping knife wound in the left side of his neck. She immediately telephoned her father's top business associate, who summoned the police. Detectives and the police chemist were dispatched. Uniformed patrolmen were sent to guard the house and yard, since the murder of a leading banker guaranteed instant headlines. Pasadena still basked in the 1935 assessment by Professor Thorndike as the "most cultural city in the Western world," deserved or not. The annual Tournament of Roses and famed New Year's Rose Bowl football game assured national publicity in this situation.

The body of the banker lay supine on his bed, the thick chocolate-colored crust on the blood indicating that a good many hours had passed since his death. His only attire was his undershorts. Certain red marks observed on his chest later proved to match up with the tines of the bent silver fork found in the sink.

Judd's daughter reported finding two empty highball glasses on the dresser when she found the body. In a state of shock—according to her story—she tidied up the bedroom and managed to wash the glasses while awaiting the arrival of the police. This, of course, completely eliminated the possibility of detecting the fingerprints of suspects who had shared this grisly celebration.

Judd's right arm was stretched on the bed above his head, the palm upturned, the elbow bent. Several tentative knife wounds traced red paths across his upper torso, as though the murderer had been seeking the feel of the blade. The longest of these preliminary wounds started just below the upturned palm, continued across the flexed upper arm, and crossed the width of the chest. Apparently, after these tentative swipes at the body, the murderer had decided to play for keeps. A single killing thrust had penetrated the left side of the neck, extending almost through to the other side. It was this wound that accounted for the large pool of blood around and beneath the body.

Following routine preservation of the scene with photos and sketches, the fingerprint search commenced. More than a hundred identifiable latent prints—some of them fragmentary, having an area as small as a quarter-inch in diameter—were dusted, photographed, and lifted. The majority ultimately matched to the victim or his family. Only a few were those of strangers. One seemed particularly significant, since it was detected on the front of the refrigerator, which the cleaning lady was certain she had wiped clean the day before.

When collection of the physical evidence was completed, including a thorough vacuuming for possible fibers, the detectives swung into action. Their first clue developed from the record division. Routine check of complaint cards revealed that one

George Judd, only months before, had been deprived of his car in a strong-arm robbery. Some person unknown to him, he reported, simply took his car from him and drove away. Interestingly, the robbery had occurred only a few blocks from Judd's home.

Crimes of this sort immediately suggest a homosexual element. The patron who buys a boy for the evening is as likely as not to end the night badly beaten and stripped of his valuables. Under the circumstances, these crimes often go unreported. In Judd's car-theft case, it appeared that Judd had severely edited the facts in his report to the police.

Discreet inquiry soon proved the banker to be a weekend swinger. He customarily frequented a notorious homosexual hangout on East Third Avenue in Los Angeles. Judd was well-known to the bartenders, who implicated five members of the trade as having left with Judd at one time or another.

An especially fascinating element of the case was the disappearance of an expensive wristwatch constantly worn by the victim. Only five copies of this watch were ever made—which, the detectives felt, eliminated the likelihood of ever locating the timepiece. This watch was just too distinctive. Only a fool would chance having it connect him with the murder.

As frequently happens once suspects reach the all-points-bulletin level, the five men identified with Judd's secret past began to surface. Two of them surrendered voluntarily. A third made the bucket on a drunk charge, and his rap sheet fingered him.

When each of these suspects was located, a tremendous flurry of fingerprint searching followed. Enormous amounts of time were consumed, comparing latent prints with the several square inches of each of the rolled impressions taken in the booking process. None of the crime scene latents could be matched with those of the three suspects.

Next, each of them was given the opportunity to submit to a polygraph test, or lie box, in police parlance. Pasadena had pioneered in numerous innovations, including both one- and two-way radio and extensive use of the lie detector. Following interrogation by skilled polygraph operator Walton Talley, each of the three suspects was given a clean bill of innocence.

Then, unbelievably, the victim's watch showed up in a New

Orleans pawnshop. The rare phenomenon of locating a fifteen-hundred-dollar watch pawned for one-hundredth its worth and then reported to local authorities was almost too good to be true. Yes, the honest pawnbroker told New Orleans detectives. He remembered the person who had pawned the watch very well. He was a dark-haired youth, about eighteen years old, good-looking in a cruel sort of way. The description exactly fitted one of the two remaining suspects, a lad with a lengthy criminal record, including several violent crimes.

With the spotlight focused on the most likely suspect, it was only days before an alert Los Angeles patrolman spotted the wanted youth in Pershing Square—melting pot of the soapbox orators, ancient loungers, and petty criminals, as well as the more overt homosexuals.

The refrigerator fingerprint matched exactly with one of the suspect's. Confronted with the evidence, Edgar Eugene Bentley admitted accepting Judd's hospitality, going with him to the house near the Rose Bowl, tossing down several strong drinks. His memory faded abruptly with the events of the late evening. He dimly remembered Judd's loathsome sexual advances and his resistance. Faintly, he recalled some sort of struggle, followed by a blank period.

Sometime later, he said, he returned to consciousness, his pounding feet leading him away from the Judd house. The valuable watch had somehow found its way into his pocket—possibly a gift. He grinned insouciantly at the interrogators.

Despite the obvious history of violent crime, the district attorney seemed ready to accept an offer by Bentley's attorney to cop out to manslaughter.

"Look at it this way," the D.A. said in a pretrial conference with the police chemist, "there'll be little sympathy for the victim as far as the jury is concerned. Our baby-faced murderer will plead defense of his honor. I know his record stinks, but we can't introduce that during the trial." He threw up his hands. "For my money we might as well buy the manslaughter plea. We'll at least have something. If we let the matter go to trial, Bentley just might beat the whole rap."

So another case was about to be copped out to expediency. The police chemist reached for his file. Maybe something in the physical evidence could change the district attorney's mind.

Chapter 3

"Let me put it this way," the police chemist asked. "If a man attacks me—threatens to kill me—and I have a gun, will the law let me shoot him?"

"Of course," the D.A. agreed. "You have a right to protect yourself against violence, particularly against threat of death."

"Well," the police chemist said, searching through the Judd file, and slowly withdrawing the autopsy report, "suppose I disable the attacker, even knock him out with a lucky punch. Do I have the right to finish him off—give him the *coup de grâce*?"

The D.A. swiveled in his chair and reached for a massive tome from his law library. He quickly found the reference, studied the case law for several minutes, then flipped the book closed. "Once you have disabled an attacker," he paraphrased, "you have no right to injure him further. A killing under those circumstances is premeditated, first-degree murder."

The police chemist smiled as he handed over the autopsy report. He indicated several marked passages which emphasized the crushed structures in Judd's throat. This proved that he was choked into insensibility and would undoubtedly have died of strangulation without further attack. "Looks like Mr. Judd was well beyond defending himself before Bentley ever brought the knife and fork into the bedroom," he commented. He slapped a photo down on the D.A.'s desk which highlighted the straight-line path on forearm, upper arm, and chest.

"I'd say this picture of the knife wounds proves that Judd didn't move a sixteenth of an inch from the time the cuts were made. He was obviously unconscious at the time these slashes were made and later when the knife was stabbed into his neck."

When Bentley's attorney was confronted with this evidence, he quickly plead his client guilty to second-degree murder, a reasonable compromise considering the nature of the case.

Only three hundred years ago man lived in virtual ignorance of the structure of his world and the materials which surround him.

But the lust for unlimited wealth—gold transmuted from grosser materials—drove the alchemists of those days into a frenzy of experimentation. In 1669 Hennig Brand discovered phosphorus. Still other alchemists are believed to have increased man's knowledge by adding arsenic, antimony, bismuth, and zinc to the known chemical building blocks.

True, even medieval men used other of the basic elements, including gold, tin, copper, and iron, but they did not think about the elemental nature of all materials. Those who practiced philosophy were still caught up in the ancient Greek concept that the universe consisted of only four basic elements—earth, air, fire, and water.

Not until Robert Boyle bucked these "inviolable laws" was progress made.

Antoine Laurent Lavoisier further refined Boyle's concepts until, by 1789, he'd added a total of twenty-three elements as we know them today into the sum of man's knowledge.

By 1808 John Dalton systematized the gathering of elemental data and enunciated the basic theory that, in the smallest units which act chemically, all elements consisted of atoms, which are immutable in chemical changes. He added that all atoms of a given element weigh the same and have a different weight from that of any other element.

The systematic sciences of chemistry and physics gradually emerged. Although theories were propounded, these disciplines remained largely empirical; that is, well-known relations, like hydrogen's ability to combine with oxygen to form water, could be measured and relative values obtained. Chemical "cookbooks" could be followed with predictable results. The causes were something else.

Then, in 1897, Joseph John Thomson discovered the electron. In 1923 Robert A. Millikan won a Nobel prize for determining that the electron had a mass just 1/1,840 the mass of the hydrogen atom. Millikan's atom contained a nucleus of one proton, with, theoretically, a single electron orbiting around the nuclear center much in the way the earth and other planets orbit the sun.

The pursuit of atomic knowledge accelerated. Niels Bohr broke with all tradition by asserting that the whirling electron would not dissipate its energy as claimed by the classical physicists. He expanded Max Planck's radical concept that radiant energy was never emitted as a continuous stream, but rather in small discreet packets called quanta.

Albert Einstein's theory of relativity set the stage for probes to the heart of matter—nuclear exploration—which continues at an astounding pace even today.

The increasing complexity of atomic exploration boggles the mind. Take the case of Millikan's electron orbiting the hydrogen nucleus. In one sense the traditional planetary orbit concept holds true. In another, it's just a working model. The electron's real orbit is not quite like the moon revolving the earth once a month. Rather, the orbits are of the magnitude of one hundred million billion circuits every second, so that the electron may practically be considered as being everywhere, all at once in terms of our prosaic concepts of time.

A number of the latest hypotheses, however, have quite practical application. It really matters not just what the theory is; like the early chemical cookbooks, they work. One such concept is the knowledge that bombardment of compounds with radiant energy causes the electrons within the atoms to move outward into orbits which are at greater distance from the nucleus. The number of electrons which may be located in any given orbit seems a function of inexorable law. There may be as many as thirty-two electrons in the most populous of the seven concentric orbital paths, though never more than two electrons in the innermost or outermost orbits.

What matters here is the unique way given molecules absorb radiant energy as it thrusts them into orbits further from the nucleus. Equally important is the fact that the outer orbit is an unnatural circumstance for the electron, which flings itself back to its usual path at the earliest possible billionth of a second.

Accompanying the electron's trip home is a release of the stored energy in the form of a *photon,* or wave of energy. This light packet has characteristics of a wave which are uniquely related to the parent substance. The waves differ—again uniquely —within the electromagnetic spectrum, that marvelous continuum starting at the shorter end with gamma rays and increasing in length through visible light to heat, microwave, and radar, finally soaring with radio waves, which are miles long.

The photons that the forensic scientist deals with vibrate in and near the visible light range, straddling it on both sides. On the highly individual qualities of these photons depends much of what happens in the near-magic instruments of the crime lab.

Typical of the inventive genius constantly at work is the marriage between two scientific instruments whose hybrid offspring holds marvelously exciting potential. The two are the workhorse of today's crime lab—the gas chromatograph—coupled with the mass spectrometer, which is capable of enormous sensitivity in analyzing the specific make-up of organic compounds.

The GC, as the gas chromatograph is affectionately called, is itself a relatively recent development which earned its perfectors a Nobel prize in 1952. Over sixty thousand of the instruments are presently in use throughout the world.

The GC has innumerable possible uses in the crime lab, but one of the most common is preliminary analysis on human blood samples, which comprise the major portion of most crime lab workloads. A tiny amount of blood—one hundred times as much would make only a single drop—is pulled up with a hypodermic syringe and squirted into the intake port of the instrument. There it rushes into a flowing stream of inert gas such as nitrogen or helium. In minutes, each organic compound found in the blood sample identifies itself by a characteristic squiggly graph drawn by a lightweight pen on slowly moving recording graph paper. Responding to electronic controls, the pen may trace the typical peak for such chemicals as paraldehyde—a forbidden drug today, but commonly sold over the drug counter only a few years ago.

Paraldehyde is used medically to reverse the often fatal symptoms of alcoholic withdrawal. Frequently the wino who considers canned heat the *pièce de résistance* of his liquid meal will swill it for a cheap drunk when the other dainties are not available.

The paraldehyde peak on the grinding GC graph appears earlier than the trace of such interesting common substances as ethanol, methanol, or isopropanol—three of the alcohols often found in the blood of dead bodies. Ethanol is the pharmaceutical name for the alcohol found in legal beverages. The other two, wood alcohol and rubbing alcohol, are chemical country cousins sometimes found in illegal beverage alcohol. Enormously toxic, they cause violent reactions ranging from bellyache to death.

The world around, the common denominator in tragic death is alcohol. Whether murder, suicide, falls, burns, drowning, asphyxiation, motor vehicle accidents, or other circumstances surround the death, over half of these individuals are legally drunk at the time. According to the Department of Transportation, the abusive drinker accounts for more than thirty thousand of the over fifty-five thousand annual highway deaths. The current Alcohol Safety Action Program (ASAP), administered in thirty-five locations, has conducted a series of random surveys of the extent of alcohol use and abuse. In Albuquerque about 27% of the drivers checked during the evening hours had been drinking, with 6% legally intoxicated. In Portland, Oregon, the figures were 42% and 4%, respectively. In San Antonio, between 1:00 and 3:00 A.M. 50% of the drivers had been drinking, 20% were legally intoxicated, and 10% had blood alcohol readings in excess of 0.15%, which indicates in the average problem drinker a hard alcohol consumption close to one fifth of a gallon.

Demonstrably, the alcohol abuse problem is number one, nation-wide. Yet agencies vary widely in their ability to detect and remove the drunken driver from the roadway. A recent comparison by the California Traffic Safety Foundation revealed that the top drunk-driving arrest rate in the Golden State was enjoyed by the city of Los Angeles, with a ratio of 12.6 drunk-driving arrests per thousand population, annually. San Francisco's score on the same scale is one per thousand.

In the last decade, the city of San Diego has increased drunk-driving detection and arrests from about two thousand cases per year to almost ten thousand.

These skills can be sharpened, as most of the thirty-five ASAP localities are discovering. These pilot programs offer hope for the future. Meanwhile, in most American communities, the situation is both muddled and muddied. Take lovely Honolulu. There, unless Mother Nature enforces her natural law, one has the greatest chance of escaping drunk-driving punishment of any city in the nation. For the decade of the sixties, average arrests for drunk driving were well under fifty per year. In recent years, with the enactment of additional supporting legislation, there has been an unsurge in drunk-driving arrest activity—Hawaiian style. Latest reports show progress—with over one hundred drunk-driving arrests annually. San Diego, you will remember, arrests one hundred drunk drivers to Honolulu's one.

The crime lab is the first to feel the impact of a genuine increase of drunk-driving arrest action, particularly where alcohol levels are determined through measurements of blood or urine. This is the situation in both the Santa Clara and Orange County crime labs, discussed earlier. In each, the analysis of biological fluids takes close to half the total available time of the criminalists. As in other drug-abuse cases, no legal basis for trial exists until the scientists authenticate the specific drug alleged to have caused the loss of driving ability.

When the Santa Clara GC registers the presence of ethanol, further testing is in order. For the most part, these are coroner's cases or those in which there is some question of whether some other substance was involved in the impairment of the driver's coordination.

Given the preliminary GC analysis of a blood sample, the toxicologist then charts his course for further tests, such as wet chemistry (using test tubes and other laboratory glassware as opposed to instrumental analysis), determining the quantity of ethanol for the highly important backup evidence in drunk-driving cases. Some crime labs also use the GC for quantitative as well as qualitative analysis of blood specimens. Progressive coroners routinely check all bodies for alcohol content, and sometimes for other drugs. California law, for example, requires that all coroners check for blood alcohol and barbiturates.

Early researchers believed that the human animal had a built-in mechanism to prevent death from intoxication—namely, the inability of the intoxicated hand and arm to lead the glass to the mouth. Clearly, the mechanism is not failsafe, since recent studies indicate an increase in deaths from acute alcoholic intoxication. In most states in the United States, blood alcohol level presumptive of legal drunk driving is 0.1%, although the actual median for arrested drunk drivers around the world is

0.23%. With the exception of enormously experienced alcohol abusers, most people tend to become greatly intoxicated and extremely sleepy somewhere between 0.25% and 0.3%, passing out with a slight increase in this level. Most individuals cannot even reach 0.2% even in forced drinking without becoming ill.

In one case involving a routine blood alcohol determination in a coroner's toxicology lab, the toxicologist noted that the blood alcohol reading was 0.56%, an unusually high reading even in a dead body. Further check revealed that the victim had been known to limit his drinking to beer. Contrary to the popular belief, it is possible to become intoxicated on beer alone. But the amount which must be consumed to reach 0.56% blood alcohol is so great as to raise serious doubt that anyone has that capacity.

Further investigation revealed that the beer drinker had recently married a widow with a teen-age boy. Not unexpectedly, the family situation had been strained, with the teen-ager caring little for the unsolicited advice of his stepfather. The detective on the case, alerted by the toxicologist's report, burrowed into the events of the evening before the body was discovered, finally unearthing the following story:

The victim was enjoying another of many bottles of beer at the kitchen table when his stepson lurched through the kitchen door accompanied by a friend. The stepfather remonstrated with him, saying the boy should wait until he learned how to drink before "trying to act like a man." The boy reacted predictably, and challenged the stepfather to a drinking bout. The friend went out to the car and returned with a nearly full bottle of vodka.

Clearly, the stepfather had been well steeped in brew before the contest commenced, since even an entire fifth of 86 proof vodka, chug-a-lugged, would not have elevated his blood to the fatal 0.56% alcohol level. The match began, with the older man determined to rout the lad.

Before he had finished off the bottle, the stepdad had yielded to gravity and slumped to the table. The youthful contestant smirked at his lopsided victory, and with the friend's help, hauled the older man to his bed and eternal rest, unaware of the lethal booze dosage.

With the full story revealed, there appeared no criminal intent. Other values were established, however, including the possibility of accidental death benefits in the insurance payoff. Little doubt remained that this was no normal demise.

In mating the GC with the mass spectrometer, the Finnigan Corporation of California developed a tantalizing instrument. The GC is used to separate the various families of materials which might be contained in an unknown (scientific jargon for material of questionable makeup). As each of the family groups emerge from the column of the GC, they swarm into the ionizing chamber of the mass spec, where they are separated into segments with a characteristic fracture pattern according to the dispersal of the subparticles by molecular weight. For example, water's atoms are oxygen and hydrogen, with atomic weights of 16 and 1, respectively. Since the chemical sign for water is H_2O, this means there are two atoms of hydrogen and one of oxygen, the molecular weight of the compound being 18. When the fragmented water molecule is recorded by the mass spectrometer, it shows characteristic weights of 1 and 16, with twice the amount of the lighter, hydrogen atom.

Since the organic compounds this instrument ordinarily analyzes are infinitely more complicated, the recording graph will present itself in a typical series of peaks, each representing a molecular weight ranging from 1 to 260. The entire rig is coupled to a computer, which takes an electronic look at the thirty most prominent peaks, searches its memory, and then prints its decision as to just what stuff it was analyzing. All this in seconds.

In one case, the investigator was a deputy coroner. And he was stumped. The drowned youth had been known to be a thoroughly experienced scuba diver. His father was a professional diver, who had frequently used his teen-age sons to assist him on diving jobs that called for several people.

True, the boy had violated a basic safety rule in diving by himself, a no-no with both skin divers and those who use self-contained underwater breathing apparatus. Obviously, neither the boy nor his father had envisioned any hazard in the calm and shallow waters off the boat dock. The boat had seemed sluggish lately, and in scraping off the barnacles on the bottom, the boy was under none of the hazards encountered in the surging currents found around coastal rocks where so many scuba divers foul up. What could possibly have happened? When the boy failed to surface, a search revealed his body on the bottom of the bay underneath the boat. His air tank was still full and the breathing apparatus worked perfectly.

"When had the air tank been filled?" asked the investigator. "And who did it?"

The father wasn't sure who'd filled the tanks. Three of five tanks had been exhausted on the last commercial job, and the diver's contract called for the company hiring his services to replace the empty tanks with full ones containing the nitrogen-oxygen mixture customarily used by divers.

The autopsy revealed nothing unusual, no lung collapse or cardiac arrest, but only some nonspecific indications consistent with drowning. The deputy coroner enlisted the help of the toxicologist, filling him in on the background and the lack of clues as to the death.

When the toxicologist ran preliminary GC analysis of the victim's scuba tank, he could scarcely believe the read-out. There was complete absence of oxygen, and the nitrogen reading was unbelievably high.

Armed with this knowledge, the lab sampled the gas in the other tanks and found them to contain nitrogen also. Clearly, the youth had selected a scuba tank with pure nitrogen. After he was underwater, two or three breaths would have exhausted his residual body oxygen, with unconsciousness setting in instantly.

The boy was gone. But thanks to the detective's detective—the forensic lab—the misfilled bottles were taken out of service and other lives were undoubtedly saved.

A few crime labs are directing yeoman efforts toward keeping up with drug case requirements. One such, the Santa Clara County Laboratory of Criminalistics, met this challenge head-on by developing a facility to concentrate entirely on the problems of drug analysis. Administratively, this California operation serves all Santa Clara County agencies under the office of the district attorney.

Very much in mufti, the drug facility is hidden in a small residential bungalow in a neighborhood, which has gradually yielded to the encroachment of small business interests. The bungalow next door houses a small real estate business, with cleaning establishments and other one- or two-man enterprises nearby. The existence of the lab is so secret that their neighbors have no inkling of the mysterious processes performed within its walls. This is just as well, since the principle reason for concealment is to prevent destruction by arson or bombing. Organized crime's drug pushers and some of their fanatic customers would scarcely hesistate to eliminate this threat to their nefarious trade.

Yet the very existence of this lab creates an almost impossible case burden. As in other areas offering a high degree of accuracy in blood-alcohol analyses, most drunk-driving suspects are asked to offer blood to be tested instead of choosing the alternative tests of breath or urine examination. The case load is further increased by the California legal provision that makes it a misdemeanor to drive under the influence of a combination of alcohol and other drugs.

All of this creates an unbelievable flow of blood samples to the drug lab. Rapid evaluation is essential in order to prevent the lab from becoming engulfed in blood, literally.

Here's where the screening gas chromatograph leaps to the aid of the criminalist—particularly in coroner's cases. As we saw earlier, the GC can process a minute amount of blood and give quantitative analysis in short order, so that decision can be made on the need for further processing. Since this lab receives large numbers of blood samples from dead bodies as well as those from the living, it must search for substances beyond mere alcohols.

The versatile gas chromatograph operates on the principle of partition between a moving carrier gas and a stationary solvent material. This results in travel times through the GC which are highly characteristic of specific compounds. In *liquid* gas chromatography, with which we're dealing, a number of variables affect findings. First is the diameter of the column in which the absorption and subsequent release of the materials is to occur. The column may be as much as an inch in diameter or larger, or as small as a tiny capillary tube. In general, the smaller the column, the greater its ability to distinguish sharply among similar compounds.

Solvents used are varied, and much of the skill in gas chromatography depends upon choosing the solvent which will achieve the desired distinction among sometimes similar substances. The choice of temperatures selected to coax out compounds with more favorable conditions introduces still another variable. Column temperature varies between 100 degrees centigrade for the alcohols and similar compounds to around 400 degrees in arson cases, where trace remains of inflammables used to start a fire are sought.

Choice of column diameter should compromise between the need for a larger solvent area and the need for close separation of chemical look-alikes. The bigger the column, the more alternate paths open to the carrier gas in traveling through the solvent-bearing pellets. Sharp recording peaks help distinguish between similar substances. When some of the molecules meander and others follow the straightest path, emergence time will spread out, giving broader peaks.

Another broad-peak problem comes from lack of a tight plug of the unknown being evaluated. The GC operator will prefer to inject the testing material all at once, for tight grouping. If the injection is slower, then a broader peak results.

From a practical point of view, the gaseous compounds are quite selective in two respects: the way they dive into the solution, and the time they choose to emerge. While a number of different compounds may have similar emergence times, if all the GC conditions—carrier-gas flow rate, temperature, and solvent—are identical, any specific compound will have a *precise* emergence time under the same GC environment. Separation of chemical neighbors takes skill in introducing variables so that emergence times will be different. Findings can be replicated within an accuracy of plus or minus one percent. Since GC graph libraries contain charts for tens of thousands of reference materials, it's little wonder that the GC is the workhorse of the scientific world.

While the individual molecules of the sample act in a highly complicated manner, diving in and out of solution, from a practical viewpoint their activity averages out, so that the whole troop arrives at the detector end of the GC in predictable order. The arrival is signaled by an electrical reaction, which activates the recording pen. This in turn immediately traces its squiggly lines on the moving graph paper.

Standard graph patterns are developed by sending known

materials through a given combination of column, temperature, carrier-gas flow rate, solvent, and solvent base. From the precise patterns of these standard graphs, the identity of an unknown is readily determined.

The detectors themselves are enormously interesting. The most common type uses thermal conductivity. One of its two filaments is bathed in a bypassed portion of the carrier gas, the other in the material emerging from the column. The electrical signals from the two filaments are balanced to a neutral point on the recording dial before any materials are introduced into the GC.

As the unknown molecules emerge, they surround the one filament, temporarily insulating it and preventing it from discharging its heat. This also changes its electrical properties, with current differential activating the recording pen and tracing the characteristic graph of the particular molecules. The thermal detector uses a test sample of about ten microliters, which is the equivalent of one-quarter of a small drop.

The hydrogen flame detector is a thousand times more sensitive. Much smaller samples are used, with only one part per thousand introduced into the column, the balance saved for other uses. As the molecules of the unknown reach the hydrogen flame, they form *ions*—electrically charged fragments of the original compound—which are attracted to charged collector plates connected to recording instruments. This technique is so sensitive that great care must be taken not to overpower the registering mechanism with an oversupply of the unknown. The test sample used is in the order of one-tenth of one microliter.

Electron capture uses a still more sensitive detector, from 100 to 1,000 times as discriminating as the hydrogen flame device. It is particularly valuable when dealing with the hyperactive molecules known as the polar functional groups—members of the halogen chemical family, such as bromine, chlorine, and iodine.

Because of the enormous numbers of cases, lengthy wet chemistry methods of blood-alcohol analysis have been replaced with a modified Kozelka-Hine method. First, the sample containing preservatives and anticoagulants is washed and chemically scrubbed until the protein matter of the blood precipitates out. Next, it's distilled with a mixture of potassium dichromate, which clutches the alcohol to its chemical breast. The dichromate not needed for the reaction is finally measured by a spectrophotometer sensitive to the amount of chromic ion. Standard titration methods, formerly used to measure remaining chromic ions, eat up time. The spectrophotometer uses a fraction of a second for its reading.

While even faster automated techniques are available, these methods result in considerable speed-up when compared with the laborious, one-at-a-time procedures too often used in blood-alcohol analyses.

Drug handling in this well-organized lab reaches even more efficient levels. Having escaped the blood flood, the lab would drown in a sea of drugs if enormously important speed-up techniques had not been perfected by Cecil Hider. The fact that the Santa Clara criminalists are convicting drug pushers by the gross is testimony to their effectiveness.

Two congenial business friends recently agreed to meet for drinks at the travelers' posh bar of the airport hotel. Bill and Jim checked their luggage with the bellman, started the thirst-quenching process, then glanced around at the scenery.

The background included two most attractive young ladies who just happened to be passing by when one of them stumbled and almost fell into Jim's lap. Amused at the fortuitous accident, Bill insisted on assuaging the young ladies' embarrassment with a drink.

Instant compatibility set in. Jennie and Jill were delighted to meet Bill and Jim, who soon realized that fate intended this to be a most unusual evening.

Not too much later, Jill suggested that since they were all getting on so famously, wouldn't it be nice if they made a real party of it? How would the darling men like to engage a couple of rooms in the hotel, preferably adjoining with a connecting door?

The orgy was as good as under way.

While the "boys" reclaimed their luggage and rented the adjoining rooms, the girls ordered one more round of drinks. Jennie proudly presented the drinks to the boys on their return. Not only were the drinks delicious, both Jim and Bill quickly felt a warm euphoric surge spreading happiness throughout their bodies. What a fun evening this was going to be!

The hotel bedroom whirled, the windows bright with the sun high in the sky pierced Jim's eyes, burned into his throbbing head. He was hung over. He fought the urge to vomit as he swayed to the bathroom. All he could remember was the last drink the lovely girls had bought for them and the delightful euphoria accompanying it. Perhaps if he brushed his teeth. . . .

His shaving kit was missing from the expected position on the marble lavatory table. He started to shrug his shoulders, but couldn't move his neck because of the horrible pain brought on by the motion. Of course. He probably hadn't unpacked the three-suiter he traveled with.

Painfully, he worked his way back to the bedroom, lowering the lids over his bloodshot eyes in reaction to the stabbing morning light. No suitcase! Maybe the bellman had put the luggage in Bill's room. Jim shuffled to the connecting door, and rapped twice, even though the noise pounded on his brain. Perhaps Jenny was still with Bill. This matter called for delicacy.

When there was no answer, Jim called to his friend. Still no answer. He called louder. Finally, he opened the unlocked door and entered the other bedroom. No luggage was visible, his or Bill's. Nor were there any of the usual traveling man's paraphernalia on the dresser such as wallet, jewelry, or watch.

Bill lay still on the bed, his face a peculiar bluish color. Jim hurried to his side, recoiling as he felt the cool body. Bill was dead.

Chapter 4

The police investigators seated a stricken Jim in the interrogation room. Jim's hand was palsied as he tried to examine the pictures of known prostitutes, call girls, and females whose speciality was robbing their victims after enticing them to a hotel room.

Jim, the investigator noted, could scarcely focus on the pictures at a normal distance.

The investigator quickly glanced into Jim's eyes. The pupils were dilated. This medical condition, known as mydriatic pupil, is a common sign of several of the illegal drugs, as well as an indication of excessive consumption of alcohol. Still, Jim was relatively sober, though hung over. It could scarcely be the alcohol widening his pupils.

Jim insisted he was taking no prescriptions or other legal drugs. He was incensed at the suggestion he was some kind of drug abuser. But the investigator asked Jim to accompany him to the hospital, where blood and urine samples were obtained.

The toxicologist examined the two GC graphs—one with high peaks, taken from Bill's blood, the other with similar but lower peaks, representing the considerably lesser amount of the drug still remaining in Jim's body. The drug appeared to be the same in each specimen, but this GC tracing pattern puzzled the toxicologist. He couldn't remember ever having seen one like it.

Since the roistering days of the Barbary Coast, recruitment of seamen on the San Francisco waterfront traditionally began by adding knockout drops to the victim's drink. Minutes later, the slumped victim was hustled through a trapdoor into the rowboat tied to the wharf underneath the waterfront dive. Next stop—Shanghai!

The practice of adding chloral hydrate to the drinks of overly boisterous saloon customers found its way into the folkways of bartenders in tough bistros, and undoubtedly continues throughout the world to this moment. With impolite behavior chemically diminished, the knockout-drop victim is unceremoniously booted from the saloon's front door, or in some cases dragged to the back room to sleep it off. Usually he awakens. On those regrettable occasions when the drugged victim slips over the great divide, he is quickly dispatched to a gutter some distance from the saloon, to be tallied as yet another of the Skid Row unfortunates who froze to death.

Chloral hydrate, then, was the logical drug to test for in the blood samples from Bill and Jim. To make sure his memory wasn't fooling him, the toxicologist ran a known chloral hydrate sample through the GC. His memory was correct. This graph was nothing like those made from the bloods. The puzzle now was to find a drug which produced the clinical symptoms described by Jim and observed by the doctors who had examined him at the hospital. The inquiry began by consulting pharmocology reference books, seeking a drug known to both dilate the pupils and induce a euphoric state.

Meanwhile, failing to find a suspect in the photo ledgers of known prostitutes and other females who rolled their unconscious male victims, the police spun a web in which they hoped to trap the homicidal dolls. Essential to their success was complete suppression of the news of Bill's death, which would surely frighten Jennie and Jill into instant flight. Teams of detectives and the surviving member of the original business duo planned to check out the major hotels in the area that catered to traveling businessmen. Presumably, neither Jill nor Jennie were aware their knockout drops had killed one of the two suckers they'd fleeced the night before. If they continued to ply their trade, there was hope Jim might identify them.

The problem was compounded by the number of possible hotels within the service radius of the airport. All they could do was cross their fingers and hope the teams would not only encounter the felonious females, but that the witness might be able to identify them. The search would begin that very night.

The toxicologist studied the enormous reference book listing tens of thousands of drugs and their possible psychological and physical effects. Anyone who has read the disclaimer the manufacturer encloses with physicians' drug samples will have an idea of the complexity of the task. Page after page, the search went on.

A memory bell rang when the toxicologist arrived at the "S" section of the directory. He scanned down the column. "Scopolamine aminoxide," he read, "widely used in proprietary sleeping compounds." (Proprietary medicines are those sold over the counter, as opposed to drugs available only on prescription.) He read further, his excitement rising. A nearby entry listed pure scopolamine, which had enjoyed a flurry of medical popularity a few years ago as a sedative in its hydrobromide form. It was best-known as an adjunct to certain narcotics in producing twilight sleep used, during its vogue, to alleviate pain in childbirth. It soon proved too potent and much too toxic for casual employment and fell into relative disrespect.

Pure scopolamine was unthinkable as a knockout potion, because of the extreme danger of its use. Even the most callous call girls and roll artists would hardly welcome a trail of dead victims. Robbery is one thing, murder quite another. The possibility existed, nevertheless, that the girls had confused scopolamine aminoxide—widely used in sleeping medicines and relatively safe—with its explosive cousin, pure scopolamine.

The sentence that excited the toxicologist was, "Scopolamine is noted for producing a euphoric state as well as mydriatic pupils."

A supply of scopolamine was quickly produced for examination on the GC. The graphs matched. Since scopolamine could only be bought with a prescription, its possession by the suspects meant the D.A. now had probable cause necessary to charge them with murder.

The detective and Jim begin their search at the nearest hotels which catered to the swinging travelers, choosing an inconspicuous spot in the lounge from which to check the action. Possible suspects were plentiful. Word of the better pickup bars travels rapidly through the swingers' grapevine, resulting in ample patronage. Not all the females were professional hustlers, of course. Many were just lonely women looking for a fun evening.

Business was good—for pickups, not for the investigative team. Couples continually met and left for other activities. Still no sign of Jennie or Jill.

After an hour in one hotel, the team moved to a second location, doubling the scope of their coverage. Then they returned to the first spot to check the continuing action. By the end of the evening the pair was tired and discouraged.

"You think there's any hope?" Jim asked.

The detective smiled wryly, "We know this is a long shot. That's the way things are in police work—wait and hope. You never know. Maybe the gals had another date for tonight. Or maybe they're fencing the loot. We can only trust that they aren't running."

The second night was the same—nothing.

The third evening seems an eternity as it dragged on. By now the team was easily recognizing the regulars—girls who concentrated on a particular bar. But still there was no sign of Jennie or Jill.

Jim and his investigator finally extended their search to a hotel almost twenty miles from the airport. While it seemed unlikely the girls would move so far from their known base of operations, this particular place enjoyed a twenty-year-old reputation as a swinging spot.

Jim and the detective were hardly seated when Jim stiffened. "There they are," he whispered hoarsely. Both men watched intently as the girls approached a table with two well-dressed travelers. Oblivious to the observing eyes, Jill and Jennie reenacted the approach Jim remembered so well, stumble and all. In short order the girls were seated laughing at the table of their prospective victims.

Now it was clear why Jill and Jennie hadn't been located earlier. This hotel so obviously encouraged the love-in-bloom theme that the girls had a virtually unlimited market.

Quietly, Jim and the detective circled the noisy room, swooping down on the two girls before they were aware of their presence. The newly-found lovers' initial protestations died completely when the detective identified himself. He asked Jill and Jennie if they'd mind accompanying him, and they consented. Outside, he informed them of their rights and placed them under arrest. In a few minutes they were joined by a roving policewoman summoned by radio.

The policewoman's search of the girls' handbags produced two curious vials of a well-known eye remedy, advertised for erasing the red in tired eyes. Normal enough, particularly in a trade which called for hard drinking, except that the over-the-counter eyedrops are tinted yellow and flow freely. The contents of these two bottles were colorless and flowed thick and syrupy. These were both characteristics of scopolamine.

Jill and Jennie were interrogated and their statements recorded. Then they were duly booked. Complete search of their purses produced two hotel keys from a cheaper hotel, where the girls admitted they were staying.

A search warrant was secured and the hotel room entered. There the detective found half a dozen suitcases loaded with watches, wallets, and other stolen goods, including those taken from Jim and Bill. Clearly neither of the girls suspected how hot they were. No felon worth her salt would pack a knockout drop that could kill its victim, nor would she keep in her possession evidence which so clearly incriminated her in a series of robberies. These were amateurs.

The GC analysis of the contents of the eyedrop bottles brought the anticipated results. Squiggle for squiggle, the lines on the graph were identical with scopolamine. Now the tox lab had the proof desired for court use. Jill and Jennie were charged with grand theft and murder.

The goal of an entirely different class of criminal is not loot in the ordinary sense. He seeks negotiable securities, payroll checks and check protectors, blueprints, and trade secrets. He's adept at quick entry and slick in disposal of stolen goods, frequently popping them in a mailbox so rapidly that even when he's pounced upon, he manages to appear empty-handed.

If forced entry is necessary, he's a great improvisor, using makeshift methods and leaving the borrowed tools behind, eliminating the tool match possibility. He takes care to protect against leaving fingerprints, although he'll occasionally slip up and leave heelmarks on polished surfaces or spilled papers.

Some gangs specialize in floating loans on stolen securities, then vanishing before the theft is even reported. Often the airlines are utilized to transport negotiable paper to another section of the country, where it can be converted into cash long before word of the disappearance reaches the buyer.

Such a suave and speedy professional recently invaded several offices in a prosperous financial district. The burglar's major mistake was not selecting a location where such a crime would be kissed off or inadequately investigated. This Orange County city was fortunate in having a top-notch crime lab as well as first-rate evidence investigators. In this instance the burglar chose one of those cities where the criminalist personally checked as many crime scenes as possible.

Fickle fate also intervened by interjecting an alert patrolman whose sixth sense told him there was something irregular about the well-dressed man who was leaving the business quarters a trifle late in the evening. The thief had been clever enough to pop his loot in the building's mailbox before ever leaving the premises. His glib story of seeking an old friend he believed worked somewhere in the neighborhood almost held water. Nevertheless, the policeman's antenna quivered just enough for him to demand proof of identity and record the information on a field interrogation form he routinely used.

When the crime was later reported, the criminalist first examined the probable entry door. A professional burglar can easily open most building locks by slipping a flat, thin, and flexible tool around the doorlatch. Modern credit cards seem made to order for this purpose and attract no attention in the course of a police shakedown, such as happened in this case.

The weatherstrip on the entry door showed indications of tampering, with an almost microscopic powdery trace still clinging where the burglar's credit card scraped across the lock. The criminalist preserved the nearly invisible evidence, and also called the detective bureau to alert them to the possibility that a plastic card had been used for entry.

Meanwhile the investigators discovered the routinely filed interrogation report, noted the nearness of its location to the burglary scene, and decided to call on the possible suspect. They also obtained a search warrant so that any evidence they might obtain would not later be kicked out in court.

Because of the criminalist's notification, they were particularly alert for a credit card which might have slipped the lock. When they discovered the suspect owned such a card and that slight wear was visible along one edge, they seized the card as evidence and brought it to the crime lab. Microscopic examination revealed that the credit card had picked up a material similar in color to the weatherstrip at the crime scene.

Now the possible matching depended on two problematic factors. First, there was a relatively small quantity of material available for testing by any method. Until the development of microtechniques, one incorrect test would have used up the entire sample, leaving the case unsolved. This ruled out virtually all wet chemical methods, since they require quantities too large for the evidence at hand. The second rub was the difficulty of analyzing a mixture of two polymers—the enormous man-made molecules of which most plastics consist. Tests that are highly successful in other evidence matters, such as infrared photo-spectroscopy, could not distinguish between the ingredients in a mixture of polymers.

Even though by now the investigators were convinced that their suspect was the slick professional who had committed the office burglary, their hunch wasn't good enough to go to trial. Nor would there be any trial unless some technique could be found to accurately analyze the mix on the weatherstrip and prove that it contained the same ingredients as the mix on the credit card.

Dazzling straight-arrow light, squeezed through a ruby, smashes through space to strike a bull's-eye the size of a silver dollar on the moon. With the delicacy of an angel on tiptoe, the same beam can slip inside the human eye to weld a slipped retina with exquisite accuracy. Or it may roar its fury in a death ray capable of exploding stone.

Its name—laser; its future—unlimited.

Ordinary light dashes about wildly, dispersing itself in a thousand directions. Laser light can be condensed into a disciplined beam comparable in size to that of a scanning electron microscope—as small as twenty-five millionths of an inch in diameter. Used together with spectrographic analysis, the laser beam is only semidestructive. The tiny pit exploded in micro-spectroscopy allows dozens of tests, even on microevidence. In experimental use, a sample less than a five-thousandth of a cubic millimeter has been analyzed. Its mass was so slight it could not be weighed with the most sensitive scales.

Scarcely visible to the naked eye, the tiny sample is centered in the cross hairs of the high-power microscope, and the subsection to be tested is brought into critical focus. Now the laser microprobe shoots its sizzling beam against the material, using the optical system of the microscope to strike its target. It vaporizes the minuscule portion of evidence, which reacts with a characteristic photon emission that is in turn recorded by the spectroscope.

Using this technique, the criminalist spectroanalyzed the two polymer mixtures—that found on the weatherstripping and the trace removed from the edge of the credit card. And while the polymers found in credit cards may be common enough, the strength of the case would rest upon the unlikely possibility of an ordinary credit card being contaminated with a polymer identical with that of the weatherstripping.

Next came the development of the spectrogram and the line-by-line comparison of the two spectra.

They matched exactly! And enough material was left over for verification if needed by another scientific examiner.

Thanks to the new laser microprobe and the miniaturization of the technique, another clever burglar bit the dust.

Still another technique has been moving closer to forensic use in Raman spectroscopy. Lacking adequate sensitivity for crimi-nalistic application initially, the capability has been gradually improved, as instrument manufacturers strove to make Raman spectroscopes sensitive enough to make measurements in micrograms.

Spectrophotometry, using either ultraviolet or infrared light, detects a substance on the basis of the light waves absorbed by the unknown, the results being arrived at by subtraction from the known spectrum of the light source. Raman spectroscopy uses light scattered after striking the material being examined. Greater intensities of light are used, mostly in the visible range.

While in its criminalistic infancy, Raman parallels the laser microprobe in the extremely small amounts of material it now promises to analyze for chemical make-up. Its laser beam can be concentrated into an unbelievably thin spotlight as small as ten to twenty microns in diameter. Raman spectroscopy appears particularly valuable with analysis of plastics and drugs, detecting trace contaminants that may identify sources with far greater refinement than is possible with the more conventional methods. Perhaps in the future, when evidence is collected more carefully, it may play an invaluable part in analyzing evidence that resists other methods.

Many pieces of wondrous instrumentation are currently begging for practical forensic uses. Indeed, a major problem in almost any crime lab, other than the giants, is lack of the latest space-age equipment. Even the FBI thinks twice before acquiring certain high-cost, low-usage instruments.

Most modern crime labs have certain standard types of instruments such as gas chromatographs, spectrographs, ultraviolet and infrared spectrophotometers, and paper and thin-layer chromatography equipment. In addition, they have those items standard since the earliest crime lab days, such as magnifying devices for evidence examination, black-light lamps, camera equipment for photomicrography and photomacrography, wet chemistry, and, naturally, fingerprint-processing equipment.

Some highly desirable modern equipment—the crime lab mink coats—represents sufficient cash outlay that only a few labs in the country have the price. Mass spectrometers start around thirty thousand dollars and easily exceed the hundred thousand mark. Where cost-effectiveness can be demonstrated, such as in semiautomated drug analyses, cost-conscious public administrators can sometimes be persuaded to authorize such expenditures.

Still other exotic and expensive gear is clearly out of the reach of most regional labs. Mind-dazzlers such as atomic reactors to provide neutron flux essential for neutron activation analysis, or the electron-scan microscopes (costing up to half a million dollars each) cause scientists to salivate. The most useful equipment is obviously within reach, but consider that a six-thousand-dollar hunk of scientific gear opening tremendous avenues in subtyping bloodstains is found in only a single crime lab in the entire United States!

Occasionally, time on such instrumentation can be begged, borrowed, or rented on nearby installations. Industry is extremely generous in helping crime-busters. Though certainly better than nothing, unfortunately, shared time often delays vital investigative leads.

While crime labs bog down in the enormous load of drug cases, the state of the criminalistic art continues to grow and blossom. The international, national, and local meetings of associations of criminalists are constantly producing new and better techniques.

Forensic journals and conferences contribute immeasurably to the goal of learning about the latest scientific breakthroughs with forensic application or the development of new instrumentation. The prestigious American Academy of Forensic Science publishes a learned journal, as does the British Forensic Society. (The British journal, interestingly, also serves as the official publication for the California Association of Criminalists.) In addition, an international journal published in Switzerland carries the latest developments of the Forensic Science Group in South Africa. Among the fascinating articles, for example, was one on the ability to identify a specific socket wrench used to strip a vehicle of accessories by identifying the unique tool marks left on the nut head by the wrench. Another described the possibility of sex determination from "exfoliated epithelial cells." Practically, this meant that the microscopic shreds of tissue found under a victim's fingernails can be used to determine the sex of the individual they scratched.

The California Association of Criminalists makes excellent efforts toward sharing the know-how so vital to progress. The group meets at least quarterly, and holds a well-publicized semiannual meeting, with several days of formal presentations, mingled with informal exchange of shop talk and an opportunity for exposure to vendors of new equipment.

During the most recent annual conference, the problem of locating suspected dead bodies arose. A Sacramento criminalist touted the efficacy of a long, hollow metal probe connected to a methane detection meter. Methane, or swamp gas, is the companion of organic decomposition and is readily detectable in the soil around bodies for months—even years—after burial. "Beat's digging up several acres," the scientist laughingly commented. A few weeks later, when I visited another crime lab on the track of pioneering instrumentation for in-depth analysis of dried bloodstains, the criminalist I was seeking was out in the field with a methane probe, searching for a dead body.

The American Academy of Forensic Science also holds annual

meetings, and there are international meetings where scientists from all over the world share current information. All of these are ongoing mechanisms for spreading the use or application of newest methods.

An early example of the payoff from continuing scientific communication occurred in southern California during the mid-1950s, when the gas chromatograph was just entering the scientific world. P.Y.E., a British corporation, was sharing its advanced GC experimentation in a series of meetings which invited interested workers in a variety of scientific disciplines. A local criminalist took advantage of this opportunity for exposure to gas chromatography. At that time it was the strange new term in the scientific lexicon and basically a misnomer, suggesting that the art has something to do with color determination.

The P.Y.E. experts mentioned that the Aerojet General Corporation was feverishly developing portable GC instrumentation for use in lunar exploration—that far-off impossible dream. The whole concept of gas chromatography fired the imagination of the criminalist, who tucked the new information away against some distant day when it might be useful.

The day proved to be the next week. A young secretary working late in the offices of a noted research organization was locking up for the night when she was grabbed from behind by a stocking-masked assailant, who pressed a sweet-smelling rag over her nose and mouth. Even though she fought valiantly, she was shortly overcome by the anesthetic fumes.

When she regained consciousness miles away—which constituted a kidnapping under California law—she discovered she'd been raped. The responding police found and preserved the rag used by the rapist to render her insensible.

Good police work quickly uncovered a suspect. In his possession was a small container, holding a few drops of volatile liquid similar in odor to that of the rag. In short order this highly perishable evidence was in the hands of the same criminalist who'd just learned of the existence of gas chromatography.

The familiar odor of ether suggested the logical substance used to subdue the victim. Certainly the criminalist was familiar with the smell of ether, since it plays a prominent role as a solvent in chemistry. He was equally aware of ether's extreme volatility—when placed on the skin it evaporates so rapidly as to give the sensation of freezing. Worst of all, this was typical scorching southern California summer weather. The rag was enclosed in a glassine envelope, which gave scant likelihood of containing any of the remaining ether.

The criminalist knew that nothing in his bag of tricks was capable of detecting the minuscule amounts of ether remaining on the evidence rag. Equally, the mere act of examining the two or three drops of ether left in the container would substantially reduce the residue.

Still, for the D.A. to have a case, the ether on the rag and the ether in the container had to be chemically matched. Odor identification simply wasn't good enough for court. Then the criminalist remembered the P.Y.E. conference. Aerojet General, supposed to have one of the new miracle gas chromatographs, was only a few miles away.

The burning sun, penetrating the lab, stirred him to action. He wiped the sweat from his forehead and headed for the phone.

Chapter *5*

Sure, they'd be happy to try the GC on the evidence, boomed the Aerojet General scientist on the phone. "Better get the stuff on dry ice as soon as you can and hurry out here."

Shortly after the phone clicked, a police car's siren screamed toward a plant that sold the precious refrigerant. The dry ice—the solid form of carbon dioxide—was able to restrain the surging ether molecules in their feverish efforts to fling themselves away from the parent liquid on the rag and in the container found on the suspect.

The sweating criminalist furrowed his worried forehead as the Aerojet General scientists led him to the gas chromatograph. He handed over the ice-beaded container with the dry ice and the evidence. "Can't be much left on the rag," he fretted. "What's the minimum the instrument can detect?"

The GC operator smiled. "We only need head space," he explained, showing how the GC worked. In most scientific instruments, the unknown material must be placed in solution before chemical examination can be attempted. But the GC inlet could "sniff" material directly from the air. Its detection capability was incredibly sensitive compared with then existing instruments. Even though there was no apparent trace of the ether detectable by the human nose as the glassine envelope was opened near the entry port, hopefully there would still be a few million molecules kicking around to enter the intake port and mix into the solvent material.

As the moments dragged toward the expectation time, when known ether would activate the detection unit, excitement was high. The criminalist sucked in his breath when the recording pen sprang into action at the exact predicted second. The squiggles of the pen were quickly checked against a standard graph. Unquestionably, the material on the rag was ether.

Now for the remaining drop or two immobilized in the container by the dry ice.

This test was a cinch. For a device capable of identifying a mere whiff of molecules, the remaining evidence was plentiful. Best of all, the GC tracing was an exact duplicate of the tracing from the ether on the rag. Had they come from different sources, trace contaminants would probably provide minor deviations in the GC peaks to raise questions about common origin. None were present in the two materials tested. *This* evidence would stand up in court.

Seldom is the forensic profession an easy one. Many kinds of evidence hint but slightly, others somewhat more so, but still far from conclusive. Still better is the occasional case where the evidence is, as they say, strongly suggestive.

One type of evidence that demonstrates such strong probability that nearly any jury will instantly accept it is the jigsaw fit. Such cases come in many sizes and shapes. One, from the eminent Centre of Forensic Sciences in Toronto illustrates one of the more elementary jigsaw fits. In this instance, foul play was suspected when an adult male was reported missing. After a couple months of careful investigation, evidence probers were led to search for the missing man's body in the back yard of a gentleman friend of the victim's wife. The body was quickly located, dug up, and proved to be wrapped in a length of plastic sheeting. A partial roll of similar sheeting was found in the wife's home. The plastic had been whacked off in apparent hurry, leaving a zig-zag scissor path, which neatly fit a complementary path in the plastic wrapped around the body. This jigsaw fit helped convict the wife's gentleman friend of murder.

Another such case involved an ordinary drunk-driving suspect—not entirely surprising since drunk-driving stops are fruitful sources for criminal arrests.

In this instance a small element of mistrust was suggested by bloodstains noted on the drunk driver's clothing. Skepticism is a highly desirable quality for the investigator, and in this case the policeman exchanged the driver's clothes for prison garments, sending the bloody garments and shoes to the crime lab for a check.

While they were being examined, another agency was working on a murder, in which a man living in a remote desert area was beaten to death. Physical evidence secured at the scene included a fragmented, bloodstained liquor bottle. By a curious coincidence, search of the shoes worn by the drunk driver revealed a torn fragment of bloodstained liquor label.

The bloodstains alone might have offered valuable leads in placing the drunk driver at the scene of murder. Certainly, a lack of blood-type match would have tended to eliminate him. But even with highly skilful detection of many subfactors in addition to the standard ABO blood types, this evidence alone is only strongly suggestive.

The label fragment was something else. Snuggled into a hole in the label on the murder-weapon bottle, the match was unquestioned. This jigsaw fit left no doubt as to the drunk driver's presence at the murder scene.

Burnt paper matches are often found at crime scenes which prove that either the burglar forgot his flashlight or he's a compulsive smoker. Now it's possible, under some circumstances, to mate the crime scene match with a matchbook found in the criminal's possession. Sometimes, the match will be torn from the book with such a unique and jagged tear that a jigsaw fit can be discovered. In the average case, however, the mating technique depends on the process used to manufacture book matches. A normal-sized paper matchbook contains twenty matches, in two rows of ten each. The manufacturer forms the individual matches by cutting ten in one operation. This cutting procedure actually cuts and tears at the same time. Most matches have a fairly good-quality paper front. The remainder of the match consists of a mixture of miscellaneous materials and is like pressboard or particle board. This material is torn apart when the individual matches are formed.

The key to this technique is locating two matches which were adjacent to each other. Every effort should be made to obtain the matches that may have been torn from the book, since the original match was left at the crime scene. When two are located which once were one, before cleaving, the particle board portion may slip together in perfect jigsaw fashion.

Because of the manufacturing process, small inclusions of paint chips of various colors or metal foil or other foreign material may have been present in the initial mix. When the matches are formed by the cleaving process, these inclusions may be cut apart. When adjacent matches are submerged in a benzine solution, the inclusions can easily be observed. If a large enough portion of the match stem is unburned, numerous points of comparison can be found by matching cut-apart inclusions. In addition, an examination of the backs of the matches can often reveal matching fibers that were cut apart when the individual matches were formed. Under these circumstances, positive or near positive identification can be made.

With improving miniature technique, jigsaw evidence is getting so tiny it would scarcely irritate one's eye. In one case in my experience, however, it took a man and a boy to even move the evidence, let alone lift it.

Following a rending collision, the entire side of the negligent driver's car, including a bumper and license plate, was literally ripped off. A quick call to the motor vehicle department, and a policeman was awaiting the hit-and-run driver at his home. A perfect jigsaw, it was easy in this case.

Most evidence is somewhat smaller. Broken headlight shards and fragments of auto-body trim quite frequently fit into the investigator's shirt pocket. One type of evidence with enormous potential is so minute the eye scarcely can see it, since it burrows into fabric at crime scenes, and leaves with the criminal—to his later undoing.

When clothing is brought into the crime lab, it is usually first examined under low-power magnification to locate and chart stains or clinging evidence, which is set aside for later examination. When obvious possibilities are exhausted, the search continues into the world of the microscope.

Techniques for extracting such diminutive material are the subject of some quarrel between laboratories. Some prefer a modified vacuum cleaner, with a trap near the orifice, which collects the evidence on filter paper. Other labs claim the vacuum removes not only the evidence but also a year's supply of fuzz and irrelevant dust and fibers, which only confuse search for forensic material. The FBI, for example, bangs away at such fabrics with a stout tool resembling an old-fashioned tire iron. The material is hung over a clothes line for an old-fashioned whaling of the sort Grandma gave her rugs during spring cleaning, and a large sheet of new wrapping paper spread underneath catches the chaff of evidence.

Once collected, the evidence is first examined under relatively low magnification. Most criminalists favor equipment in which the power can be increased rapidly, zooming in for a tighter look as something interesting comes into view.

In addition to glass, paint chips, and other inert material, localized flora—a plant growing only in the Florida Everglades or a weed seed uniquely found in the high western desert country—suggest possibilities often overlooked in evidence search.

In our airborne society, a fleeing criminal can easily span the country in a few hours. In one murder case the suspect relaxed as soon as the plane landed him some fifteen hundred miles from his victim. He was almost amused when an alert investigator scooped him up the next day for interrogation. He claimed he'd never been in the part of the country where the murder had occurred—but a check of the suspect's ear wax identified microscopic seeds of a plant found only in the vicinity of the murder.

A unique breed of grass makes New York's Central Park its exclusive habitat. Seeds from this grass were found on a blanket in which a murdered victim's body was stored before being transported elsewhere for disposal. The suspect had an alibi that covered the spot where the body was ultimately discovered. Proving the body had been in Central Park, even for a short time, would blow the alibi apart.

Again, the proof that the Central Park seeds were connected with the corpse resulted in a confession.

Almost equal in importance to the evidence itself is proper record-keeping of the exact discovery site and subsequent possession. Whenever practical, photographs should be taken of the evidence *in situ*, with appropriate labeling and notes regarding the relative location to other crime scene elements.

Suppose a case involves a forced entry, in which the bar prying open the window dislodges chips of paint, which fall into the burglar's trouser cuff. Perhaps there's even a minute transfer of paint on the right knee of the trouser leg, where the burglar dragged himself over the high sill while climbing in the window.

Possibly a few threads are wedged in the rough wood of the sill, just past the spot the knee rubbed hard enough to dislodge surface paint.

Unless the evidence collector at the scene and the criminalist in the lab keep careful records of discovery sites and subsequent processing, the credibility of their case is damaged.

In this idealized example, a chemical match might be made of the sill's paint and that exchanged on the trouser knee. The fiber pattern dragged into the sill could show identical thread count to the trousers' fabric. The few threads torn from the trousers could be matched—thread by thread—to their frayed counterparts on the trousers. Add the bonus of a jigsaw fit between the paint chip caught in the cuff and the window site it broke from, and any jury will accept the evidence as proof of the burglar's presence. Lacking proper site data, the evidence becomes much weaker. Furthermore, site information that accurately located gives a better chance of reconstructing the crime.

Much of this benefit is lost when the evidence is gathered all in a jumble on a piece of brown wrapping paper or adhering to the filter from the crime lab vacuum. Not that the microevidence isn't valuable, but it takes intense inspection for evidence that cannot be connected with a precise discovery location. The specific collection, though harder at first, is always better than the general one.

Once in a while the searcher under the microscope is rewarded by that tiny jewel in miniature, a microscopic jigsaw fit. The smallest fragment of splintered wood may offer as good a jigsaw match as a telephone pole torn from its base. If the pieces fit, they fit! Even the layman concedes a match when broken fragments slip together exactly, one into the other.

Still another sort of match is possible with multilayered evidence. A classic example is the artist-owned dwelling which was covered with twenty-one layers of wildly varying paint. One season the artist enjoyed his mauve period; the next cerise. The odds against some other house having successive layers of violet, magenta, and Spanish red, stagger the imagination. In this case, all twenty-one layers gave the burglar cause to regret his entry. Who could ever doubt the source of paint chip from that house!

New muscle is being brought to forensics by the scanning

electron microscope (SEM). The SEM gradually evolved from the electronic revolution of the last thirty-five years, but not until 1965 was a commercial model available. While a cheapie copy lists as low as fifteen thousand dollars, the starting price-tag for those usually in service runs about seventy thousand dollars, so there's little likelihood of a runaway demand. Yet the SEM opens horizons undreamt of in conventional optics. Nearly any feat performed by the highest-powered optical microscopes can be bested by the SEM. In two capabilities, magnification and depth of field, the SEM wins by a country angstrom (the angstrom, one-hundred-millionth of a centimeter, being the unit used in measuring light).

The power source for the SEM is usually a tungsten filament, zapping a stream of electrons toward the target with an electrical pressure ranging from one to twenty thousand volts. On its way to the target, the electron beam is demagnified by three electromagnetic lenses, until the beam measures only a hundred angstrom units, an infinitesimal spot less than a ten-millionth of an inch in diameter.

A few limitations save the SEM from optical perfection. First, on most instruments the sample size is limited to not over two inches on a side. Second, because the instrument operates in a vacuum, only nonvolatile materials are easily examined. (However, researchers report that some volatile substances are currently being examined, though with considerable difficulty.) Finally, nonconductive material such as plant leaves must be plated with an electrical conductor such as aluminum or gold before examination. The conduction layer is only some four hundred angstrom units thick, which is not enough to affect the value of surface detail. As with most ultramodern instrumentation, there is constant improvement, and a recently developed field-emission SEM is reported to operate with nonconductors that have not been precoated.

As the powerful electron beam collides with the target, its energy is converted into heat, back-scattered electron reflections, and secondary electron emissions. Emerging with tremendously reduced energy, these secondary emissions are detected by the receiving end of the mechanism, which translates them into a pinpoint of light affecting a cathode-ray tube. All the while the electron beam is scanning the viewing area in typical TV raster pattern. For visual inspection, the scanning rate is fast enough to maintain a picture on the cathode-ray tube. For photography, the scanning rate is cut by as much as five-sixths, which gives greater resolution.

The upper limit for optical examination of a highly polished metal surface is about twenty-five hundred magnifications. With the SEM, this increases to as much as fifty thousand or more. Most technicians find themselves completely lost in this unfamiliar world, feeling a little like Alice in Wonderland the moment some three thousand enlargements is exceeded.

Probably the most important contribution of the scanning electron microscope to forensics is the extreme clarity of its pictures and the great depth of field, which permits access to places forbidden by the laws of optics to refractive lens systems. The SEM opens entirely new dimensions to criminalists, letting vision slide into depressions such as those made by a gun's striking mechanism, or along a length of wire severed by a cutting instrument. While soft metals such as lead do not afford the extreme resolution possible with brass and iron, still the perennial ballistic problem of looking around the edge of a bullet is now duck soup with the SEM.

Another exciting application of the SEM is examination of biological evidence for detail hitherto unknown to forensic science. To choose an exotic example, the eye of an ant at twenty-one hundred magnifications shows tiny hairs growing between each of its multifaceted lenses. The very existence of these hairs was unknown before the invention of the SEM. Undoubtedly, as further experience is gained, the SEM will revolutionize the use of submicroscopic evidence.

In spite of complaints of unfamiliarity, the new world of the ultratiny holds much forensic promise. Fingernails, it appears, have characteristic ridge patterns which may persist for life. Coated with gold, the underside of a fingernail examined under the SEM looks like a furrowed field plowed with a gang-plow. At ninety-three hundred magnifications, paint develops a whole new characteristic of cracks and weather traces never before recognized under optical microscopy.

Excitingly exact measurement of multilayered evidence is

possible with the SEM. Viewed edge-on, the miniyardstick potential may be accurate to a micron—one-millionth of a meter.

Used as a microprobe, the SEM allows virtually nondestructive analysis of the chemical make-up of each portion of multilayered evidence. Since the material is examined in cross-section, the microprobe searches each layer, one at a time, by bombardment with an enormously stepped-up stream of electrons. Voltage pressure is increased, until the electrons colliding with the sample drive off photons in the X-ray spectrum. Analysis of these photos reveals the basic elements contained in each layer.

Since each thrust of the microprobe knocks loose a sample something less than a hundred angstrom units in size, the material is unconsumed from a practical point of view. The presence of trace elements, and the variance of these trace elements from one layer to another, suggests much future usefulness for the SEM microprobe.

Piggyback evidence, like drug synergism, often packs a greater wallop than the sum of its parts. Add barbiturates to alcohol and the result may be fatal overdosage. Forge evidential bonds together and the chain far exceeds the strength of any of its individual links.

There's a cause-and-effect relationship between factors limiting vision—inclement weather, inadequate headlights, shortened days—and traffic accidents. In autumn dusk, a speeding car can travel a thousand feet before the driver recognizes the shadowy pedestrian. Add a pinch of frosty blast, causing the pedestrian to lean into the wind; top with several generous libations, including one for the road, and the curtain lifts on tragedy.

The deadly, all-too-real drama played one fall afternoon in upstate New York. The sixteen-year-old girl probably never knew what hit her as the speeding car flung her into the air.

Had the driver stopped and attempted to render aid, the tragedy might have been held excusable. With the driver's merciless abandonment of the bleeding girl, public opinion was instantly aroused.

Superintendent of the New York State Police, William E. Kirwan, is both a pioneer in the field of forensic science, and a

Fellow in the American Academy of Forensic Science. Of this type of crime, he says, "Our emphasis on the technique used to solve hit-and-run cases is based on the intense interest and emotion that the public displays whenever such an incident occurs."

With the boss a graduate of criminalistics, it's little wonder the New York Police Crime Lab enjoys such an enviable reputation. His lab is well aware that success in criminalistics is a partnership largely dependent upon the thoroughness of the investigating officer at the scene. In this case, the comprehensive evidence gathered presented the crime lab with a tremendous challenge.

The girl had been struck with such force that the suede coat she was wearing revealed two faint round outlines, which were identified as the imprint of dual vertical headlights, together with a partial grill print.

These imprints were photographically enhanced through the use of appropriate filters and special photographic techniques. To determine the approximate height of the vertically aligned headlights, the coat was draped on the shoulders of a woman the same height as the dead girl and measurements taken.

The vertical headlight arrangement narrowed the search to twenty-nine automobile models, and firmly established that the car had to be of 1968 vintage or older.

While the investigators might hope that the felonious driver lived nearby—since most traffic accidents occur within twenty miles of one's home—this probability could not be relied upon. In a state the size of New York, search of the motor vehicle records for all possible listings on twenty-nine car models would certainly produce too many vehicles to be checked out. Time was of definite concern, since a hit-and-run killer frequently mounts monumental efforts in trying to alter the damage so neither police nor concerned citizens can detect traces of the accident.

Using the enhanced photo, the crime lab added another stout link in the chain of evidence. Careful measurement of headlight diameters, distance between lights and other elements of the imprints were laboriously compared with the extensive library of identifying data maintained concerning similar data for all domestic and most foreign cars. Most such searches serve to eliminate rather than to identify, but they greatly narrow the possibility of the candidate vehicles. Searches of this sort are unromantic and have none of the derring-do the TV viewer associates with policework. Nevertheless, the great majority of successful investigations depend on just such patient, thorough, plodding concern with detail.

In this case the study paid off. Now the Albany scientists knew that the configuration and exact styling details of the car in question would be found only in vehicles made by the Ford Motor Company.

So the slayer car search narrowed down to Fords made before 1968. Still, during each model year, Ford produces millions of cars. New York doubtless had a greater share than any other state except California. If only there were some way to specify the precise model and its present color, recognizing that cars as old as five or six years, frequently have been repainted.

Now it was time to delve into the world of the microscope.

Chapter **6**

The microscopic quest roved over and round the tiny nubbins of the suede, past the hills and valleys permanently impressed by the killing pressure of the car's twin headlights.

Suddenly an object popped into the view of the stereo eyepieces. The operator adjusted the instrument and zoomed in closer until the minute speck assumed boxcar proportions. With a surgeon's skill, he extracted the infinitesimal fragment, and delicately grasped the chip with tweezers whose ends were dwarfed by an ordinary sewing needle.

Seen in side view, the minuscule chip clearly was multi-layered—almost certainly a tiny fragment of paint ruptured from the area around the headlamps. Carefully charted and preserved, the chip stood ready for further examination. Yet it was so very small! If only more chips could be discovered.

When the exhausting search was completed, three more chips were added to the evidence, all multilayered, all with the same color in each of the layers. Fortunately, two of them were much larger than the first chip.

Now, painstaking analyses could be made of the layers representing the manufacturer's original paint job, since the top layer of paint was obviously added to the original factory finish.

Let us quote Superintendent Kirwan's account of the technique used to pin minute chips such as these to specific knowledge about the year—and possibly the model—of the vehicle:

> The control paint reference file consists of plaques
> of original paints used by the four major United States
> automobile manufacturers. The first step in identifying
> an unknown auto paint sample is to painstakingly compare
> the color of the paint against this reference file. By
> this simple technique the possibilities are usually
> narrowed down to less than a dozen plaques. Comparative
> chemical tests are then conducted on the unknown paint
> and these dozen or so possibles. These tests include

chemical solubility, chemical color reactions, emission
spectroscopy, infrared spectroscopy, pyrolysis gas
chromatography, and thin-layer chromatography. The number of possible tests is frequently limited by the
sample size.

In previous chapters we've discussed many of the techniques
and instruments mentioned by Superintendent Kirwan, and will
cover others later. One particular method, often helpful in this
sort of comparison, is pyrolysis gas chromatography. With this
technique, the solid sample, such as the smallest possible portion
of the evidence paint chip, is placed in the pyrolizer—an
attachment connected to the opening port of the GC. This
consists of a small plate containing a heating coil which can be
controlled and recorded exactly. The heat of the plate is
gradually increased until the solid sample literally turns to gas
and is sucked into the entry port of the GC to be analyzed as in
other GC determinations, with just the right combination of
column diameter, solvent base, solvent, column temperature, and
detector.

Following the tests possible, considering the size of the
specimens, the examination of the hit-and-run paint chips
narrowed the choice down to only a couple of the reference
plaques. Check was then made of reference charts by make, year,
and model which used paints with these qualities. Under the
skilled eye of the experienced examiner, the likely car models
were further narrowed down.

Now the criminalist was certain the most probable car was a
1967 Ford, repainted a light blue.

Media were soon screaming the message to the public that the
wanton killer of the sixteen-year-old girl had driven a 1967 light
blue Ford. At the same time, New York state troopers continued
combing the car registration records. Hot as the suspect was,
every possible alternate activity had to continue until he was
located.

In twenty-four hours the suspect gave himself up. The fatal
car—as promised—was a 1967 light blue Ford.

This successful solution of the case was no fluke. The
partnership between the New York State Police investigators and
their criminalists produces a remarkable batting average. During

the thirty days preceding my visit to this facility, eight major hit-and-run cases were reported to the state troopers. Already, seven of the eight were cleared up by apprehension of the suspect.

The second most common denominator in criminal cases is the motor vehicle. Alcohol is the first. Some criminologists feel that as high as eighty-five percent of major crimes are committed under the influence of alcohol, by itself or in combination with other drugs. The same figure—eighty-five percent—is attributed to the involvement of motor vehicles as one aspect of major crime commission.

The getaway car is a traditional tool in holdups. Wheels provide access to the majority of the burglaries and the ability to remove the loot. A kidnapping without a long and tortuous ride through the country with the victim gagged, blindfolded, and trussed on the floor would be laughed right off the TV screen.

A major interdisciplinary study of fatal traffic accidents in Massachusetts revealed the startling intelligence that as high as one out of ten highway deaths may be murders! These investigations disclosed the incidence of slashed hydraulic lines, tampered steering linkage, and other malevolent meddling with safety and control features, clearly indicating a new and ominous direction which investigators should pursue. The project director warned, "Every traffic fatality should be regarded as murder until proven otherwise."

Regrettably, police competence in traffic investigation is in even sorrier shape than in nontraffic crimes. Wholesale numbers of traffic crashes are kissed off by leading jurisdictions under claim of other pressures, even though the economic losses from traffic accidents rank much higher than the equivalent losses from crime.

Add to that the admitted fact that the best criminalistic work holds little promise of recovery of missing goods in most criminal cases. Not so in traffic investigations. In most states, the money riding on an injury collision is in excess of fifteen thousand dollars and may be as high as half a million. There's little likelihood of justice being done without adequate police investigation. If the traffic investigator does not record conditions at the time of the crash, make appropriate photos and measurements, locate and properly interview witnesses, and find and preserve physical evidence, no one else probably ever can. Mere movement of the vehicle may eliminate possibility of establishing blame or credit for skid marks and other elements which make reconstruction possible.

There are a great many enforcement agencies which do perform nobly in traffic investigation. But for every first-rate operation, there are dozens which are inferior, haphazard, catch-as-catch-can. Ironically, as major crime surges into prominence, investigation of traffic accidents backslides still further, with the very agencies which were mediocre in the beginning moving backward most rapidly.

The majority of traffic cases, even when investigated with reasonable competence, never become the concern of the crime labs. Only where the stakes are elevated by death is the criminalistic potential realized.

Certain types of evidence, however, are there for the taking. A simple example is where skid marks start before an intersection and continue past the red stop sign, right up to the wheels of one of the crashed vehicles, positively proving failure to make the required stop.

Others, less obvious, are there for detection by reasonably skilled policemen.

Headlamps—burning or not? This puzzler frequently surfaces in collision investigations. Lack of lighted headlights during darkness hours not only contributes to crashes but may be pivotal in resolving financial responsibility.

The glowing filaments of headlights operate only in inert gas or a vacuum. Burst the lens when the filament is glowing, and the tungsten rapidly combines with the oxygen in the air. If power continues uninterrupted, the filament will quickly burn through. Often enough, the crash force which shatters headlights is violent enough to knock out electrical power. Then, determination of the headlight status at the time of crash cries for the experience of the criminalist who is fully conversant with the scientific principles involved. It doesn't hurt, also, if he has experimented with a variety of crash simulations and has also compared headlight evidence in a host of known real-life crashes. Such an expert can tell whether the lights were burning and within hundredths of a second how long illumination continued after fracture of the glass. He tells all this by the relative size of the filament, its color, and the conditions of the other portions of the headlamp.

One of the greatest lacks in traffic evaluation is the basic inadequacy of data-gathering systems. A car plunges through a traffic control signal, according to a witness, striking another vehicle traveling with the green light. In investigating, the officer attributes the crash to the motorist's "failure to observe the traffic signal." In fact, the red light may not have been burning at all, since the witness knew only that the other light was green, but never actually observed the red indicator to know whether or not it was lit.

Substantial numbers of traffic signals are poorly designed and inadequately maintained, so the motorist often has no opportunity to observe the light. Perhaps a truck or bus hid the signal, or maybe the setting sun overpowered it. Possibly, the signal light was lost in the competition of the neon signs in the background. Any and all of these conditions are the norm rather than the exception in this land full of engineering booby traps. Yet the investigating officer will unswervingly indicate "failure to observe traffic signal" as the cause of the crash.

Or take vehicle equipment. An enormous tug-of-war has been fought for years between interests which demand compulsory vehicle inspection as the cure-all for the traffic ills of the country and others who feel this single solution is not the way to attack a problem of such tremendous complexity. As of this writing there is not sufficient evidence to draw valid conclusions that periodic motor vehicle inspection pays its way.

One difficulty is the inadequate records system for causal determination of traffic crashes. In the traditional record-keeping process, causes are determined by the policeman responding to the incident—if indeed there is a response. The policeman, as often as not, instructs the involved drivers to exchange identity information. He checks to see that none of the vehicles are stolen and that the drivers are licensed. If this so-called investigation includes a routine, walk-around check of the vehicles, he may test the horn, light, steering wheel play, brake pedal, and windshield wiper. Should any of these fail to work, the report will indicate equipment failure as a cause of the accident—even to the ridiculous extent of stating that windshield wiper failure was significant on a dry day or that taillight failure explained the daytime crash. Even where the rain was pouring or the night ink-dark, the equipment failure may have no relationship to the events leading to the crash.

On the other side of this coin, scarcely ever are vehicles examined with sufficient thoroughness to truly establish equipment failure.

In the previously cited Massachusetts study—in a state having compulsory inspection—over eighty-five percent of the vehicles examined by teams of automotive engineers and master mechanics proved to have serious equipment shortcomings not detected or corrected by the compulsory vehicle inspection program.

Since the enactment of the Highway Safety Act of 1966, the Department of Transportation has contracted with interdisciplinary investigative teams to attempt discovery of the proper role of equipment failure in vehicle crashes. Adequate scientific evidence is accumulating which offers much promise for intelligent countermeasures.

A landmark case concerns a Thunderbird which on two occasions ran amok, swerving off the road without warning and killing its occupants. In each case the car itself was only slightly damaged, and after the first fatality it was patched up and sold.

After the second killing, the insurance investigators brought the car to expert mechanics, pleaded with them to discover any mechanical malfunction. Better to destroy the vehicle than to allow it to kill another time.

The mechanics used every trick in the book, yet nothing could be found to explain the mysterious swerving and loss of control.

Computerized diagnostic equipment had just been developed. Fortunately, one diagnostic center was available to these investigators. Without revealing the car's sorry history, they turned over the T-bird to the mercies of the machine.

When the examination was concluded the operator examined the computer print-out. "Only one thing wrong," he commented. "There's a pinhole leak in the right front wheel hydraulic line. When the brakes are applied, a small amount of the hydraulic fluid might squirt on the brake lining."

"Wouldn't that fluid be detectable if the brake were stripped down?" the investigator asked.

"Not likely. There's such a small amount, the first real braking effort would burn it off."

The investigator stared at the computer report, then lifted his eyes to the operator. "What might happen if you applied the brakes where there was a squirt of hydraulic fluid on one of them?"

Ominously, the operator shook his head. "Wouldn't recommend it. Brake would probably grab and make you lose control. Probably throw you right off the roadway."

The fingerprints of the motor vehicle—its tire tracks—seldom find their way into criminalistics, even though they offer a major source of identification. Like the equally neglected footprints left at a crime scene, tire impressions offer a fertile source for crime reconstruction and identification of the vehicles involved in the crime.

Admittedly, not every murder will occur at the beach cottage or near impressionable surfaces ready to record their history for the discerning investigator. Nevertheless, the frequency with which cars are involved in gaining access to the crimes, for transportation of the loot—or the body—for the rapid escape, including flight from the law, all strongly indicate a search for tire tracks which may have left a signature.

Several avenues may be pursued once the evidence has been preserved. At least a hint of make and model of the vehicle is possible when tracks are left by new equipment. Beyond that, the very fact of wear and tear may provide possible jigsaw fit comparison between a tire track and the tire originating it. As in the case of tennis shoes or rubber heels and their impressions, the differences are what counts, not the class characteristics of the manufacturer.

Tires are exposed to brutal forces as they bounce off jagged pavements, pound against curbings, are slashed by ragged debris. In addition, assorted pebbles, twigs, soils, and other materials lodge within the caverns of full tread. Each of these irregularities offers potential for matching against impressions left at the crime scene.

. 71 .

Soil from a unique locale will occasionally lodge in the tread of a tire driven on hard surfaces and accumulating the soil only at the crime scene. Together with tracks, this would add strength to establishing the vehicle's involvement in the matter. Practically speaking, this seldom ever happens.

A statistical advantage accrues with each element of individuality, particularly in sets of tire tracks. Take the example of the burglar's pickup truck that had tires of two different sizes and four different makes. Even though one or more of the tires may have left insufficient impression to register fine details such as cuts, lodged pebbles, and the like, the similarity of class characteristics such as the number of groves in the tread, the antiskid design, wear on the inside or outside of tread, and similar features can mutually reenforce matching elements on the tire tread from the same car. Given a suspect car in which each of the recognizable features has its opposite number preserved in the evidence tracks left at the crime scene, and the term *vehicle fingerprint* becomes very clear. It's a pity so little use is made of this type of evidence.

The stylized concept of a traffic accident includes the ear-splitting wail of tires dragging over pavement, then the crunch of metal demolishing metal, immediately followed by the tinkle of falling glass.

Both at the time and in retrospect, the shrieking of the tires seems interminable, yet it is a rare skid indeed that actually takes as long as two seconds to lay down. The crash itself occurs in such a limited time framework that it's virtually impossible for an eyewitness to know what occurred, unless he was staring directly at the point of impact at the moment of collision.

Pioneering studies by the Institute of Transportation and Traffic Engineering at the University of California at Los Angeles demonstrate how really brief this time lapse is. In a head-on collision between one vehicle traveling at 37 MPH and another at 23 MPH, the beginning-to-end impact took slightly more than one-tenth of a second.

Swiveling one's head at the sounds of a crash, on the other hand, takes nearly twice as long as the impact. So what the witness thinks he sees is scarcely what happened. His version is the byproduct of his sets, his prejudices, his imagination.

The burning summer sun lashed the solid stream of cars crawling antlike up the four-lane highway leading up into the Santa Cruz Mountains in northern California. On the far side of the mountain range lay the surfer's mecca, the waves crashing almost under the dormitory windows of the University of California at Santa Cruz.

Further down the coast, a thick fog carressed the fields of the Watsonville district, giving the ideal climate that made the area the center of the nation's artichoke production. Only a few minutes further south were the attractions of Monterey, California's first capitol and tourist-rich locale of Steinbeck's *Cannery Row*.

Long known as Death Alley, the jammed highway leading to Santa Cruz twisted its tortuous passage through the mountain valleys. In spite of the steep climb, the vehicles swarmed along in excess of 50 MPH, unmindful of the wall of moving steel headed down the grade only inches on the other side of the double center line.

Suddenly a Porsche veered from the lane next to the center line and swerved over the yellow stripping, slamming head-on into a southbound Studebaker. A violent second later, three people were dead, with one occupant of the downhill car surviving.

Traffic ground to a screeching halt, plugging the artery both ways. Well-intentioned bystanders attempted aid. A motorist with a citizen band radio tried to summon help.

Before too long ambulances and the highway patrol arrived at the scene. As soon as the dead and injured were headed away from the scene, one of the patrol units pushed the Porsche to the side of the road, then the Studebaker, clearing a detour path through which the stagnated stream of traffic could proceed. At the same time, the officer radioed for a new type of help, only available since the National Highway Traffic Safety Administration began underwriting in-depth investigations of selected crashes.

The early moments of the investigation revealed no reason why the Porsche driver should have swerved abruptly onto the wrong side. There were none of the usual indications of causes for a loss of control such as an animal in the roadway, a dumped load, or tire failure. Perhaps the new multidiscipline investigative team could explain the mystery.

In the garage, the engineering member of the team started by stripping the steering components of the Porsche into their respective units. Every nut, bolt, washer, gear, lever, and piece of linkage was visually inspected, then magnifluxed to reveal any hidden flaws. When the exhaustive investigation was completed, the mystery was as opaque as ever. The steering seemed flawless. The wheels and tires were in mint condition. Up to now, detailed interrogation of the witnesses added nothing to solve the puzzle. The engineering investigation, thus far, only increased the enigma.

While the logical sites of failure had been unrewarding, the engineer wasn't about to give up. There had to be a discoverable answer, even though several days of intensive investigation had not produced even a hint as to the underlying causes. He shrugged his shoulders and returned to the fray. There was still a lot of Porsche left to examine. As a scientist, he knew that accidents are no accident. The actual factors which caused the collision ought to be detectable.

Chapter 7

Every dent, scratch, paint exchange on the Porsche was mercilessly scrutinized, photographed, and evaluated. Nothing was accepted until its source was determined.

The dynamics of head-on crash occur in a few thousandths of a second. High-speed motion pictures of instrumented crash vehicles have clearly established how very rapidly large-energy crashes rend and distort metal, smash glass, fling components from under the hood over the countryside. A rear seat passenger may be dashed into the front windshield and rebound to the rear seat before any knowledge of the crash can penetrate his brain. The elapsed times are frighteningly brief.

To account for the twisting damage done in this head-on, the Porsche had to be examined inch by inch, with every mark matched to its source. If any question arose, there would be laboratory analysis of paint and paint exchanges with spectrographic instruments and microscopic examination.

At last the detailed examination was almost complete. All of the markings had been accounted for except for two relatively small pieces of damage. Slight impressions in the rear body and on the rear bumper could not be explained by any known information concerning the collision. In addition, the right rear fender was slightly distorted, bent forward as though a sky hook had caught it and swung the rear end of the car to the right, forcing the front of the car to head to the left—and over the divider line.

Could these two unexplained markings have somehow accounted for the loss of control of the Porsche? They just didn't seem to have any relationship with each other. Still, they were all that was left.

The engineer asked for a consultation with the highway patrol officers who had investigated the crash and originally requested his help. When they arrived, he pointed out the two unanswered pieces of damage. Did the officers have any idea where either of them might have originated?

They were able to resolve the bumper and rear body markings. One officer remembered pushing the Porsche off the roadway to release the dammed-up traffic stream. Further examination with the matching scars on the highway patrol unit's push bar proved that the rear-end damage originated from that source.

Now for the right rear fender.

The investigation centered on all persons and vehicles known to have been at the scene. The investigators started a methodical check of all the witnesses and their own vehicles. They started with the closest witness, who had been driving alongside the Porsche the instant before it swerved across the center line into the Studebaker, which was driving down the hill. Did this driver remember anything that might have a relationship to the bent right rear fender on the Porsche? He didn't.

The engineer asked if he might examine the Plymouth this witness was driving that day. The driver was happy to oblige. Certainly, he had nothing to hide.

Now that the involved car had been located, however, the stark evidence was plain to see. There was a slightly bent wraparound rear bumper, pulled out where it had hooked the Porsche's fender. And there were paint traces still in evidence on the bumper, where it had wrenched loose from the fender after tossing the Porsche out of control. Spectrographic analysis would prove the match between the two paints.

The mystery was solved, with no one more amazed than the driver who had caused it all.

Fifty-five thousand people are killed every year in traffic crashes, with another two million seriously injured. In most crashes, the causes are never determined, yet in virtually every collision the evidence is there for the finding. What *is* lacking is the investigative know-how and persistence.

Glass is a special material that gladdens the heart of the criminalist. First, it is bounteously available, ready to involve itself at the first inkling of force, from smashed shopwindows to shattered headlights. Nemesis of burglars who break and enter, it finds a home in cuffs and pockets, and snuggles into fabric folds. Its lacerations shear flesh, drawing blood, whose stains point fingers of suspicion toward the culprit. When violence occurs, it flings itself far and wide, clinging tenaciously in unnoticed particles. Or it spears into yielding surfaces, then breaks off to later gleam its presence under the microscope, where it can be scientifically mated with its source. In vehicle crashes, it lodges in the skin and bones of hit-and-run victims and adheres to their clothing.

"He shot first!" screams the survivor of a shoot-out in which gunfire was exchanged through a window. "I saw him lurking outside, waiting to kill me. After he fired through the window I had no choice but to defend myself."

Likely story? Maybe. But let's look at the window and the tale it has to tell. The two bullet holes are surrounded by radial and concentric cracks. Indelibly imprinted in the glass is proof of the direction from which each shot was fired and their sequence, far more accurate than any eyewitnesses.

Fractured glass shows two characteristic stress patterns, each related to the strain which bent the glass past the breaking point. Radial cracks spread out from the center of strain in a sunburst configuration. Concentric cracks, like ripples radiating from a pebble dropped in still water, surround the center of impact. Viewed edge-on, stress lines permanently record the direction of the breaking force.

The stress lines of radial cracks start like a lazy parenthesis, commencing nearly parallel to the side from which force occurred, then curving to exit almost at right angles to the far side.

The reverse is true of concentric stress lines. Their near right angle starts at the surface where stress occurred and flows to be almost parallel to the opposite surface.

Using these physical indicators, stories can be confirmed or refuted. The staged crime where the so-called victim steals from himself and then breaks the window to indicate burglary, comes a cropper when the window proves to be broken from the inside.

In the shoot-out, the glass fractures told the investigator two things. First, the direction from which each shot was fired. Second, the order in which the shots were exchanged.

The concentric fracture lines from the first shot fired will have a chance to be complete circles, surrounding the bullet hole like a bull's-eye target. Those from the second shot will stop when they come to one of the preexisting fractures.

The examination clearly revealed the shot from the inside was fired first. A closer look at the second shot, in relation to the location of the marksman inside, suggested that the true victim was falling to the ground as he returned fire, since the bullet wasn't even close. Further investigative work on the relationships between the men established that the man inside had been threatening for some time to 'shoot that bastard on sight.' He had, and then opportunistically tried to accuse his victim of firing first.

In another case a policeman told of the horrendous gunfight with a getaway robber. "Damn lucky I wasn't killed," the officer exclaimed, pointing to the bullet holes in his windshield.

Admiring friends clapped his shoulder in congratulation at his miraculous escape. Superiors seriously considered nominating him for the "Officer of the Month" award.

But the criminalist was increasingly skeptical at the combination of agility and luck which enabled the policeman to escape unhurt. Finally he took out his pocket magnifier and examined the windshield for tell-tale stress patterns. Sure enough, all of the bullets had been fired from the inside. The chagrined "hero" exchanged his proposed commendation for some time off for falsifying a report.

Four principle techniques are used to match glass evidence. The first and most conclusive is the jigsaw fit, whether it be between a headlight fragment as large as a fist, or the smallest imaginable chips pieced together under a microscope.

Given a jagged jug and a thousand chips exploded in every direction as the bottle shattered over the victim's head, it takes patience to find both the single chip and the correct presentation to slip the chip into the jigsaw fit. Patience the criminalists must have. Time he does not, however; so glass matching is seldom done. Still, occasionally, the glass puzzle is completed in time for court, providing evidence juries can easily understand.

A second type of glass identification is the byproduct of the wildly dancing electrons of material burned in the searing arc of the spectrograph. The heavier the nucleus of the element, the more radiant energy it takes to drive the whirling electrons into more distant orbits. Conversely, when they return to their normal orbits, sometimes in several interorbital leaps, the photons produced are progressively stronger and of shorter wavelength, as the electrons come closer to the atom's nucleus —all of which results in photo emissions unique to each of the basic elements.

These spectrographic emissions are directed either through a prism or reflected from a fine-line grating with as many as fifty thousand lines per inch. This spreads the light, as in a rainbow, separating each of the wavelengths into a precise position in the spectrum, which is then photographed. The lines produced by any given element and their respective position on the spectrogram are always the same and make identification of each basic element possible.

Glass spectroscopy relies on the presence of trace elements for personalization of a given sample. The traces can be analyzed qualitatively and amounts determined by the density of the individual lines on the photographic spectrogram. A larger amount of the element will produce more photons, which precipitate more silver in the photographic negative. Measured by a densitometer, the types and quantities of such trace elements permit determination of the possibility that the evidence glass and that of the exemplar are of common origin.

A third testing method relies on the familiar bending of light that occurs in transparent materials. A pencil placed in a glass of water seems to bend because of this phenomenon. This effect, called *refractive index*, occurs when light enters glass. The amount of bend is a characteristic of the physical and chemical make-up of the glass. If the evidence glass still has one smooth surface, its refractive index can be compared with that of the known glass, or exemplar, for refractive index match. This test is sensitive to the third decimal—for example, 1.484 is distinguishable from 1.485.

In crime lab practice, the refractive index of the exemplar is measured with a refractometer, then compared with the evidence using the Becke line technique. A liquid with a slightly greater density than that of the glass is placed on a microscope stage with a heat control, and the samples to be compared are put alongside each other in the liquid. As the heat is increased in the warming stage, the glass is viewed through the microscope, with the eyepiece moving up from the samples. The Becke line is a halo of yellow which appears in the liquid and which moves toward the material having the greater refractive index as the microscope eyepiece is raised. When the exact refractive index between glass and liquid is reached, the Becke line appears stationary. At that instant, the glass disappears from view. It reappears shortly as the increasing heat lowers the refractive index of the liquid. Now the Becke line will move in the opposite direction.

If all these phenomena occur simultaneously in both glass samples, then the samples have identical refractive indices.

A fourth comparative technique measures the density, or specific gravity of two materials. Liquid bromoform has a specific density of 2.89, which means it's nearly three times as heavy as water. The bromoform is diluted and layered in a transparent comparison tube, with pure bromoform on the bottom and successively diluted layers on top, allowing them to settle overnight so that there is gradual change from one density level to the next. In testing, the exemplar is first allowed to reach its own level in the calibrated tube; then the unknown is added. If density is the same, the two pieces will end up floating side by side.

A thermal variation of the density test uses a tube about two feet long, heated to produce a temperature differential of about 5 degrees centigrade from the bottom of the tube to the top. This creates a highly sensitive variable gradient density. As in the bromoform test, the exemplar is allowed to find its natural level in the fluid column, and is then compared with the evidence glass. This method is considerably more sensitive to minute differences in density than the bromoform method.

All of these tests are particularly valuable in eliminating evidence. Most authorities agree that different specimens of glass are quite dissimilar in trace element content as well as refractive index and density. However, the difference may scarcely be detectable in items manufactured with extremely high quality control, such as sealed-beam headlights, which are very similar in physical and chemical properties from batch to batch. The variance will be much greater, of course, in different brands of such lights.

The criminalist must also be aware that refractive index and specific gravity may vary slightly within the same piece of glass.

This is because glass has considerably different characteristics from most other materials.

Solids, modern science demonstrates, are mostly crystalline in structure. Glass, however, is in reality a viscous liquid which becomes increasingly solid in appearance as it cools.

This hardening may be compared to the freezing of water. At the moment when glass becomes an apparent solid, there is frequently uneven stress within the glass, resulting in portions of the same piece having slightly different refractive indices and densities. Because of this, it is important that exemplars be chosen as close as possible to the site from which the evidence glass was broken—a tough chore to do without a crystal ball, which itself would probably have stress differences.

In spite of the ubiquity of glass evidence, it is virtually ignored in the vast majority of felonious crimes. The largest volume of glass evidence results from traffic crashes, with the usual concomitant shattering of head- and taillights. An exception is found in those cases where the offense is notorious enough to have political significance.

A crack over the noggin with a vodka bottle is possibly the quickest way to destroy a beautiful friendship. When the blow is sufficiently powerful to kill the victim, the glass elements involved have a better than usual chance to come to forensic attention.

In one particular case, it appeared that an extended drinking bout had preceded the assault. According to extensive preliminary investigation, the two men had begun drinking in a local pub, the liquid adhesive cementing a casual friendship until the victim-to-be made the mistake of inviting his new-found comrade to continue the festivities at his home.

Evidently the level of camaraderie deteriorated as the party continued. The guest exercised his indignation by smashing the vodka bottle over the head of his host. He was apparently sober enough to recognize this gauche behavior as a breach of manners and precipitously took his departure, just ahead of the sheriff's deputies, who had been called by neighbors unable to sleep because of the increasing hilarity.

The party-pooper might have escaped the consequences of his deed entirely, save for the fact that his compass was somewhat erratic and led him in a circular course, where he was swooped up by the investigating deputies. Actually, there appeared little to connect him with the murder, except for his presence in the vicinity. Still, he was intoxicated, which justified holding him for further examination. As a precaution, his clothing was sent to the crime lab for examination.

Meanwhile, investigators carefully gathered the remnants of the vodka bottle upon which so much rode. The unshattered neck was carefully preserved, and assorted glass fragments still lodged in the victim's head were gathered for comparison. No other evidence could be located to pin the suspect to the scene of the crime. This was one case where the entire investigation depended on the crime lab.

Examined under magnification, the clothing of the suspect proved to contain numerous microscopic shards of broken glass, with a couple of particles large enough to be examined for refractive index. Compared with glass fragments collected near the victim and with those imbedded in his scalp, the glass proved to have exactly similar physical qualities insofar as refractive index and gradient density were concerned.

The neck of the bottle proved to be a veritable horn of plenty. A lovely identifiable latent fingerprint was raised on the bottleneck, matching one of the suspect's fingers. Finally, an unbelievably lucky jigsaw fit was made between one of the larger fragments found on the suspect's clothing and the location from which it had chipped, as the bottle crashed over the victim's head.

Chapter *8*

Except in the asphalt jungle, a most plentiful source of physical evidence surrounds us on all sides—literally by the ton. In a high percentage of major crimes, tracks are left in it. It clings to shoes and clothing, to hair and hands, and under fingernails. Within limits, it is responsive to half a dozen identification techniques in the crime lab.

Unwanted, we call it dirt. As evidence, it is known as soil.

The evolution of the top covering of the earth is almost as old as time, beginning with nature's primordial heavings as the planet cooled. Continents broke the surface of ancient seas and mountains were squeezed upward to be attacked immediately by the deluge from constantly storming skies. The eroding forces of running waters were doubled when the water froze in crevices and split rocks into fragments. The breakdown was speeded by the weak carbonic acid which nature continually produces from water and carbon dioxide from the atmosphere. Relentlessly, winds ravaged the surface of rocks, rasping biting sand particles over the surfaces. All of these forces working together resulted in the first thin soil coverings, to be further enriched by the contributions of the evolving plant and animal life.

Crime lab use of soil evidence is complicated by two diametrically opposite considerations. First is the relative sameness of soils. Ninety percent of the earth's crust consists only of oxygen, silicon, aluminum, and iron. Soils, for the most part, consist of varying mixtures of four principal substances. These are: humus, which is the residue of decayed organic materials; sand, mostly weathered quartz particles; silt, made up of microscopic sand grains; and clay. There are three principal types of clay: kaolin, illite, and montmorillonite, all of which are indistinguishable from each other by the testing methods used in most crime labs, if soils are, indeed, tested at all.

The other side of the coin is that in a sample small enough to be contained in a thimble, the soil may vary substantially. While a truckload of soil may contain approximately the same

. 83 .

distribution of the common materials, a spoonful may lean heavily to one or another of the basic constituents.

Soils also vary both laterally across the ground, and vertically, as in samples taken from various levels of a grave. Two qualities affect a particular soil: the mineral make-up of the rock underneath, from which the indigenous soil was formed, and the portion which is imported by man or nature, by floating dust, plant and animal life, flood waters, or truck.

Two additional difficulties face the forensic scientist who would analyze soil. First is the difficulty of obtaining a sample adhering to the criminal or possessions associated with him which is pure enough to permit reasonable possibility of matching with exemplar soil gathered from the crime scene. Where soil is soft and clinging, the mix is likely to change with each pounding footstep as the criminal flees the scene. So placing the criminal at the crime scene on the basis of soils lodged in crevices or clinging to shoes is a herculean task.

The second problem is finding exemplar soil near enough to the location where evidence soil originated that there is hope of a match.

Nevertheless, on occasion, a match can be made. Suppose a burglar jumps from a window, his heel jamming into the spaded flowerbed below, ramming soil into an open part of the heel pattern. His next step may protect the purity of the initial sample by covering it with a leaf, or forcing a pebble on top of it. Under such conditions, a pure piece of soil can be compared with exemplar soil gathered from the heel print where the burglar landed.

Sometimes soils may cling to shovels or other implements used in digging a grave. Or a small clod may lodge in a pocket or pants cuff. Even where multiple layers of soil cling to a shoe, it may be possible to dry the evidence and then separate the layers for individual analysis.

As an occasional boon, a soil will have a relatively high percentage of a particular mineral element. One of the oddities of soils is that they tend to concentrate the trace elements of the rocks from which they were formed. The underlying rock, for example, may have only one-hundredth of one percent of copper, yet by the time the rock becomes soil, the copper concentration may be one hundred times stronger.

Rarely, the mineral content will be local enough to give valuable case assistance. In a hit-and-run fatality, dirt was dislodged from the fender which struck the pedestrian. A suspect car was located, and comparison samples of the soil still clinging to the underside of the damaged fender were sent to the FBI laboratory. Both soils contained measurable quantities of zinc ore and silver. These metals were not found closer than 125 miles from the crime scene, in a mining area the suspect was proven to have visited recently.

In collecting exemplar soil, the investigator should gather the sample from the location most likely to have provided the evidence soil. Additional samples should be collected in the immediate vicinity and in the general neighborhood. Two methods are generally followed in preserving samples showing the soil characteristics in a given locality. In one, the exemplar is considered to be the hub of an imaginary wheel, and the other samples are collected along its radiating spokes. The other uses a grid pattern for collection. The number of samples and their distance apart depend on the judgment of the evidence collector and the obvious soil differences. One soil specialist says that he uses color as his primary indicator, since color variances the eye can detect are likely indicators of fundamental differences in soil make-up. The same man insists on collecting his own samples, since they must be faithfully labeled to identify the precise location where they were secured—a task he will not trust to others.

Not until after World War II was much work attempted in soil identification for forensic purposes. In 1886, a researcher in Ireland used a gradient density technique for geological purposes. The technique was apparently rediscovered by Linderstrom-Lang in the forties and adapted by others for crime lab use. The method used resembles the gradient density testing of glass particles, except that the liquid medium in which the particles are floated must encompass the full range of densities of the material likely to be found in a soil sample. After the initial applications of the gradient density techniques in crime scene soils, the technique enjoyed a flurry of popularity which has since subsided in most crime labs.

Most soils connected with crimes are topsoils, usually containing about five percent humus. In low-lying areas the soils tend to have a greater percentage of clay. In the mountains the parent rock material will be represented to a greater extent, and in deserts the sand content will be much greater. While the density gradient method may provide some insight into the composition of soils by separating clays from lighter or heavier minerals, many authorities feel that density gradient testing for soil samples has been oversold. The clay minerals which may predominate in many soils have a nearly indistinguishable particle density. In addition, most soils contain quartz in the sand and silt fraction. Since this mineral is represented in most soils, its occurrence, even in matching density gradient tubes, is of no probative value.

In the FBI laboratory, soil is removed from shoes or other material it may be clinging to, and dried. The color and texture of the clumps of soil are noted, along with any peculiarities such as plant matter, mottled coloring, or other ingredients such as cinders, slag, or building materials.

If the soil appears to contain sufficient clay, a portion will be removed, and evidence and exemplar samples compared on the differential thermal analyzer. The basic types of clay vary in their ability to be exothermic—giving off heat, or endothermic—taking in heat.

Other soil samples are washed in an apparatus which utilizes high-frequency sound waves to scrub each individual grain, and are then compared with the gradient density methods already mentioned.

Next, the examiner studies the mineral fractions, identifying the minerals present. This technique is limited, however, to soils with a high content of minerals other than clay minerals, since the clays are so minute (less than two millionths of a meter) that they cannot be resolved by an optical microscope. Such an examination could be made with a scanning electron microscope, but no such application is known at this time.

The mineral fraction determination is slow, tedious, difficult work which cannot be performed by present instrumentation. As far as we know, in North America only the FBI laboratory and the Toronto, Ontario, Centre of Forensic Sciences undertake this painstaking, time-consuming petrographic analysis of soil samples.

Only in the last fifty years have scientists discovered that many of the qualities of a solid were due not so much as to what the solid was made of, as the way its molecules were arranged. Virtually all solids are, in fact, collections of crystals, which assume classical shape if the material is pure enough. All crystals take one of seven basic shapes which offer a clue to the mineralogist as to the particular substance present in a soil sample.

Theoretically, the examiner can identify the crystal in part by its shape. Actually, crystals are seldom pure, and a completely perfect crystal has yet to be found in nature. Some feel that constructing such a crystal in the laboratory would rank with splitting the atom, since a perfect crystal would be the strongest substance known.

The very inability to find perfection actually works to the benefit of the mineralogist, who would make forensic comparison of two soil samples, since a crystalline imperfection of a particular type is quite convincing when matched by exactly similar imperfection in the comparative sample.

The laborious process of physically counting the number and type of each particle in a soil sample is a staggering burden. The possible combinations run into the hundreds. Using a petrographic microscope, assisted by special light sources such as ultraviolet or polarized illumination, the soil inventory is begun—so many plagioclase particles, so many microcline, so many hornblende, and so on.

The resulting evidence is vastly more convincing than elementary gradient density comparison. The fact that only two North American labs both have the time and take it to practice this art speaks volumes for the present level of crime lab soil examination.

Only recently, a whole new avenue opened up for crime lab use of the good earth. The techniques promise exciting possibilities for personalization undreamed of in previous soil work. Still on the drawing board, however, it will probably be a few years before these methods find widespread application in practical forensics.

Home base for this immense potential is humus, that five percent portion of topsoils. Most people—criminalists included—have thought of soil as dead and inert. Nothing could be further from the real state of affairs. True, the make-up of the ninety-five percent portion is relatively stereotyped. But what's left is alive with activity, teeming with countless living organisms that vary enormously with the environmental conditions which brought them into being.

A typical soil sample of only one gram—about half the weight of a dime—may contain the following living organisms:

1. *Three billion bacteria*, microorganisms which contain no chlorophyll and which multiply by simple division. While some bacteria threaten the human system, man could not exist without the partnership of bacteria, since dozens of strains live in his body and perform functions vital to his life force.

2. *A million algae*, members of the plant kingdom containing cholorphyll, the miracle substance that converts carbon dioxide and water to carbohydrates, creating the ecological balance by which plants and animal life complement each other.

3. *A million mold organisms*, fungus-like growths living on the surface of organic matter.

4. *Thousands of single-celled animals*, of the phylum Protozoa.

5. *Carbohydrates*, the products of the decomposition of plant starches and cellulose.

6. *Amino sugars and amino acids*, breakdown products of starches and proteins.

7. *Enzymes*, or biochemical catalysts necessary for reactions taking place within the cells of the microbes.

Dead and inert indeed! The real promise for soil use lies in this exciting microworld. The variables found in the living portion of the soil are far greater than those in the inorganic portion, and more likely to reflect environmental conditions that might be unique to a given location.

The amount and quality of humus-forming plant life depends on a host of different factors. Changing wind currents transfer soils and distribute plant seeds, as do birds and animals. Amounts of moisture and sun and average heat control germination and plant survival. Anyone who has noticed the way desert plants limit themselves to available water, staking out a plot sufficient to maintain life as though planted by a master landscaper, will appreciate this aspect of plant distribution. Compared with the teaming growth of a rain forest, the range of plant life becomes an obvious function of the other environmental qualities.

Given this variety of affecting factors, it's reasonable to assume considerable individuality in the plant growth that results in the humus content of a given soil.

Within the humus, the microorganisms clash, devour one another, multiplying until the food source becomes in such short supply that the ravenous foragers themselves nearly become extinct. This continuing change in the micropopulation, in turn, leaves indelible traces in soil, principally through very small concentrations of the enzymes produced by the life processes of the microorganisms.

The soil detective is able to measure these infinitesimal enzyme quantities by a clever method of amplification. Since enzymes have considerable specificity in the reactions they make possible, the criminalists can introduce a measured amount of a substance such as glycerol. One of the enzymes, lipase, performs the task of hydrolyzing fatty acids and glycerol from lipids, or fats. By measuring the amount of fatty acids which result from the soil enzyme action with the lipase, the scientist can deduce the quantity of lipase, amplified some hundred thousand times in this process.

Repeating the procedure for dozens of other enzymes results in an enzyme profile that is infinitely more sensitive to soil variance than are the tests for the inorganic qualities. The question now is when these exquisite techniques will move off the drawing board and into the real world of forensic science.

D. M. Lucas, director of the Ontario Centre of Forensic Sciences, puts it this way: "Soil evidence by itself is rarely sufficiently strong to resolve a case, but more frequently it provides corroboration which together with other direct or circumstantial evidence will assist in resolving a case. In this respect, it is not unlike a great many other types of physical evidence."

In one Ontario case, a young woman was walking along a residential street, totally unaware of any threat to her well-being, when she was seized from behind by a man who seemingly emerged from nowhere. Before she had an opportunity to cry out, the man struck her a brutal blow on the side of her face, which fractured her cheekbone and caused a deep laceration. The man then led the dazed girl to a bushy area nearby and raped her. Incongruously, he then walked with her to a nearby hospital and left her at the door.

The girl's appearance in the emergency room was relayed to the police, who immediately started searching the area. In a short time, the officers located a suspect, who admitted having led the young woman to the hospital, but insisted that he'd done her no harm. Quite the contrary! The poor girl had been bleeding badly and wandering around in a dazed condition when he'd happened by. Much as he hadn't wanted to become involved, common decency had required that he render assistance.

This certainly didn't have the ring of a story a rapist would tell. And the young man *had* led the unfortunate girl to the hospital. What was more, no impartial witnesses could be found.

Still, there was a trace of dirt on the right knee of the suspect's trousers. The investigators held the young man for further questioning and submitted his trousers for inspection to the Centre of Forensic Sciences. In addition, they gathered evidence from the scene of the alleged rape. Nine other soil samples were taken at the scene and within a fifty-yard radius of the area.

One of the most interesting items submitted in the rape case was a large lump of soil taken directly from the attack location. There was a distinct fabric imprint on the surface of this lump, which was compared with the dirt-smeared area of the suspect's trousers. A close examination of both the impression in the lump and the fabric of the trousers proved that the thread count and other characteristics were the same. Although this was not conclusive evidence that the suspect's trousers had made the impression, it at least kept the case alive. Had the thread count and fabric design been different, it would almost certainly have cleared the suspect.

Now came the matter of the soils themselves, the slow and methodical comparison of each of the nine soil samples with that remaining on the suspect's trousers.

One thing became clear from the outset of the soil comparison. There was considerable difference in each of the soil samples collected from the area immediately adjacent to the spot where the pattern-bearing lump had been located.

The moment of truth was at hand when the soil from the crime scene itself was compared with that clinging to the trouser knee. These two soils were found to be indistinguishable.

Until this time the suspect had kept his composure, adopting a hurt attitude that his Good Samaritan deed could have been so misinterpreted. When the investigators confronted him with the similarity between the fabric pattern left on the soil lump and that of his trousers, his façade of innocence began to crumble. After reviewing the evidence showing that the soil on his trouser knee was the only one of nine which matched the crime scene soil, he broke down completely.

At his hearing, he changed his plea to guilty and was sentenced to five years in the penitentiary on a charge of indecent assault.

Today's man-made fibers dazzle the imagination as polymer chemists exceed nature's alchemy in creating ever-increasing varieties of test-tube filaments. This surfeit brings complications to the forensic specialist, who would maintain reference files of all possible kinds of evidence he may be called on to identify.

The star of this fiber show, however, is the most abundant of the natural fibers—human hair, which so often plays a critical part in the solution of cases of violence. When the hair is found clutched in the hands of a rape or murder victim, the crime can be partially reconstructed.

There are approximately a hundred and twenty thousand hairs on the well-endowed human head, something in the order of a thousand per square inch. These hairs vary from spot to spot in the same head, and more so from head to head.

Hair begins its growth in the papilla or root. When forcibly wrenched from the head, the bulbous portion of the root still clings to the base of the hair. The hair shaft that protrudes through the skin is composed of three parts: the medulla, or central canal; the cortex, a layer which surrounds the central core; and the external sheath or cuticle, which consists of an outside layer of scalelike growth.

Each of these sections is of particular interest to the criminalist, since they vary in thickness, diameter, shape, and color. Even the scale pattern of the cuticle can contribute significantly in identifying origin of a particular hair or group of hairs.

Criminalists much prefer to work with hair in quantity, for a variety of reasons, one of which is that a clump—if large enough—can sometimes lead to a site on the suspect's scalp from which the hair was wrenched. Another is that hair color varies from top to base and from hair to hair. This is particularly true if the owner has been altering nature's gift with bleaches or dyes.

The cortex carries the basic pigmentation, which determines the untampered-with hair color. The amount of pigmentation sometimes differs at separate locations in the same hair. In some hairs, the medulla may be pinched out of existence, giving a unique cross-section. The relative amount of coloring changes from hair to hair as, for instance, with those who are starting to become gray. In spite of all these variables, the range is usually limited enough to provide reasonable accuracy in determining a suspect's hair color from evidence hair.

The diameter of the hair shafts varies from one four-hundredth to one fifteen-hundredth of an inch. The cross-section may be oval, kidney-shaped, circular, or triangular. All of these factors permit the criminalist to determine whether the hair is of Caucasian, Negroid, Indian, or Oriental origin, if the donor is of reasonably pure extraction. Quite often the age, sex, and portion of the body where the hair grew can be determined with reasonable accuracy.

Microscopic examination of the hair ends often reveals other telling information. If the hair is dead and fell out naturally, it exhibits the telltale symptoms of shrunken root and frayed, broomlike ends. Cut hairs have sheared ends if done by scissors, or chisel-shaped if a razor was the trimming instrument. (In days past, the nature of the cut was a hint as to the sex of the donor, but not today.) Hair from a bludgeoned victim may have crushed and splintered shafts.

Since the emergence of nuclear physics, considerable effort has been directed toward techniques which would permit the "individualization" of hair, so that an identification can be made that is as conclusive as a fingerprint.

One apparent star appeared on the forensic horizon when neutron-activation analysis was directed toward hair identification. With only a few million dollars and a captive neutron pile, scientists theorized, it might be possible to analyze a single hair in such detail that its entire life history would be revealed. Since each of us lives in an environment which is singular and unique, it was reasoned that any particular lifestyle would be reflected in the growth structure of our hair. Thus, the woman who had Wheaties and rye toast today, bacon and eggs tomorrow, and listened to the music of Brahms would possess different enzymes, produce varying proteins, and develop a crowning glory like no other female.

Some precedent exists for such Buck Rogers logic. In the year 1840 Marie Lafarge undertook a campaign to sever relationships with her husband. It commenced with a gift of arsenic-spiced cake, which she sent to him in Paris. This irritated him, but not to the point of fatality. Whereupon she put the poor man to bed and systematically fed him arsenic-laced food until he finally obliged her and died.

Regrettably, her ploy was eight years too late, since one James Marsh had spoiled her game by discovering a way to detect arsenic in 1832. Sure enough, it was found that arsenic loved to settle in the hair.

From this humble beginning, the forensic ability to detect poisons in the system has grown increasingly sophisticated—to the point that only recently it was found that Napoleon was treated to arsenic tidbits during his terminal years on Saint Helena. Medicines of the time were impure and frequently contained trace amounts of arsenic, so the doctoring may not have been deliberate. No doubt the poison did nothing to insure Napoleon's longevity, so history may be incorrect in attributing his death, on May 5, 1821, solely to cancer.

Chapter 9

The concept of neutron-activation analysis is relatively simple, even if its execution is complex. Expose any object to the swirling flux of a neutron-generating atomic pile and the smallest imaginable traces of any element become detectable.

All radioactive elements have a known half-life, which means that time it takes for one-half of the sample to be flung away through radioactivity. This half-life ranges from one ten-billionth of a second for subatomic particles produced in nuclear research to four and a half billion years in the case of uranium.

When exposed to a radioactive source of neutrons, our old friend arsenic becomes radioactive itself. This produces some ten forms of arsenic, ranging in weight from 70 on the elemental scale to 79, with half-lives from 52 minutes to 265 days. Arsenic 76 has a half-life of 26½ hours and starts returning beta ray emissions, after irradiation, at three specific energy levels. If these energy levels are present, and if in 26½ hours there is a distinct loss in the quantity of the emissions by one-half—bonanza—that's arsenic!

By means of sophisticated channel counters, the assorted ingredients of a given sample are extractable on a qualitative basis—arsenic, sodium, bismuth, and so on. Elements can be quantified by including standards which have shared the neutron flux with the sample being tested. Thus, if there are two thousand clicks from the known arsenic and only five hundred from the unknown sample, it may be reasoned that the amount present is one-quarter that of the standard.

The only problem with neutron analysis and the personalization of hair is that it doesn't work very well. After a first flush of enthusiasm, during the course of which a couple of gentlemen went to jail, it was agreed that the technique works better with nonorganic materials, such as the lead and antimony detection of the murderer's hands discussed in Chapter 10.

Surprisingly, the drawing board has recently produced another technique using an entirely different principle, which comes one step further toward the specificity goal. This method was developed by Dr. Peter Jones of the Aerospace Corporation, so it is another dividend of space technology.

Most of us have observed luminescence resulting from a beam of black light—ultraviolet radiation—produced by a low-pressure mercury lamp. Frequently used in theatrical productions, and a must for exciting display of many mineral specimens, the black light arouses photons in the visible spectrum for some thrillingly beautiful color effects.

Black light is an old friend of the criminalist, since it helps ferret out invisible materials such as semen, urine, and certain laundry marks.

Dr. Jones's method uses a high-pressure Xenon lamp to produce intense ultraviolet emissions. The UV beam is screened for selected wavelengths by a device called a monochrometer.

Two phenomena may occur from UV radiation. The first, fluorescence, is a glowing reaction of extremely short duration, decaying in .00000001 second. The second, phosphorescence, may last slightly longer, with a decay time of 0.000001 second. Or it may linger for several seconds.

Choosing a single input wavelength, the scientist measures the entire UV and visible spectrum of emitted light, for fluorescence, phosphorescence, and the length of decay time for each phenomenon. Repeating this procedure for each segment of the input spectrum produces a mass of highly individualized data.

Hair is protein and contains three principal amino acids that fluoresce and phosphoresce—phenylalanine, tyrosine, and tryptophane. Researchers into chemistry of hair tell us it is very sensitive to diet, atmosphere, exposure to sun, and other environmental factors, all of which affect hydrogen bonding. Early work in the field indicates that as long as the relative lifestyle continues pretty much the same, so will the content of the hair. One experiment with fifty individuals showed consistent ability to identify the particular hair owner every time. The tests take only two minutes each and can use a length of hair as short as one-half inch, preferably of the root end, since it offers best replication of results.

While correct determination in one out of fifty is not exactly as individualized as fingerprint identification, still the technique offers much future promise. In its present level of development, it could serve as an excellent screening test, if only for elimination of a suspect.

In too many localities, evidence is turned in to the crime lab with only the sketchiest accompanying information. In hair diameter comparison, it is particularly important that the examiner be as familiar as possible with all aspects of the case. In one rape case, the examiner was able to find identical similarity in all features of the evidence and exemplar hair save in diameter, the evidence hair being only half the thickness of that secured from the suspect.

Before eliminating the possibility of match, the criminalist checked with the investigator. Yes, there had been a tremendous struggle, with the girl fighting valiantly. She tried to discourage her attacker by tugging at his hair. In the course of the struggle she finally pulled the hair out in a clump. Then the rapist cut her throat with his switchblade knife and fled, leaving the lock of hair still clutched in the girl's fist.

The criminalist experimented with the exemplar hair. Under severe stress, the hair stretched. Remeasured, it now was very close to the diameter of the evidence hair.

While human hairs have occupied our spotlight, those of other species can be invaluable as evidence. The allegation that the hair lodged under a suspect vehicle in a fatal hit-and-run case was really that of a rabbit proved the driver's undoing. Not only was the blood singularly *not* rabbit; it turned out that in this case the victim had been the unfortunate carrier of two very rare scalp conditions which had never before been known to occur together on one human scalp. Exit rabbit alibi, enter a long jail term.

Animal fur as well as its blood is frequently claimed for alibi. Serology and microscopic examination of the suspected fibers make or break such an alibi with ease.

In a recent Canadian case, police arrived at the scene of a car crash to find a smashed car, a broken pole, and two quite inebriated gentlemen who, bystanders said, had emerged from the vehicle immediately following the accident. Each claimed the other had been driving.

Examination of the vehicle showed a small tuft of hair clinging to the broken windshield on the driver's side. Comparison of the hair from the two passengers instantly eliminated one candidate. Since the tuft quite matched the other's hair, he reluctantly admitted he must have been the driver, although he still wasn't entirely sure.

In addition to hair fibers and their frequent exchange in crimes involving physical assault, the enormous family of textile fibers contribute substantially to the arsenal of tools available to the criminalist. While detection and use is minuscule in most of the country, the likelihood is extremely great that physical contact with other individuals, points of entry, vehicles, and the crime scene itself will produce a fortuitous transfer of fibers from the criminal to the crime scene and vice versa. The trick is to find them, identify them, and connect them with the criminal.

This phase of criminalistics fills libraries of reference materials as well as scholarly texts on the differences among the tens of thousands of different fibers and fabrics found today.

Fabric evidence can almost rise to the jigsaw fit league when crime scene evidence is mated with evidence found on the suspect. Given exact fit of threads of different length, by color, type of material, and twist of thread, and little doubt remains that the torn pieces once were one. Fabric patterns, imprinted on entry sill or indelibly impressed on a bumper or other part of a vehicle make impressive evidence in burglary or hit-and-run cases.

Fabric dyes provide another source of identification. While enormous quantities of fabric are produced, there may be minute and measurable variables between dye batches to help clinch a case.

Criminalists continue research aimed at improving the evidentiary value of fibers, with emphasis on hair. The Contra Costa crime lab recently developed a simple technique for hair reproduction which permits much higher photographic magnification than is possible in ordinary microscopy because of depth-of-field problems.

The layman encounters this law of optics when he tries to get a nice clear picture of Aunt Martha's face while simultaneously keeping a sharp image of the top of the Empire State Building in the background. Since the larger the magnification, the narrower the field of sharp focus, microphotographs of hair scale detail always pose a problem.

This California crime lab found that the coating liquid

enclosed with black-and-white Polaroid film can be spread on a microscope slide and the hair pressed into the quick-drying transparent material. In half a minute, the hair is gently pulled from the casting plastic, leaving a perfect impression of its scale pattern, which can be flattened out and magnified many times more than could be done with photos of the original hair, since there no longer is a depth-of-field difficulty.

A liquor store was stuck up by a single armed bandit wearing a silk stocking mask. The investigators found such a mask in the immediate vicinity. The victim was reasonably sure that the robber was a young black, but he could describe only the clothing and build of the robber, since his face was distorted by the stocking mask.

A short while later, a young black man was arrested nearby. He was flustered at being interrogated, but vehemently denied any connection with the robbery.

Before the days of criminalistics, the principal evidence would have been eyewitness identification. Given a bad track record—particularly a previous arrest for suspicion of armed robbery—and the suspect usually would end up charged with the offense.

In this case, the suspect was brought back to the liquor store to see if the victim could identify him. This very process inevitably superimposed the suspect's face over the victim's memory of the robber. The victim looked over the trembling suspect for several seconds before saying, "That's him, all right." The frightened youth was on his way to jail.

Under the circumstances, the liquor clerk can hardly be blamed for making this quick identification, confused as he was by his own fright and passion over the very real danger always present in armed robbery.

The next day the clerk was asked to come to the police station. There the suspect was placed in a line-up, and the victim was asked to pick out the suspect from several other individuals. With last night's memory still fresh, he had no difficulty in reenforcing his identification of the horrified suspect.

The travesty of too many line-ups is that no care is taken to insure that the group is even remotely similar in appearance, as we mentioned before. This situation came to legal crisis in California when one John Caruso, who was six feet one inch tall and who weighed 238 pounds, was fingered in a line-up with four other men who were each a hundred pounds lighter and a head shorter. The California Supreme Court rendered a 1968 judgment voiding this practice, but this ruling is not binding on the other 49 states.

After the second identification, the suspect was hustled back. to jail while the legal machinery ground along which would charge him with armed robbery.

Fortunately for justice, the stocking mask had been turned in to the crime lab. Under the microscope the criminalists discovered a single human hair clinging inside the silk stocking. At a greater power, it became clear that the hair was Negroid. Comparison with exemplar hair from the suspect showed general similarities. So the suspect was still on the hook. Had the class characteristics been significantly different, the microscopic examination would have cleared him.

As it was, since both the immediate postrobbery identification and later line-up recognition were positive, there remained only one possible avenue of escape before the suspect was on his way to the penitentiary. This was a newly discovered technique which offered the promise that, in some cases, hair could be tested for blood type. It was a slim chance, but this criminalist was determined to give it a try. In common with most scientists, he distrusted the ancient practice of sole reliance on eyewitness identification. This test might add another element indicating the guilt of the suspect. Or there was the remote possibility that it might prove him innocent.

The criminalist regarded the single Negroid hair with the utmost seriousness. The test he was about to undertake was certain to be destructive. Whenever possible, criminalists prefer examining methods which leave at least a portion of the evidence for reexamination by an *amicus curiae*—friend of the court—if original test results are challenged during the trial.

Prior to the critical test, the criminalist made photomicrographs of the hair, showing each of its physical qualities. He also measured the outside diameter and thickness of each of the layers. Finally, he counted the scales in a given area.

Now he carefully placed the hair between two highly polished steel plates. The steel sandwich was inserted in a hydraulic press, and the pressure increased to twelve thousand pounds per square inch. This crushing action breaks down the stout hair structure, making it possible for typing factors to interact with the serums used in blood typing.

After crushing, the hair was carefully divided into two samples and the normal procedure for blood typing commenced.

The tests worked! The ABO blood type of the hair's owner was determined positively. Most important, it was *not* the type of the suspect in custody, who was promptly released.

A short time later, another suspect was located. *His* blood type proved to be the same as the evidence hair. Confronted with this positive comparison, he confessed. Once more, forensic science helped protect the innocent and convict the guilty.

From the time Lady Macbeth cried, "Out damned spot," until the present, literature has been pervaded with the notion that bloodstains can't be removed. But this is not so except when dealing with very old stains. Many of the most frantic efforts to eradicate blood stains do fail only because of the emotional atmosphere likely to prevail following a brutal killing. The labor expended in attempting concealment of these damning spots ranges from repeated scrubbings and bleaching to covering with paint. And even today a criminal occasionally tries to explain away the stains by claiming them from a butchered animal.

In the early annals of crime detection it was a blundering criminal indeed who forced his wrongdoings into attention. Instances abound in which a spouse lost a number of mates to mysterious death, indulging in such blatant behavior as placing poison in the victim's cup in the presence of witnesses. Yet, even then, the muddied minds of the observers were slow to suspicion. In one classic case, a murderess choked half-a-dozen children to death, being caught virtually in the act in a few cases. Not until the pattern became undeniably obvious was she finally brought to account.

So it was with blood identification until the turn of the century. For every blood-dripping assassin held accountable, a hundred escaped scot free. Not until the emerging forensic sciences added chemicals such as benzidine and luminol to the detective's tool bag was real progress made in unearthing buried traces of blood. It took companion discoveries by biological scientists to develop blood analysis into the extraordinary tool it has since become.

With no pun intended, 1901 was a red letter year in the field of forensic serology. On February 7, Paul Uhlenhuth announced a method for determining whether blood was of human origin—the so-called biological precipitan test. Not only could the test be used for fresh blood; it also served to identify the human origin of dried bloodstains, "no matter how small the traces were," according to Uhlenhuth.

The second major discovery that year was the outgrowth of medical tragedy, when pioneering blood transfusions were attempted, with death resulting for over half the patients. Autopsy revealed that death had been caused by sudden coagulation when the donor's blood intermingled with the patient's.

This quality of agglutination was pursued by Dr. Karl Landsteiner. His work, published November 14, 1901, ultimately won him a Nobel prize for medicine. It also laid the foundation for identification of bloodstains at crime scenes.

Dr. Leone Lattes applied Landsteiner's findings in a 1915 criminal case and developed a method which was employed in criminalistics for many years. His textbook on the topic soon came into international use.

By the 1930s the Lattes tests were even further refined by the work of Dr. Frank Holzer, who developed the absorption-inhibition testing method.

From these early beginnings the art and science of blood typing have grown immensely. Landsteiner's discovery of the basic ABO system at last made it possible to eliminate, if not identify, individuals suspected of being involved in crimes where blood was spilled.

With the passing years numerous additional factors have been discovered in typing wet blood. In one of the favorite cases of the chief serologist for the FBI, a bank robber was wounded in an exchange of gunfire and managed to deposit a fairly large pool of his blood on the floor of the bank before making his getaway.

This was criminalistic break number one. The amount of lost blood indicated the robber would need surgical attention before too long. And the wet blood offered the serologist opportunity for much greater depth in typing than ordinary dried bloodstains afford.

Break number two was the relatively rare combination of factors detectable in the robber's blood.

Starting near the robbery scene and spreading out as time passed, authorities notified hospitals and medical authorities to be alert for a gunshot wound with the robber's particular combination of rare blood groupings.

This combination of evidence was strongly suggestive that any patient meeting these specifications would be the wanted bank robber. One did, and he was!

At this moment there are something in excess of five hundred identifiable blood groups and subgroups, creating the hope that in time to come, the state of the art will permit replacement of our social security numbers with our blood types.

However, few serology experts expect to live long enough to realize that possibility. In the past, even ABO typing was delicate, calling for exquisite care and sensitive technique. Most of the problem stemmed from the difficulty of obtaining adequate antiserums. As recently as World War II, more than fifteen percent of the typings for our military personnel were found to be in error. Happily, in actual surgical situations, blood was tested for compatibility. In compatibility tests one introduces the donor's cells to the patient's serum and observes microscopically for clotting, since even blood of the same type may not be compatible. In addition, commercial serum sources have greatly improved, lessening the likelihood of typing error.

But dry bloodstains are something else.

Chapter 10

The initial step, origin testing, seeks to determine the species of creature that made the stain. Let the suspect cry "animal blood," and the criminalist needs to affirm or deny the alibi. The test for this determination depends on nature's boundless ability to repel invaders of any biological system.

Serums for such testing are produced by injecting the body of a laboratory animal, such as a rabbit, with blood of domestic and wild beasts likely to be chosen for alibi. The animals run the gamut from aardvark to zebra, with all the likely beasties in between.

The injected blood causes the laboratory animal immediately to produce substances known as antibodies. Most of these antibodies will cause clumping or agglutination, when mixed with cells from the blood of the same animal strain.

Sometimes a false positive reaction occurs between the agglutinins of the serum and the cells of the blood under examination—wherein lies the rub. A failsafe antiserum for deer blood is the toughest to make. This is because all antiserums react (although more weakly) with closely related species. In forty-eight out of fifty attempts to produce deer antiserum, the material will respond with false positive clumping with nearly related creatures. The FBI, for example, still produces its own antiserums, simply because no commercial source is able to meet its severe standards.

In preliminary testing of bloodstains, the benzidine-hydrogen peroxide technique is used with a minute speck of the suspected stain. In the words of one noted serologist, "If you can see it under a low-power microscope, you can test it."

A positive benzidine reaction leads to further screening procedures to see if the initial reaction could have been caused by some agent other than blood. Both the hemochromogen or Teichmann's hemin tests are quite specific for hemoglobin, the factor which is common to all bloods, human and animal, and which imparts the characteristic reddish color.

Satisfied that the substance is blood, the biological searchlight is now directed toward the determination of species orgin. The questioned blood is placed in successively diluted solutions, which are compared with antiserums of each of the possible species. A couple of drops of the thinned blood are added to antiserums, using tiny test tubes the length of an ordinary wooden match and only slightly larger in diameter.

If of the same animal type—human animals included—the biological warfare at the junction of the liquids, or interface, produces a cloudy precipitation. This biological precipitan test quickly provides the means to verify animal source, or to blast such an alibi.

As the space age accelerated miniaturization, criminalistics increasingly moved into the world of the microscope to practice its magic. Evidence totally overlooked in the past now generates important solutions with the help of microchemical and micro-physical methods.

One fascinating serological procedure coats a microscope slide with a thin layer of agar gel, the same material used to grow bacterial cultures. A blood speck no larger than the shaft of a straight pin is placed on the solidified agar gel. Slightly larger reservoirs are cored in the gel about three pin-thicknesses away, surrounding the blood like the cardinal points of a compass. Microdrops of appropriate serums are placed in these minicups, the slide moistened with distilled water, and nature allowed to take her course.

In about twenty-four hours, the miniature warring troops span the minichasm in the direction of the antiserum of the same origin. Where the battle is joined, a thin threadlike line appears in the gel, at right angles to the line of travel, giving cloudlike proof of their common source. This technique has been used to establish the nature of bloodstains over nineteen years old.

Confirmation of the human origin of blood is but a first step in a process where blood typing becomes increasingly valuable with the identification of each blood group. First in the testing sequence comes determination of the basic ABO grouping.

Holzer's absorption-inhibition method, so welcome to detective agencies in 1930, is based on the blood's absorption of the antiserum, which is then unable to react with known blood cells. In practice, the sample is successively diluted until it fails to react with the antiserum. The next stronger dilution is then divided into two parts to which anti-A serum and anti-B serum are added separately. Typing is arrived at from the following table:

#1 (A cells added)	#2 (B cells added)	Blood Group
Clump	Clump	O
No clump	Clump	A
Clump	No clump	B
No clump	No clump	AB

In most locations the later absorption-elution technique has supplanted the absorption-inhibition, since it is some one hundred times more sensitive. In absorption-elution, the antiserums are added to divided portions of the stain solution and allowed to absorb. The solutions are then thoroughly washed to free them of any nonabsorbed antiserums.

Now the samples are heated to a temperature of 56 degrees centigrade. At this heat the antiserums break loose from the stain, and can be used to agglutinate known types of cells.

In many individuals, blood type can be determined from other body fluids. In theory this promises much serological potential. In practice, numerous obstacles must be overcome.

Perspiration stains fire forensic fancy when bloodstains are unavailable, as when the criminal leaves behind some article of his clothing. Testing the clothes may, in fact, provide valuable investigative leads, but is less helpful in nailing the criminal to the scene. This is because nobody sweats selectively. The armpits, star of TV commercials, are the main culprits, unless inhibited by your failsafe deodorant. One might predict that a fair majority of criminals involved in blood spilling would forget to protect their dainties before charging off to the bludgeoning. The catch is that most people sweat all over if they sweat at all. Palms also moisten and forearms glisten. The amount of perspiration differs only in degree.

What's more, there's a possibility that other substances in or on the garment, such as dye or detergent, might produce a false negative reaction in typing.

Which brings us, head-on, to another forensic must, and the reason perspiration testing is not very helpful. Before any stain analysis can be considered certain, identical testing must be done on the background on which the stain was found. The background must *not* react to the test before the stain reaction can be affirmatively accepted. Such control testing usually demonstrates the ubiquity of perspiration. It is hard to find a spot on a garment that does not have at least a little perspiration, so the background material can never be isolated. Thus, sweat is not generally useful in deciding blood type except for investigative leads.

Semen is something else. Not only are seminal stains important evidence in sexual crimes to establish *that* element, but the stains are excellent for determining blood typing because the strength, or titer, of the antigens in seminal fluid is exceptionally high. Such typings in sexual attack cases may give immediate investigative leads which both protect the innocently accused, and strengthen the case against the guilty.

Authorities agree that forcible rape is the most under-reported major crime in the nation. Embarrassed and ashamed, the victim suffers the likelihood of leering interrogation further complicating the physical and psychic trauma. The opposite side of this coin is that accusations of rape frequently are unfounded; for example, when the inept prostitute, having failed to collect in advance, discovers her cohabitor had thought his fun was free. Nor is the cry of rape necessarily directed at the guilty individual, even though the forcible attack was genuine enough. In rape cases, the intense emotional factors add substantially to the usual unreliability of eyewitness identification. Considerable experimentation with eyewitnesses shows that recollection of a traumatic situation will contain elements of pure invention in at least fifty percent of the cases.

One such incident involved the positive identification of a rape suspect who insisted he was innocent. Vaginal swabbings from the victim established the presence of type A secretions. Both the victim and her accused assailant, however, were blood group O and incapable of producing A type secretions. So the unjustly accused man was released from suspicion and the search continued for the real rapist.

Saliva, under the right conditions, yields blood type, particularly on the fine-textured rice paper of nonfiltered cigarettes. Such plain cigarettes, smoked in a normal manner, provide the best opportunity for typing residual saliva.

The just-right amount of spit needed is a matter of delicate balance. The sloppy smoker louses up possible testing by introducing an intermingling of spit and tobacco juice. Absorptive tips soak up the saliva so that typing become impossible. But given the right combination of ingredients in the saliva, the criminal smoker may well leave evidence which will help detect his blood type.

With secretors—some eighty-two percent of the population—the basic blood-typing factors may well be found in most of the other biological materials, such as ear wax, urine, even hair. Blood groups in hair are not related to secretor status—ostensibly, all individuals except O have blood group substances in their hair, although much more needs to be learned about this phenomenon. With dead victims, the list can be augmented with tissue specimens, bile, and spinal fluid.

From a criminalistic point of view, however, blood is still the best substance, although the specimens ending in the crime lab may literally be too small for the eye to see.

Finding the blood, particularly where there is only suspicion of foul deed, sometimes proves to be a considerable challenge. Where location of possible spots is reasonably certain, tests such as the ultrasensitive benzidine reagent still are used to narrow the search. When larger areas require examination, spraying with luminol produces fluorescence in contact with residual blood so that detailed examination may proceed. The luminol tests must be carried out in total darkness, which limits its potential use, but under the right conditions it may save hours of search.

More commonly, however, the problem is not discovering the blood but proving whose blood it is—or isn't.

The woman freely admitted stabbing her man, but she claimed it was self-defense. Her deft knifemanship had severed the victim's aorta, with resultant profuse bleeding. The woman's dress was drenched in blood, creating some elements of doubt in the investigator's mind concerning her protestations of self-defense.

But she stuck to her story. The beast had creamed her, she claimed, before she had ever thought of the nearby knife. What else could she do in resisting his brutal assault? First, he had smashed her nose until it gushed blood. Then he hung a couple on her jaw. When he lunged at her for the third time, she snatched up the knife and let him have it.

The blood on her dress, she said, was her own, from the nosebleed. The minute she saw her attacker slump from the slash across his neck, she ran away.

The dubious investigator brought her clothing to the crime lab, to confirm or deny her story.

Blood typing of the dead man, the woman, and the blood on her dress was of little initial help. The woman and the man were both type A, as are forty-five percent of the population. But the lab didn't stop there. They attempted a seldom-used technique to try and measure the Kell factor, one of some sixty factors which can be tested for in wet blood but which have resisted detection in dried bloodstains until the most recent times.

The test succeeded. The woman and the dead man had different Kell factors. The blood on the woman's dress matched hers in Kell factor, but didn't match his. Her self-defense alibi was corroborated, and she was released.

Typing from dried blood beyond the common ABO groupings is far from easy, and few crime labs routinely dig more deeply. The first additional blood groups, M and N, vex and confound because they are difficult to identify and sometimes produce misleading findings. In any case, a high degree of proficiency is called for.

Paternity cases are evaluated with in-depth blood typing from liquid samples. A recent report in *Medicine, Science and the Law* comments: "However, an investigation which does not include ABO, MNS, Rh (D,C,c,E,e) and at least three or four of the other systems, cannot be considered adequate."

So much for liquid bloods. It's a different ball game with dried stains. Fortunately for justice, the following case occurred within the jurisdiction of the only laboratory in the United States using an AutoAnalyzer capable of testing dried blood for the Rh factors.

The confrontation, an extension of a feud of long-standing, took place during the evening. The two men started quarreling within earshot of the victim's friends, who were waiting in his car.

As the prosecution later reconstructed the case, the verbal fight heated up. The defendant was carrying a gun, and several witnesses who saw him just before the showdown were willing to swear the gun was on his person. He drew the gun and the victim grappled with him, seeking to prevent its use, but one shot was fired without damage.

Then the victim attempted to run away.

The defendant raced after him, firing one additional shot which struck the victim in the back. The bullet entered the victim's leather jacket in the back, struck a rib, tore up through the lung, struck another rib, then exited, to disappear forever.

The victim, bleeding profusely from the chest and hemorrhaging from the mouth, staggered to his waiting car, collapsed on the back seat, pleading with his friends to take him to a hospital.

The assailant followed the victim to the car, climbed in the rear seat after him, and acted as though he were going to shoot him again, but was persuaded to leave by the other occupants.

A short time later the victim died.

In court, the defense story, not surprisingly, offered a different version.

First, the defense claimed, there really wasn't any gun belonging to the defendant, certainly not at the time of the quarrel, in which the victim had been the aggressor.

The prosecution countered with the results of analysis of swabbings of the defendant's hands when he was arrested, using neutron-activation analysis. This technique has replaced the discredited paraffin test, wherein melted paraffin is poured over the hands and stripped off when solidified. Using wet chemical techniques the paraffin can then be tested for nitrates, but this method is no longer believed valid because of the almost universal distribution of nitrates.

In neutron-activation analysis the sample is exposed to neutron bombardment in an atomic pile. This creates secondary radiation in the sample, which can then be evaluated by techniques of extreme sensitivity to trace amounts. When first announced, neutron-activation analysis underwent a flurry of promise in hair identification, which it failed to live up to. But for items in the heavy metal category, it has no equal in sensitivity of detection.

In this case, the neutron-activation analysis showed definite traces of barium and antimony, primer constituents which escape in the exhaust blast when hand guns are fired.

The defense then changed its tune. There had indeed been a gun, which had been fired in the course of a struggle between the defendant and the victim. The bullet had bounded off a nearby wall and returned to enter the victim's back with the sad result.

Expert testimony was presented which proved conclusively the impossibility of a ricochet returning as claimed. Other tests showed the gun had been at least several inches from the victim's jacket, since there was no powder residue on the leather. In addition, the defense's allegation that the gun had fired accidentally in the course of a struggle was demonstrably wrong. The human wrist can bend only so far, and in a face-to-face struggle, it is patently impossible to turn the wrist sufficiently to fire directly through the victim as the defense claimed.

Now came the pivotal point: "I never came near the victim after the shooting," alleged the defendant. "It's ridiculous to charge that I followed him into his car and threatened him further."

The defendant's story deserved honest consideration. As we've pointed out before, cases of unreliable eyewitness accounts are legion. Without solid physical evidence proving that the defendant had followed his victim into the automobile, the story of the witnesses was challengeable.

Which brings us back to the blood. There was blood aplenty—in the car, slathered over the back of the driver's seat, soaked into the rear upholstery behind that seat.

Far less conspicuous, an ultrathin stain had been found on the sleeve of the defendant's waterproof coat, another slightly larger stain on the front of the coat. Because of the repellent coat, only the slightest traces of blood remained. These, the prosecution alleged, had been transferred to the defendant's coat as he climbed after his victim in the back seat of the car.

So, once again, it was up to the crime lab to develop proof that the coat bloodstain had come from the victim, and the third lie would be shown up, clinching the murder charge.

All of the bloods involved were tested—defendant's, victim's, and the ultrathin layers on the coat. Once again there was a standoff.

All bloods were of exactly the same ABO type! Another variable had to be found.

Infant mortality, particularly stillbirth, seemed largely a matter of cruel fate until the twentieth century. Even with the growth of modern medicine, the occasional stillborn infant whose blood seemed to have simply decomposed was considered an insoluble mystery.

After Karl Landsteiner emigrated to New York in 1921, with the help of the Rockefeller Foundation he continued his trail-blazing work in the study of agglutination. This work was ultimately recognized in 1930 with the awarding of a Nobel prize. Many of the subsequent developments in the field of serology were discoveries of students and associates of Landsteiner. One such associate was Alexander Wiener, whose interests extended beyond the pure research, to which Landsteiner confined himself, into practical administration.

In 1935 Wiener was appointed head of the Blood Transfusion Unit of the Jewish Hospital of Brooklyn, where he became increasingly involved with serological experiments and with the practical use of bloodstains in criminal matters.

One of the components Landsteiner had discovered in his blood research was the M factor. In seeking to produce an anti-M serum, Wiener and Landsteiner used Rhesus monkeys whose blood contained a factor which corresponded to human M. The usual antibody technique was applied: Rhesus monkey blood was injected into rabbits in anticipation that the rabbits would develop an anti-M serum, which could then be used for M determination in typing human blood.

Surprisingly, the new serum not only clotted blood with M

. 111 .

factors, but clumped red blood cells that lacked the M factor. Still another blood element had been discovered, called Rh after the Rhesus monkeys.

Further work showed that about eighty-five percent of the population had blood with the Rh factor. Such people were said to be Rh positive; those lacking it, Rh negative. When an Rh positive man sired a child with a Rh negative woman, he passed on his positive quality to the offspring. In some cases, generally after several pregnancies, the Rh negative mother's blood started producing Rh antibodies, which fought with the blood of the unborn infant, resulting in coagulated blood and the death of the baby.

The goal of increasingly sophisticated blood typing is the greater ability to match or eliminate crime scene bloodstains and suspects. In the ABO system distribution throughout the population of each type is as follows:

Type	Distribution (%)
A	45%
O	42%
B	10%
AB	3%

Obviously, the AB type blood improves odds in fingering a suspect. Add the additional groups M and N, and the odds improve. Still, identifying M and N factors from dried bloods is quite tricky, so these qualities seldom are used in forensics.

The Rh subgroupings opened up a whole new avenue in forensic potential. Rh factors are, as other blood aspects, genetic in origin, with one set of predisposing genes inherited from each parent. Like the traits of blue eyes, skin color, or curly hair, the various elements of the blood are individualistic and unchangeable. Given enough detectable subgroupings, the many combinations offer exciting possibilities of blood identification as accurate as fingerprints.

Rh factors are classified by the designations D,d, C,c, and E,e. With random selection, three alternate combinations exist for each pair of factors. A particular blood, for example, may be DD,

Dd, or dd. Mathematically, the possible variations of subgroups is three to the third power, or 27. Practically, there's no present test for the d constituent. Even so, the Rh factors add another eighteen groups to blood analysis.

Electrophoresis, the latest analysis method just on the forensic horizon, promises immensely greater subdivision of blood factors. In the London Metropolitan Police Forensic Laboratory, Brian J. Culliford, senior principal scientific officer, is one of the leading serologists in the world. At present, routine analysis of a dozen protein factors expands the scope of blood examination in this operation, with enormous hope for ever-increasing possibilities as research continues.

Electrophoresis is based on the varying rates of the migration of protein molecules under the influence of an electric current. In combination with highly complicated chemical methods, which accelerate the electrophoretic movement of some molecules and impede others, the relatively heavy protein molecules are physically separated under electric prodding. Once apart, analytical techniques permit identification of hundreds of these blood proteins.

Until recently, typing dried blood for Rh factors was virtually impossible from a practical point of view. Too many steps were necessary in the enormously complicated procedures for the crime lab even to give it consideration.

In the meantime, a piece of marvelously complicated laboratory equipment called the AutoAnalyzer was developed by the Technicon Corporation. The first report of the adaption of the AutoAnalyzer to the detection of blood-group factors was made by R. Douglas and J. M. Stavely, working in New Zealand. Margaret Pereira, working in England, developed a number of improvements to increase the sensitivity of the instrumental method, and reported successful determination of all the Rh factors in bloodstains.

In most jurisdictions in the United States, any murder case which hinged on blood identification beyond ABO and MN would have been stymied when those factors proved identical in the bloodstains involved. In a handful of cases there had been determination of other factors, even of Rh, but the inherent difficulties of such laborious manual analyses discouraged virtually all of the crime labs from even attempting such analyses from dried bloodstains.

Returning to the waiting defendant, it was fortunate for forensics that this particular murder took place in Contra Costa County in northern California, the one location in the country possessing an AutoAnalyzer. Thanks to a grant from the Law Enforcement Assistance Administration administered by the California Council on Criminal Justice, Contra Costa's crime lab had already painstakingly evaluated the AutoAnalyzer, verifying its accuracy in the enormously delicate detection of the Rh factors.

The AutoAnalyzer is an intricate maze of pumps, reagent dispensers, reaction and settling coils, and other analyzing devices complicated enough to bring joy to the heart of a Rube Goldberg. Peristalic pumps shove the samples through the system, which adds antiserums here, scrubs it there. Agitating, agglutinating, and precipitating processing affect the swirling liquid as it moves through a precise array of procedures controlled by the fully automated machinery. Ultimately, a colorimeter activates a recording pen, which reports the findings of this amazing instrumentation.

Meticulously, the criminalist prepared the device for its first major operational test. At last the five antiserums were in place in their holding cups, waiting for the elaborate preparation of the bloodstains before they were added to the AutoAnalyzer. Now the instrumentation took over. Fluids surged around dizzying coils, reacting with the antiserums, agglutinating on meeting their opposite number, and at last dropping to the bottom of a settling coil to be analyzed and counted in the final steps of the process.

Finally came the critical moment, the recorder tracing, which held the decision in its moving pen.

The AutoAnalyzer came through in the clutch. The Rh factors differed between the suspect and the victim. And the blood on the murderer's coat exactly matched that of the victim in Rh factors.

Confronted with this evidence, the defendant admitted his pursuit of the victim into the car. The allegations of the defense were proven false.

The jury found the defendant guilty of murder.

Chapter 11

Since the days when Eugène François Vidocq commanded the French Sûreté, the police have relied heavily on memory for identifying criminals. Vidocq's own men were selected for their recall of known criminals. With such a tradition, it is little wonder the police had high regard for eyewitness testimony.

Without the ability to use alternate methods, little choice was open to them. Occasionally, the suspect would be apprehended with the loot still in his possession. More often, however, he would be known in the community as a violent lout, or a chap with taking ways. So when a crime occurred, it seemed only natural that the witnesses would finger the more churlish members of their group. Psychology had not yet discovered that all of us see the world through filters which distort the facts according to our own peculiar longings, fears, and prejudices.

With the growth of forensics, the possibility of physical evidence back-up ought to have lessened the police's reliance on eyewitnesses. When eyewitness testimony exists, however, the old failure to search for physical evidence persists to this day.

Numerous studies establish beyond question that there's less than a fifty-fifty chance of correctly remembering trivia after a couple of days. In one experiment, children were shown postage stamps of various colors and sizes. For several successive days, they were quizzed on what they'd seen. Their memory proved increasingly incorrect. If we consider the passion and terror involved when eyewitnesses are present at a major crime, the wonder is that they are ever correct. In spite of all this, the eyewitness is given as much credence as in the past in most police circles, and the physical evidence search, which could prove the truth conclusively, is almost totally neglected.

In a recent case in Miami Beach, a gang of holdup men forced entry into a bank and held four employees at gun-point while they proceeded to loot the premises. The robbers were not disguised, and the captive bank employees had ample opportunity to memorize their features during the considerable period the holdup was in progress. During the holdup, the leader of the group vaulted over a four-foot counter, his ungloved fingers pressing on the top as he easily surmounted the barrier.

When the police arrived, the terrified employees gave full description of five bandits and excitedly pointed out the counter on which they believed telltale fingerprints might be found. They described the athletic gang leader as "in his forties," even though such physical agility seemed unlikely in most individuals that age.

Fortunately, hidden spy cameras were grinding away during the entire holdup, recording the scene on motion-picture film. While of considerable assistance in identifying bank robbers, these action movies suffer a major drawback—the delay of processing and comparing against mug shots of known bank robbers. Standard practice calls for the films to be shipped to Washington, with as much as two weeks' delay before local police are able to search for the suspects—ample time for the robbers to be long gone.

In this instance, thanks to a grant from the Law Enforcement Assistance Administration, the Miami police department was equipped with a high-speed photoreproduction machine, which can grind out literally hundreds of photocopies in an hour, bypassing ordinary manual darkroom methods.

In short order, the movie film was developed and selected frames enlarged for examination with the help of the speedy copier. What followed illustrates both the valuable help of modern copy techniques and the fallibility of eyewitnesses.

First, there were only four bandits, not the five described in detail by the eyewitnesses. Somewhere during the holdup's progress, the witnesses created a composite image of a nonexistent fifth member of the gang.

Second, the gang leader was actually in his twenties.

Third, even though all four witnesses had been within a few feet of the event, the counter they pointed out as the site of the athletic leap was fifteen feet from the counter over which the bandit actually leapt.

Thanks to the efficient photocopier, hundreds of pictures of the bandits were in the hands of other police agencies within a few hours, together with descriptions which were accurate within an inch as to the height of the robbers. The search was so swift that within a few hours the bandits were in custody and the loot recovered.

One of the most spectacular scientific accomplishments in history was a simple photograph of a woman's hand wearing a gold wedding band. What claimed the attention of the world was the miraculous fact that you could see the bones within the hand.

In 1895 a German physicist named Wilhelm Conrad Roentgen was studying the behavior of a new scientific curiosity called a Crookes tube. In operation the Crookes tube emitted a greenish light. Roentgen wanted to experiment in total darkness, so he covered the Crookes tube with black paper. In the corner of the laboratory lay a piece of cardboard covered with fluorescent barium platinocyanide, which he was using in a completely different experiment. When he turned on the high-voltage switch to the Crookes tube in the completely darkened laboratory, the coated cardboard began glowing. It continued to glow even when a thick book was placed between it and the tube. Only heavy metals like platinum or lead cut off the mysterious rays that caused the crystals to fluoresce.

After several days of enraptured experimentation with this new phenomenon, Roentgen discovered another phenomenon of nature—an irritated wife who came seeking him in the laboratory, demanding to know what he was up to.

By this time, Roentgen had learned that the strange invisible emissions affected photographic film. He instructed Frau Roentgen to place her hand over the package of photographic film, turned out the light, and flipped the switch to the Crookes tube. The resultant photograph, showing bones and opaque wedding ring, is history.

This discovery of these recondite emissions, named X rays by Roentgen, became one of the greatest sensations of any age. More than a thousand articles and books were written on the subject within a year. Laws were passed in countries around the globe prohibiting the use of these prying rays to reveal the female form beneath her outer garments. A London firm did a land-office business peddling impervious unmentionables. Their newspaper ads screamed: "X-ray-proof underwear—no lady safe without it."

Many years were to pass before scientists realized that X rays were yet another phenomenon of the electromagnetic continuum. At the long end of the continuum the waves are called radio and may be several miles from crest to crest. Several types of radio waves continue the progressively shorter wavelengths, including AM radio, short wave, TV, FM radio, and radar. At that point the waves are known as infrared and ultraviolet, and the shortest waves are called X rays and gamma rays, the principal difference between the latter two being that gamma waves have enough energy to interact with atomic nuclei while X rays do not.

X rays are produced in a vacuum tube when the high-energy electrons, originating at the anode end, strike a heavy metal cathode with sufficient force.

Crime labs put the X rays to work in a number of interesting ways. Among the most obvious is inspection of the innards of a suspected bomb to determine how it works and how to defuse it. Another is the examination of a body, before autopsy, to determine the location of any opaque objects such as bullets, broken knife blades, nuts, bolts, nails, and other shrapnel.

The breakthrough scientists who first theorized that solid matter was in fact made up of crystals could only speculate on the internal arrangement of molecules. The nature of molecular interaction seemed to limit the possible shapes of crystals to only seven types. The outside crystalline shape of a number of materials was well-known: diamond, gold, iron, lead, copper, and silver all having cubic crystals, for example, whereas the crystals of tin were tetragonal and magnesium were hexagonal.

The inside crystalline structure, which was like a series of boxes within boxes, could only be the subject of intelligent conjecture until X-ray experimentation commenced. If a material is surrounded with lead, then bombarded with X rays through a small hole in the shielding, the rays scatter through the lattice work of the crystals and emerge to imprint a characteristic pattern on photographic film. The crystallographer is able to identify unknown materials from such a pattern. Called X-ray diffraction, the technique finds its place in criminalistics, providing the substance to be examined is pure enough.

One forensic use, developed recently by the Finnigan Corporation, analyzes the elemental make-up of paint samples. Traditional spectroscopy consumes the material being examined. This technique bombards the samples with X rays, then analyzes the resulting secondary emissions.

In one case the target samples were automobile paints from a suspected hit-and-run car. Evidence and exemplar paint samples were screened with indium foil to permit similar-sized areas to be bombarded with X rays. They were then exposed for one hundred seconds each, with the secondary emissions driven off being analyzed for characteristics peculiar to specific elements.

When the spectra were collected, they were stored in a computer memory bank, then overlapped on the same scale for comparison. At first glance, the graph patterns seemed identical. A closer inspection showed common peaks representing lead, zinc, iron, and titanium. The paint from the victim's car, however, had no strontium, while that from the suspect car did. Furthermore, the victim's paint showed a trace of selenium, which was not present in the paint from the suspect car.

Result: one suspect cleared.

Rays of yet another quality are found between the upper end of the X-ray spectrum and the beginning of that of the ultraviolet. Called Grenz rays, from the German word for borderline radiation, they have proven to have valuable qualities in treating certain medical conditions. After Dr. Gustav Bucky developed equipment to produce and control these Grenz rays, it was possible to take medical advantage of this soft radiation in skin therapy, since the rays penetrate only diseased tissue but do not harm underlying healthy tissues.

Because of this very limited penetration, radiographs can be taken of structures with low atomic weight, impossible with full strength X rays. One of the first practical uses of Grenz rays for the crime lab was high-resolution photos of watermarks in paper.

Another criminalistic use is demonstrated by the case where an underlying message had been obliterated by overwriting. The criminalist first tried ordinary photography with normal lighting; then he tried ultraviolet and infrared illumination and special film. The ink of the overwriting proved opaque to all of these light sources and the mystery remained. Exposed to the soft Grenz ray, the overlying inks disappeared and the message underneath could clearly be seen.

It was also found that under these soft rays the printing on a counterfeit bill disappeared while it remained clearly visible on a genuine bill. It was even possible to detect a watermark on the counterfeit paper which was not present on the real thing.

Many other criminalistic uses have been found for the soft-ray equipment. Among them are identification of difficult finger-prints. When prints are located on multicolored backgrounds that are also absorbent, most fingerprint operators kiss the print goodbye. Using soft rays, a fine lead powder is sprinkled on the area, then the excess gently removed by rocking the paper until the latent image becomes visible. A photo taken with Grenz ray eliminates the confusing background, revealing excellent detail of the fingerprint.

Indented writing on multicolored surfaces had defeated the most skilled photographers because of the impossibility of elim-inating background. When the same lead powder is dusted over the indentations and that remaining on the higher surface care-fully brushed away, the writing stands out under soft rays.

With the addition of Grenz rays, the criminalist developed a whole new arsenal in his attack against crime. Faded or discolored ink can be deciphered. Printing or writing can be restored from charred or burned paper. Altered writing or erasure by chemicals stands out under the soft-ray eye.

Inks can be compared, as can various soilings on paper. Letters can be read within envelopes without breaking the seals—and letter bombs can be detected. In firearms work, the metallic traces surrounding the entrance hole of a bullet in flesh or on fabric stands out like sore thumbs when photographed with the soft rays. The technique can even assist toxicologists by detecting the salts in hair which are the result of poisoning. And the rays read the minute amounts of metal left on the skin from constantly worn jewelry.

In another aspect, contaminants such as sand, glass, splin-ters, and metal shavings and detection of their distribution throughout food products become another kind of duck soup under the probing examination of the Grenz rays. Vegetables that have been sprayed with products containing salts of heavy metals stand out strongly. The interior structure of fabrics or impregnated materials such as the remnants of burnt matches may be investigated. Even the helpful chromatogram may have elevated spots, where climbing materials reached their zenith and can be rendered visible, even if they are colorless.

And, of course, no art expert can operate without the newly discovered Grenz ray as his invaluable partner in detecting forgery.

Until recently, the drawback of X-ray use was the weight of the equipment. Starting at three-hundred pounds, it was scarcely portable, and in many instances the evidence that might benefit by X-ray examination simply could not be brought to the machines.

Moreover, in certain kinds of cases, no one wanted that kind of evidence brought to them—ever. Hospitals, for instance, when asked to X ray overly ripe corpses, will generally refuse because of the health hazard.

The problem was resolved when Peter A. Bucky, the son of Dr. Gustav Bucky who, you will remember, developed the Grenz-ray equipment, created a portable X-ray unit light enough to be carted anywhere. Weighing as little as twenty-three pounds and operating off house current or a portable field generator, the Bucky miniature proved the answer to the X-ray examiner's dream.

Like a restless wave, sources of illicit drugs surge from one portion of the globe to another. For several decades heroin was almost exclusively manufactured in illegal laboratories in France. The pitch of the opium poppy, mother of all of the opiate narcotics, was principally grown in the Middle East, and found its way into France concealed in a multitude of bizarre containers. The shipping cartons ranged from bongo drums, hand luggage, and trunks with false bottoms to the structural beam of a power digger shipped from Israel.

As rapidly as smugglers invent new methods, narcotics agents develop countermeasures. In one recent incident, dogs which have been trained to sniff out illicit drugs detected fifty kilos of heroin hidden in the fenders of a car being shipped across the Mediterranean.

But as fast as local drug officials, working with Interpol, the international cooperative law enforcement organization, can destroy one stratagem for drug smuggling, another takes its place.

In one case, a Swiss banker was keeping questionable company. He spent money with abandon, night-clubbing nine nights out of ten, consorting with known underworld figures. But not until his bank failed was the full weight of suspicion directed toward his activities.

After investigation, he was arrested and spent a number of months in prison before he was finally released because of failing health. Living modestly, apparently a broken man, he was no longer the object of police suspicion. All the while, however, he was master-minding a scheme which was to result in the smuggling of many millions of dollars of heroin into the United States.

His plan was comparatively simple. First, he and his underworld associates entered the food-import business in a big way. They set up a canning factory in Spain and organized a distribution setup, including warehouses in several parts of New York. Soon they were shipping enormous quantities of canned paella, a Basque fish chowder, and tinned codfish stew into the United States. Dozens of salesmen peddled their food products.

What the legitimate end of the business didn't realize was that, in selected cans, the content was substantially richer than either paella or fish stew. Heroin had been substituted for the fish products in a secret part of the Spanish canning factory. Lead weights were added to bring the smuggling tins to the exact weight of the fish tins. The particular cases and tins were marked with a secret code known only to the smugglers and their receiving agents. Already millions of dollars of heroin were reaching the American underworld, to be cut and recut with sugar or milk, eventually to find its way into the veins of desperate addicts.

Word of the enterprise quickly spread through the underworld grapevine, reaching the ears of undercover federal drug agents. When they discovered the name and shipping dates of several Swedish freighters on which the contraband was shipped, they were ready to spring. Unfortunately, one of the freighters had already been unloaded just before the shipping intelligence had been received. Another was steaming for New York, due to dock in a day or so. Still another had just departed the Spanish port. If only all three shipments of the paella tins containing heroin could be intercepted, perhaps the back of this new drug smuggling operation could be broken.

As the second freighter was docked, the federal agents were lying in wait, ready to pounce when the shipment was claimed. Until that event, no offense could be linked with the smugglers themselves.

Scarcely had the paella crates been lowered to the docks than a new complication arose. At that precise moment, a longshoremen's strike was declared. Hundreds of cases of the suspect fish tins were standing on the docks with tens of thousands of tins of fish chowder and stew inside. And in some of them—maybe all of them—there was reported to be the richest haul of heroin ever sent to this country.

While most evidence must be brought to the crime lab for processing, there are many instances where both the criminalist and specialized equipment must be taken to the crime scene. In bullet recovery from walls and ceilings, X-ray examination can be of inestimable help. In cases like these, taking the X-ray equipment to the crime scene might result in substantially more accurate reconstruction of the event.

In the paella smuggling case, it was fortunate that authorities in charge were fully aware of the existence of miniaturized X-ray equipment. Shortly after the SOS from the field agent in charge, the paella cases were under the scrutiny of the portable Bucky equipment. Since lead is impervious to X rays, the lead weights used to equalize the tins containing heroin were real bell ringers for this equipment. Out of hundreds of cases of fish products, only six contained the multimillion-dollar heroin shipment. Even as the X-ray search was nosing out the hidden drugs, Coast Guard aircraft escorted the third Swedish freighter in its approach to New York harbor, making certain it was not intercepted before narcotics agents could examine its cargo.

After all three shipments, including one in a Queens warehouse, had been analyzed by the portable X-ray equipment, the boom was lowered on the conspirators both in the United States and abroad. Four men were arrested in New York, and a fifth seized in Puerto Rico as he tried to flee by plane.

In Geneva, police agents descended on the retired banker. Records found in his possession gave detailed instructions for processing the heroin in the Spanish canning plant.

So Roentgen's discovery, improved for medical service by Dr. Gustav Bucky, was put to yet another application.

While man—particularly the policeman—drags his heels and resists progress, science gaily forges forward, creating inventions able to ease the task of law enforcement. At present, there are at least a dozen companies manufacturing see-in-the-dark equipment, which enables law enforcement agencies—and any others—to penetrate the Stygian blackness. Not only do these remarkable devices convert the starlit scene to high noon; some of them use infrared illumination to make apparent a scene where there's no visible light at all.

Since 1961, man's voice has been seen as well as heard. And these Voiceprints© have undone many a criminal, who is brought to justice through the visual representation of the unique qualities of his vocal production. Their match with the same voice recorded under criminal circumstances means conviction for the guilty. Even more important, lack of a match speeds exoneration for the innocent.

The Voiceprint technique had its beginning during the post-World War II period when Dr. Lawrence G. Kersta, working in the Bell Telephone Laboratories in Murray Hill, New Jersey, was attempting to develop a method for presenting coded instructions to computers. He soon realized that the missing link in the project was a machine that could visualize the spoken human voice.

Fifteen years later, the sound spectrograph was perfected. Its principle is based on selective scanning of a vocal utterance, usually a single word. The vibrations of the human vocal cords generate frequencies which range from about a hundred to as much as seventy-five hundred vibrations per second. Any given vocal sound consists of hundreds of vibrations in many different frequencies. The Voiceprint equipment scans a magnetic recording of a given spoken sound, making four hundred passes over the recording tape being analyzed in some eighty seconds. Each pass measures a different sound frequency. The results are visually reproduced in a series of wavy lines, each one representing a different frequency. Volume factors are read out by the intensity of the line. Human voices are sufficiently unique, Dr. Kersta claims, that under proper conditions of recording suspected and exemplar voice samples, the method is better than ninety-nine percent accurate for positive identification.

The result is an exciting new dimension to criminalistics, as well as many other medical and industrial uses. A car manufacturer might record Voiceprints of the sounds made of each part in the motor and mechanical system when it fails. These graphs could then be analyzed and stored in a computer's memory. When a future vehicle was ailing, the computer could listen to the sounds the auto produced and diagnose the trouble, even by telephone.

Sick human bodies can similarly produce Voiceprints related to many human ailments. Such a program of collecting known sounds of body weakness is presently under way and may greatly assist diagnosis in future medical examinations.

Dr. Kersta's first acid test came in June, 1967, when Arab leaders were claiming that the United States and Britain were involved in air attacks against the Arab nations, operating from carriers based in the Mediterranean.

Meanwhile, Israeli monitors had been able to intercept a highly secret telephone conversation between Gamal Abdel Nasser, president of the United Arab Republic, and King Hussein of Jordan. Unscrambled, the conversation revealed a plot between the two Arab leaders to falsely accuse the United States and Britain of participating in these Israeli attacks.

The recordings were rushed to Dr. Kersta, together with known recordings of Nasser's voice. Were the two voices the same, various news media and government officials asked, or was the conversation itself just a hoax?

The urgent and exhausting analysis of some twenty-five equivalent sounds from the telephone conversation and the known Nasser recordings brought an affirmative answer. The conversation was genuine, with the chilling international reports verified.

Chapter 12

In another landmark case, Dr. Kersta was given the totally unintelligible recording of the voice of a Pacific Airlines copilot recorded moments before his death. The transmission was sent just before the aircraft had plunged into a hill to the east of the San Francisco Bay area, killing all forty-four occupants of the turbojet. The voice was obviously terrified. Other than that, nothing was identifiable as to content. By pulling the message apart, a syllable at a time, the Voiceprint technique finally read out the last words of the copilot as, "Skipper's shot . . . we've been shot . . . tryin' ta help. . . ."

Armed with this interpretation, authorities were able to establish that the .357 Magnum revolver found in the wreckage and registered to a passenger were proof of a mass-murder and suicide.

The Voiceprint may be recorded in two forms, one using a bar graph, the other resembling a contour map. The latter technique is more readily converted to computer readout and storage.

The forensic use of Voiceprints, as with most innovations, was slow to gain acceptance. One of the first cases involved a call to the manager of a Stamford, Connecticut, plant where a rasping voice threatened: "Get everybody out. There's a bomb in the plant. It's going to go off . . . soon!"

The plant was cleared, but no bomb was found. Playing a hunch that there would be other calls, arrangements were made by local police to record any subsequent telephone threats. And come they did, all of them recorded on tape.

Comparison tapes were made of certain employees as the investigation focused on possible suspects. At last a matching Voiceprint was found. Confronted with the evidence, the suspect confessed. He dreamed up the bomb threat, he admitted, just to get some time off.

Cases like this are frequently concluded without going to court, so it has taken some time to put the Voiceprint technique to legal challenge. In the very first case alleging a criminal offense which involved Voiceprint evidence, a policeman was charged with perjury. He claimed he had not tipped off a gambling operation of an impending police raid. The district attorney had secured recordings through a legal wiretap which included this conversation.

As Dr. Kersta approached the White Plains, New York, courthouse for the perjury trial, he was not certain his testimony would be allowed in evidence. Then, and in many future cases, he would be confronted with so-called experts, who would testify that voice identification wasn't possible. Even so-called responsible scientists gave evidence that the Voiceprint process could not work, without bothering to familiarize themselves with this innovative technique.

In this case, the judge decided that the jury would determine whether or not this evidence should be considered. Although the Voiceprint evidence might not deserve sole credit, the suspect was convicted and the precedent was set.

Since then, as of this writing, Voiceprint evidence has been entered for the prosecution in some thirty criminal cases, and in six for the defense. At present, such evidence has been held admissible in thirteen states, the District of Columbia, Canada, and Switzerland, with strong indications it rapidly will be received in evidence elsewhere.

Early in the development of the voice identification technique, Detective Sergeant Ernest W. Nash (now Detective Lieutenant) of the Michigan State Police, was trained under Dr. Kersta, and assisted in developing a voice identification unit in the Michigan operation. A recent report published by the National Institute of Law Enforcement and Criminal Justice (NILECJ) evaluated voice identification research. It comments that since the inception of the voice identification program by the Michigan State Police in 1967, 291 voice identification cases have been submitted involving twenty-seven types of crime ranging from nuisance calls to murder.

The report goes on to say: "No information was found to prove the wrong person had been identified by voice identification techniques."

Admittedly, the likelihood of correct identification will vary with the circumstances surrounding the recording. The identification problems grow more difficult when there is a substantial lapse of time between the recordings. When voice match is attempted between Voiceprints of the population at large and a single suspect's Voiceprint, an obviously far greater range of factors compounds the problem of match. In police investigative practice, however, the number of suspects in most cases is relatively limited. In the majority of cases, the time differential is small. Under these circumstances, the error factor is tiny. The NILECJ report lends strong support to the Voiceprint technique: "Given a sufficient quantity and quality of known and unknown voice records to work with, a qualified identification examiner can arrive at opinions that have an accuracy level comparable to other types of subjective examinations now made in forensic laboratories."

One of the potentially valuable, although virtually untried use of Voiceprints is in cases in which a police informant makes the contact with the suspected criminal. A reliable informant is a pearl without price in detective circles. The police will go to considerable lengths to protect him from blowing his cover, which is certain to occur if the informant testifies in court. Usually, the police will forfeit a criminal case rather than reveal an informant's identity.

Had the informant been using transmitting equipment of good enough quality, the entire conversation with the suspect could be introduced in evidence once the Voiceprint expert established that the recorded voice and the suspect's voice were one and the same. If this procedure were used, the informant would no longer be needed to establish the facts of the discussion.

Every innovative technique has had to earn its place in forensics by removing doubt as to its validity. It would seem that the Voiceprint technique has now proven its usefulness. Hopefully, the legal obstacles to its widespread use will be rapidly overcome as a result of the NILECJ evaluation.

The dreary fall day was harsh with chill winds as the conservation officer patrolled a remote area of the game refuge it was his duty to protect. Today was his twenty-fifth birthday, and he chuckled to himself as he recalled the little slips made by his young wife as she planned the surprise party which he knew would greet him at the end of his work day. How great it was to be young, full of life, married to such a wonderful girl. He slapped his gloves against the arms of his heavy coat. He was glad he had the party to look forward to, because the weather was growing beastly. Only a few more hours and he'd head his olive-drab truck back toward civilization.

At the conservation officer's home the guests had gathered. They were just a little uncomfortable when he was half an hour late in arriving. By the time darkness overtook them, the party atmosphere changed to one of grave concern. A call was placed to the sheriff's office, and an immediate search was begun.

Late that night the search party spotted the officer's truck in a far section of the game refuge. The door was open, as though he'd just stepped out of it and might return any moment, but the officer was nowhere in sight.

Calls for help brought hundreds of persons to join the search. The next afternoon the searchers made a gruesome discovery. The headless body of the young officer was found buried in a shallow grave. His mutilated head was located in another grave, about fifty feet away.

Autopsy revealed that the victim had been shot with a 30.06 rifle, with additional shots fired from a .22 caliber rifle. A number of shell casings were located, undoubtedly from the killer's guns, as well as the bullets recovered from the body. What was needed now was a suspect and the murder weapons in order that ballistics experts could match the guns to the crime.

Enormous effort was concentrated on developing a suspect, with one detective assigned by the sheriff to work exclusively on the case. Building on the suspicion that the murderer may have been a poacher with a blind hatred for the conservation officer, a suspect was finally discovered. He was known to have a violent temper and to be capable of carrying out such a brutal and deliberate killing. And he was a poacher, with many arrests, including two by the slain conservation officer.

But where was the evidence? No witnesses had been found. If the poacher had ever owned weapons of the type which killed the officer, they were not to be found now. Without help from some other direction, the investigation ground to a standstill.

Then the investigators thought of the newly developed voice identification unit of the Michigan State Police. Was there some way that the newest weapon in the crime-buster's arsenal—Voice-prints—could be used to break through the investigative impasse?

The district attorney requested and received a warrant to wiretap the telephone of the suspect for a period of ten days, all of his conversations to be recorded.

During the past twenty-five years the police increasingly have been crying foul as appellate and supreme court decisions stabbed into issues designed to protect the civil rights of the individuals suspected of the commission of crime. Crocodile tears are still being shed concerning the shackles slapped on the police which prevent them from adequately performing their duty.

Since gathered evidence supplies the grist for the crime lab mill, this aspect of a most complicated problem is well worth examining.

First, let's make a couple of categorical statements:

> One—There are good policemen and there are bad
> policemen. Most policemen respect people's dignity,
> believe that an individual is innocent until
> proven guilty; as contrasted to others who have no
> compunction about beating a confession from the
> "human vermin" with whom they deal.
> Two—Since judicial decisions have major effects
> on all evidence, a case can be lost before it starts
> by incorrect tactics in evidence gathering. If the
> evidence is not allowed in the case because the
> method by which it was gathered is subject to
> challenge, it matters not how excellent the work of
> the crime lab is.

In 1945 the Cahan decision revolved around drug evidence swallowed by the suspect. He was forced to disgorge the evidence by police actions which the appellate court stated, "revolted and shocked the conscience." The Cahan decision insists that evidence, no matter how telling, cannot be admitted under these conditions. (It might be noted that since 1914 the FBI has operated with considerable success under rules which parallel the Cahan decision.)

In 1954 the manacles restraining the police were reenforced by the Mallory decision, where the defendant was detained some four and one-half hours because a magistrate was not available.

Mallory was not advised of his right to be silent. This decision was also aimed against delay in order to secure a confession.

The next crippling handicap, which generated anguish in police circles, concerned a murder in which Danny Escobido was denied access to his attorney, who was actually waiting outside the interrogation room. The pivotal issue revolved around securing a confession partially through promises of release if Escobido would implicate a co-conspirator. In addition, Danny Escobido was not advised of his rights.

While the critics of the Escobido decision were gnashing their teeth, saying it would be impossible to make any lawful arrests, they were deliberately ignoring the fact that the Escobido decision was drawn up in such a way as to limit its effect. All of the following very stern ground rules must be met before the Escobido decision applies:

> 1. The investigation is no longer a general inquiry into an unsolved crime but has begun to focus on a particular suspect.
> 2. The suspect has been taken into police custody.
> 3. The police carry out a process of interrogation that lends itself to eliciting incriminating statements.
> 4. The suspect has requested and been denied an opportunity to consult with his lawyer.
> 5. The police have not effectively warned him of his absolute constitutional right to remain silent.

When each and every one of the above conditions has been met, *then* a confession may be excluded from a state court proceeding.

In effect, the police must bend over backwards—the wrong way—to lose the right to introduce a confession. While these conditions limit police abuse, mental and physical, they offer little obstacle to those agencies determined to live by the principle that a defendant is innocent until proven guilty.

It is easy to Monday-morning-quarterback the actions and decision of the police officer who is faced with the need for immediate action in a crisis. In confrontation situations, particularly those involving the exchange of force or weaponry, there is an understandable likelihood that some of the basic rules of evidence may be shortcut if not bypassed. No such excuse exists in the average ex post facto investigation. Here the threat of danger is nonexistent or has been put into the background before the evidence search began. So it is more necessary than ever to be certain that all of the legal niceties are followed to insure admissibility of evidence.

The ground rules change almost daily, and you *do* need a program to tell the players. Which is to say that there must be an ongoing program of recruit officer training and a continuing effective in-service training activity, if investigators are to be aware of the newest decisions and their effect on evidence collection and admissibility.

A case in point is the rule regarding evidence seized under search warrants. In all too many parts of the country, the police are judge, jury, and executioner. At this very moment, a homicide in many locations has less than a fifty-fifty chance of competent investigation.

In the more progressive sections, the judiciary is becoming insistent that the evidence gathered in the case must remotely resemble the evidence for which search was authorized in the warrant. The days of a generalized license to discover whatever wrongdoing was concealed within a man's castle are on the wane. So the narcotics detective should delineate as accurately as possible, the specific contraband which he believes to be inside the walls to be searched. To the highest degree possible, he should detail the exact portions of the quarters in which the evidence is likely to be found. Inadmissibility of evidence is the expected result of a fishing expedition following entry on a nonspecific search warrant.

In the case of the slain conservation officer, the D.A. had received court permission for the wiretap, anticipating and closing one legal escape hatch. (It is rare that such an order, if legitimate, cannot be obtained.) At the same time, the sheriff's detectives contacted many of the suspect's friends and relatives, putting the heat on the suspect in an effort to flush out his participation in the murder. As a result, the telephone calls flowed freely from kin and friends to the suspect, seeking to discover just how much the pigs knew and what it was they wanted.

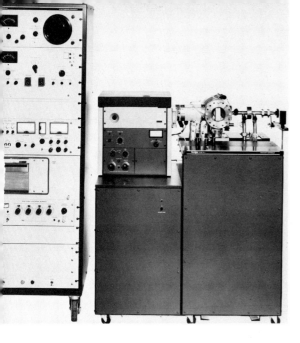

The mass spectrometer at left, and the gas chromatograph at right, have been "married" by California's Finnigan Corporation. Used in tandem, they make short work of blood analysis, detecting alcohol, drugs, unhealthy chemicals, and other byproducts of foul play.

The "bar" Voiceprint at left and the "contour" Voiceprint at right both represent the word "you" spoken by the same individual. As in ordinary writing, the Voiceprint is "read" from left to right. The vertical distance measures the pitch of the sounds at any given instant; and the volume is indicated by the heavy shading in the "bar" form—which is therefore easier for an expert to interpret. The "contour" form, however, lends itself better to computer analysis. (COURTESY DR. L. G. KERSTA, CONSULTANT, VOICE IDENTIFICATION)

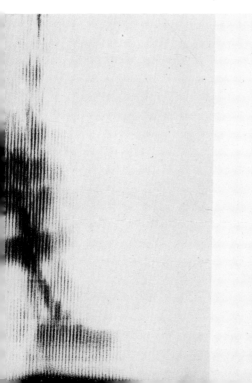

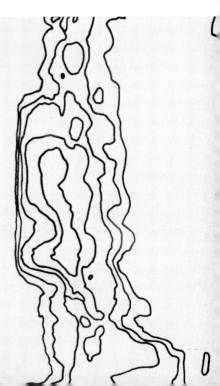

To avoid identification, criminals often file their guns' serial numbers—or just throw them away, as was this pistol recovered from a duckpond. But lab treatment can often restore serial numbers that a felon thought he had safely obliterated. Soaked in penetrating oil, chipped, brushed, forced open, and sanded, this gun revealed two legible serial numbers.

Here is how the stock of another captured gun originally appeared . . .

. . . A wax matrix was placed around the area to be examined, and the wood subjected to a corrosive chemical bath . . .

. . . With the wax removed and the surface buffed, the number "64740" is clearly visible.

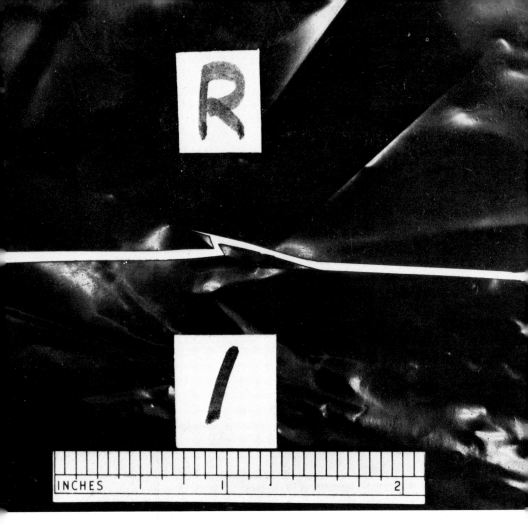

But the ideal "clincher" is the jigsaw fit between material left at the crime scene and other material still in the suspect's possession. One murderer hurriedly wrapped his victim's body in plastic sheeting, which he whacked off from a roll in the victim's home. Five jigsaw fits, similar to the one photographed above, were made between the body's plastic shroud and the remaining roll. The corpse was positively identified, and the culprit jailed. (D. M. LUCAS, DIRECTOR OF THE CENTRE OF FORENSIC SERVICES, TORONTO)

Unfortunately, jigsaw fits are not often so obvious. The scrap of liquor label at the left was recovered from the shoe of a drunk driver—whose clothes were mysteriously bloodstained. The two matching label scraps at the right were discovered at the scene of a murder that occurred the same day. (ANTHONY LONGHETTI, DIRECTOR OF THE LABORATORY OF CRIMINALISTICS, SAN BERNARDINO COUNTY)

This tiny fragment of glass, found at a hit-and-run scene, *seemed* to match a larger piece taken from a suspect's car. But it could have been coincidence . . .

. . . Until the two pieces were viewed sideways! The alignment of stress lines—formed when the glass was cooling—proved the two were once joined together. (SUPERINTENDENT WILLIAM E. KIRWAN, NEW YORK STATE POLICE)

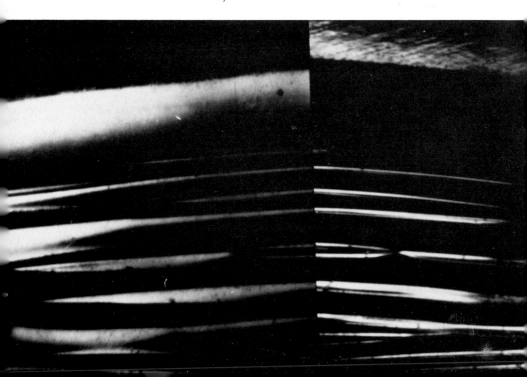

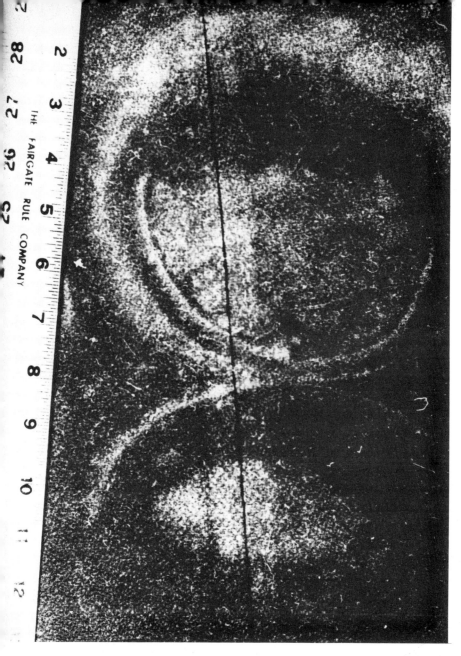

Even without glass fragments, a hit-and-run car can leave its own form of "fingerprints." In this case, the headlights left a permanent impact on the victim's suede jacket. Photographically enhanced, the pattern narrowed the police's search to 29 possible models, and a paint chip vacuumed from the same jacket provided them with the auto's color! When the killer car's probable description was broadcast, the driver gave himself up. (SUPERINTENDENT WILLIAM E. KIRWAN, NEW YORK STATE POLICE)

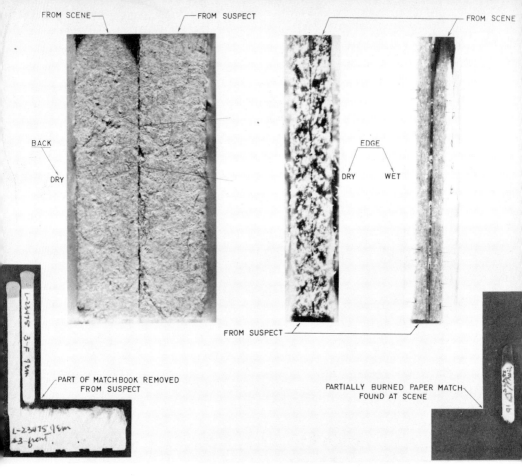

FROM SCENE — — FROM SUSPECT — FROM SCENE

BACK

DRY

EDGE

DRY   WET

FROM SUSPECT

PART OF MATCHBOOK REMOVED
FROM SUSPECT

PARTIALLY BURNED PAPER MATCH
FOUND AT SCENE

Even paper matches dropped at a crime scene can be linked to a matchbook still in the suspect's possession—if he isn't too heavy a smoker, and if his pockets are searched in time. Note that each item is marked with numbers and initials to identify it and the individual evidence collector who came across it. It is in careful evidence collection such as this that the crime lab either succeeds, or breaks down completely. (EXHIBIT COURTESY JOHN E. MURDOCK, CONTRA COSTA CRIMINALISTICS LABORATORY)

On the eighth day, the suspect had an interesting conversation with his seventy-three-year-old grandmother. During the recorded conversation, the grandmother assured the suspect that the cops would never find his guns where she had them stashed away. The same recording tape contained several other conversations between the suspect and his mother and others with his girlfriend, all of which contributed to the growing certainty that he truly was the killer. If only some way could be found to locate the cache of murder weapons.

The logical first step was to seek a search warant to examine the grandmother's property. Prior to the formal proceedings, however, the voices recorded on the authorized wiretaps were checked against the known voice recordings of the grandmother and the other individuals involved. Lieutenant Ernest Nash had examined the Voiceprint evidence and was prepared to testify that the voice which cackled as she assured the suspect that the pigs would never find the stashed guns was indeed that of the grandmother.

A hearing was called. The judge listened thoughtfully to the grandmother as she testified that she'd never made a statement to anyone concerning stashed guns and the chances of the law finding them. At the conclusion of the hearing, the judge issued a search warrant to examine the property under the control of the grandmother.

The subsequent search recovered the two rifles from the hiding place grandma thought completely secure. Subsequent ballistic work in the crime lab nailed down the weapons' connection with the murder.

The Voiceprints had one more duty to perform before this case was ended. The suspect's lips were as loose as his thinking. The recorded conversations were proven to be his by the Voiceprint testimony of Lieutenant Nash. And the warped thinking of the suspect's twisted mind, revealed by the phone calls, removed any doubt on the jury's part as to who had fired the fatal bullets. The suspect was found guilty of first-degree murder and sentenced to life imprisonment.

Increasingly, police agencies throughout the country have acquired equipment which reflected improvements in scientific technology. The polygraph, or "lie box," in police parlance, is an instrument as good as its operator. Except for interrogating the psychopath who has no feelings of right or wrong, the polygraph can be an effective tool, particularly for the exoneration of the innocent. It operates on the principle that a deliberate lie will bring detectable physiological reactions, such as increased blood pressure, sweating, and change of heart and respiratory rate.

Using the same control techniques as other scientific measures, the operator connects the suspect to the various recording devices which register physiologic changes, zeroes his instrumentation, and then asks a series of control questions to develop the norm for the particular individual.

Next, the person being interrogated is asked a series of carefully prepared questions in which key phrases are inserted among innocuous ones. All of the responses are recorded on a moving graph, which establishes time factors in vocal and body response.

In addition to the tremendous help in eliminating suspects and focusing investigative leads, the polygraph finds widespread application within progressive police agencies, which work avidly to guarantee the integrity of their candidate officers.

Many individuals are attracted to police jobs for a variety of highly unsavory motives. These range from getting rich quick by bribes to using their supposed immunity to arrest, to roll drunks, embezzle found property, even burglarize buildings they're paid to protect. Others hope to attain a status they never could achieve in ordinary pursuits by hiding behind the authority of badge and gun. Sadists salivate at the possibility of brutally beating helpless drunks and abusing prisoners on the pretext they were resisting arrest. Latent homosexuals play the same brutal game, as they overcompensate for their unacceptable sexual drives.

Whatever the odious motives of such candidates, modern police administrators agree on the need of refusing them entry into the police system. Routine background checks eliminate the majority of such persons, but psychological screening and routine polygraph examination assist in detecting the really clever imposter.·

As the work of Kinsey and his colleagues first demonstrated, most males have experienced some form of homosexual activity before achieving their majority. No enlightened person can quarrel with behavior in private between consenting adults as long as it does not affect the public weal. However, the homosexual is a high-risk policeman, not solely because of his sexual conduct, but because many such individuals are deeply disturbed and lack the maturity essential for coping with the stress commonplace in police work. In addition, even the discreet homosexual is particularly susceptible to blackmail, so that even though his life is sterling in every other respect, he would be a questionable candidate for a police position.

In one instance, an applicant's polygraph examination aroused doubt in the examiner's mind. When the examiner showed the applicant the demonstrated agitation aroused by the line of questioning concerning homosexual behavior, the candidate confessed that on one occasion long ago, he'd gotten drunk at a party and a friend offered to get him home by cab. In the cab, the friend sexually molested him—an occurrence which had caused him guilt feelings ever since.

The young man's answers seemed forthright and the polygraph examiner was tempted to skip further examination, but finally decided to try a few more questions to dig deeper into the matter.

This time the polygraph indicated such a strong degree of excitement connected with homosexually related questions that the examiner called for further background checks.

The investigation proved the applicant to be a full-fledged, practicing homosexual—who was a better than average liar, until tipped up by the lie box.

All forms of radio equipment have so proliferated in police work that it is a sad patrolman indeed who can not maintain constant communication between headquarters and his fellow officers on a minute-to-minute basis.

Miniaturized transmitting equipment has made a reality of the Dick Tracy two-way radio wrist watch. Transmitters the size of a pack of cigarettes can be carried within a shirt pocket, the antenna being run down a sleeve or looped around a coat collar, the microphone concealed in a tie clip, in a wrist watch, or beneath a coat lapel. Companion gear, located in a van within half a mile, can pick up the transmission, even when it originates in steel-clad buildings, and can amplify it a few million times to be recorded for courts and posterity.

Bugging developed into such a refined art form that the very olive in the operative's martini might be wafting cocktail conversation to eavesdropping detectives, ready to use a man's own unguarded comments against him. Virtually every modern jail cell and interrogation room maintains constant recorded vigilance of the events occurring within. The recording art, coupled with electronic data processing, makes instant replay possible for any incoming telephone conversation to the police agency, as well as logging the voice of the police operator, the radio dispatch, and the sequential time of each and every one of these steps. In the last decade recording tape salesmen became fat cats with such enthusiastic agencies as the Chicago police, which kept a permanent record of every telephonic event which transpired twenty-four hours a day, 365 days a year.

With the advent of space age technology it is now entirely possible to listen to conversations hundreds of feet distant, and take photographs under unbelievably weak lighting conditions. In true Dick Tracy tradition, wrist watch transmitters relay hushed conversations to powerful amplifiers which permanently record every nuance and inflection of confidential communications.

No argument is made against the proper use of such devices. Since attacks against property and person siphon billions of dollars and thousands of lives into criminal circles, the counter-attack with closed circuit TV or use of portable binoculars with electronic capability of fifty thousand starlight amplifications is completely laudable. We do, however, object vigorously to peeping-Tom outings by the police to enforce statutes of questionable constitutionality, and like snooping.

One of the perils of making narcotic buys is that the purchaser becomes known as a narc, which results in burning his cover. For this reason, narcotics agents, like Hollywood talent scouts, are constantly looking for new faces. The buyer must not only be a consummate actor, able to successfully play the role of a high-living, free-spending narcotics peddler. He must also talk the narcotics lingo flawlessly. His task is to convince the seller that he is part of the drug scene, ready and willing to buy the merchandise. The buyer invariably is introduced to the seller by an informant. When the seller is convinced he is not dealing with the law, the sale is made with marked money. Subsequently, the seller is pounced on by narcotics agents while still in possession of the marked bills, and if convicted, another narcotics dealer is salted away for a few years.

Fairly often buyers are drafted into the business because of their newness to the law enforcement operation. One such experience happened to a well-known criminalist and distinguished chemist we'll call Jim Jones. Jones had been working for less than a week for the state narcotics bureau, when he was approached by one of the narcotics agents. "Jim," the agent said, "I'd like you to go along with me tonight. I'm making a buy, and I'd like a witness. You might as well get your feet wet in this business."

While not overjoyed at the prospect, Jones felt he could not refuse. He and the agent then went to meet the chief of the division and the informant who would lead them to the location where the buy was to be made.

When the chief saw Jones, he told the agent, "I'm going to change the plan, Charley. I think Jones will be a natural for this buy. Get him the money and introduce him to the informant. Then you peel off." Before Jones had opportunity to let the full import of the occasion grab him, he was face to face with the seller, playing a role he didn't exactly covet.

Chapter 13

The affair went well. After a little sparring small talk during which Jones—a jazz buff—fell naturally into the jive parlance of the drug world, he passed the test and the buy was made. Now he was richer by several ounces of heroin and poorer by five thousand marked bills.

Back in the lab, Jim Jones slipped into his white chemist's jacket and began testing the material he'd bought. It was first-class, uncut heroin, worth at least fifty thousand dollars in the street market after it had been cut to the strength heroin is usually sold to the user.

The agent who'd involved him in the connection joined him in the lab. "Great work, Jim," he exclaimed. "The informant says you're a natural. By the way, don't make any plans for Thursday night."

Jones was surprised. "Why not?"

"We let that guy hang onto your five thou," the agent said. "We think he'll lead us to someone bigger. So we want you to make another buy next Thursday."

The second buy, for ten thousand dollars' worth of heroin, went off smoothly, but now Jim Jones was in over his head.

While many a narcotics agent has worked the field during his entire career without experiencing a threat to his life, there are more who've literally had to sing for their survival when their cover was blown. Since the name of the game is quick thinking and a glib tongue, such agents have often succeeded in persuading their intended executioners that they'd be smarter to let them off the hook. But not all have been successful. Each year several narcotics men lose their lives in the dangerous game of trying to reduce the unending supply of drugs.

Jim Jones's last case shows just how badly things can go wrong. This job, it turned out, was not only sudden; it was impossibly complicated. A seller had come to town a day earlier than expected. He was reported to have a large supply of drugstore goods—narcotics stolen from legitimate sources. Because of their purity, such goods are in great demand in the illegal drug trade.

Two small problems made this less than the perfect opportunity for a successful buy. The first was that Jones had never met the informant. He knew that his name was Fred, and he had a pretty good description of the man. The other problem was that the chief's office was closed, and this buy called for big money. The agent had been able to scrape up a couple of thousand-dollar bills. "Wrap these around a bundle of singles," the agent instructed Jones. "The seller won't need to see what's in the roll before you inspect the merchandise. You'll wear a Fargo [a tiny transmitter sometimes worn by the buyer to carry his conversation to the accompanying agents] and as soon as we hear you calling off the names of the drugs in those bottles, we'll move in for the pinch."

There would be three agents working on the case. They'd keep in close touch as soon as Jones met the informant and the seller. "We'll be right there backing you up," the agent assured Jones. "You just start calling off the names of the drugs, and we'll be with you in a jiffy."

The size of the first problem became evident as soon as Jones joined the informant and the seller at the prearranged rendezvous. The two men might have been related, they looked so much alike. Fortunately, the informant was on his toes and recognized Jones from *his* description. He larded the conversation with his own name in the first few minutes so that Jones was easily able to drop into the fiction that they were old buddies.

Which brought up the next problem. The seller was con-wise. As soon as he was satisfied that Jones was probably a legitimate buyer, he told the informant to get lost. Any help which might have come from that source was out the door.

Next, the seller insisted they "take a little trip" in Jones's car. He even managed to subject Jones to a quick frisk. Jones was glad that he'd put his gun in the trunk of the undercover car. He also congratulated himself that the search wasn't thorough enough to detect the Fargo. He didn't want any delay when it came close to the time he was supposed to produce the money for the buy. While he wasn't wearing his own gun, he could clearly see the bulge made by the gun carried by the seller.

As they started to drive down the street, Jones was happy to observe that he was discreetly trailed by three other cars. These would be the vehicles of the narcotics agents, who would pounce on the seller as soon as the transmitter told them that Jones was reading the names of the drugs offered him.

"Turn here!" the seller ordered abruptly. Jones turned, and the following car drove straight ahead—standard practice in tailing a suspect, since the next man in line can take up the tail.

Two additional abrupt turns later, and the following cars were all gone. Jones felt strangely alone as the seller ordered him next to turn up a dead-end alley, then stop the car. The seller had already seen his roll of bills with the large bills wrapped around the core of singles. Jones was more than anxious that the seller not be encouraged to look any deeper into that roll. He was almost relieved when the seller opened his large satchel and started to take the contraband bottles out for Jones's inspection. Slowly, Jones read the contents of the first bottle into the hidden Fargo.

During the preceding few minutes, as the seller had dictated their tortuous course, Jones had kept up a running commentary, complete with street names, hoping it would clue the trailing agents without being too obvious. Jones wasn't exactly relaxed, but he was fairly sure that the clues he'd transmitted would be adequate for the agents to catch up with his car at any moment. At the most the trailing agents couldn't be more than a few blocks away.

And so they were—but hopelessly lost. As sometimes happens with radio transmission in an area with steel-frame buildings, the message was blacked out. They circled the area frantically, hoping to pick up Jones's signal. They knew only too well how dangerous the seller was.

By now the seller was obviously impatient with Jones's dawdling inspection of each of the bottles as he read the names of the drugs inside. "What the hell is this!" the seller stormed. He waves his pudgy hand at the half-emptied valise. "The junk's all there. Just give me the dough and take it." His face clouded and he patted the bulging area under his left armpit. "I ain't got all night."

Jones smiled disarmingly. "Don't get your guts in an uproar." He reached into the valise and took out the next bottle. "You're

. 140 .

getting plenty of dough for this package. I gotta be sure it's all there."

Sweating, Jones slowly read off the name of the drug in the fifty-first bottle.

The vagaries of radio reception have plagued listeners since Marconi's invention was first improved for common use. In the beginning of commercial radio, there was always a best spot on the galena crystal where the whisker brought in the strongest signal. Modern broadcasting stations develop contour maps for their salesmen, showing the areas of top reception, those which are fringe, and the freak locations where reception is unexpectedly far better than logic would say it should be. Occasionally, a transmission will bounce off reflective surfaces, until it escapes limiting confines and then hurtles in another direction, resulting in strange reception patterns.

Thus it was with Jim Jones's Fargo messages. While his own crew were deaf to his coded entreaties for help, another narcotics agent staked out in the hill country over ten miles away received the entire transmission from the moment Jones started giving clues about the route. This agent had worked with Jones in the past and not only recognized his voice, but perceived the note of growing despair as the drug names were read off the bottles in a seemingly unending recitation. Somewhere about the tenth name, the agent decided Jones's need was greater than the case he was staked out on. His keen mind had routinely noted the street names Jones had called out. He was almost certain that he knew the very alley where they were parked at the moment.

The narcotics agent started his car and headed across town. He only hoped Jones could stall long enough for him to find their exact location.

By now the seller was definitely suspicious and was growing increasingly surly. And Jones was finding it difficult to hold down the panic which threatened to seize him. Almost certainly he was going to get no help from the outside. Clearly the agents had lost the Fargo's transmission; otherwise they'd have been there long ago. By the time Jones picked up the last handful of the bottles, his mind was working desperately. He knew that once the seller found he'd been tricked, there'd be fireworks. At the best, Jones would take a beating from the thug he was dealing with. He didn't even want to contemplate the worst.

His only hope lay in his gun, hidden in the trunk of his car.

He picked up the ninety-eighth bottle. Only two to go. He could sense the seller's fury as he read the label out loud, then read it again.

Then the last bottle was checked. And read out loud, twice. Jones started moving toward the car door. "Got to get a box out of the trunk," he said quietly.

"You ain't getting nothing . . . nowhere!" Jones found himself staring into the muzzle of the seller's revolver. "You just hand over that money. Then we'll see about getting the box."

Slowly, Jones reached into his pocket. Strange how enormous a revolver looks when it's pointed right between your eyes.

"Now jest you take it easy," a strange voice drawled at the car window behind the seller. "Come on up right slow with that gun and I won't have to shoot you with this one."

The seller rolled his head and took in the .357 Magnum aimed at his head. Slowly, he raised his own weapon and allowed the narcotics agent to slip it from his hand.

A few minutes later, after the handcuffed seller had been placed in the back of the police car, the agent smiled at the still shaking Jones. "'Fraid I wasn't goin' to make it in time. Shore glad I happened to be listening on your wavelength."

The broad smile stretched Jim Jones's mouth. "You think *you're* glad!"

The use—and abuse—of drugs is not a phenomenon unique to this decade, nor exclusive to the United States, even though our cultural patterns, mores, and the reaction of our law enforcement agencies do have certain facets not found in many other corners of the globe.

By the early 1950s, the signs and portents of increasing drug traffic were beginning to be seen. The FBI offered special training, and in cities like Pasadena the entire police department was given a better understanding of drug abuse and the countermeasures available to law enforcement. In that city, the increased knowledge and the assignment to the vice squad of specific responsibility for drug violations enforcement seemed to bear witness to a crime wave. In reality, the drug offenses had been there all along, but only with increased awareness was police action possible.

Still, when compared in simple numbers for arrest and prosecution, the drug problem in the fifties was a mere trickle compared with the raging flood of the 1970s.

Marijuana is so popular that perhaps ninety percent of today's young people have experimented with it. As many as fifty percent use it regularly. The basic pharmaceutical components of this now widespread drug resisted identification until the late fifties. Their detection in biological fluids was announced only in February of 1972—and then only by one laboratory in the country. Known as cannaboids, these active ingredients are found in the hemp family of plants, principally in the flowering blossoms and leaves. In more concentrated form, the cannaboid mixture is known as hashish, or hash. Perhaps as much as one-fifth of the world's population, excluding the Chinese, use the cannaboids routinely as a part of their daily culture. Afternoon tea, steeped from a plant of the cannabis family, is the accepted social custom from Morocco to India. A friendly, relaxed indulgence in plants of the marijuana family is as common in many Eastern cultures as is our use of chewing gum.

Whole peoples gone to pot, you may exclaim. Hardly. While the final score isn't in, the most recent research suggests that the *moderate* use of marijuana is considerably less harmful than moderate use of alcohol. Continuing research may soon produce authoritative answers, but presently many scientists believe that THC (delta-9 tetrahydrocannabinol), the cannaboid which seems to be responsible for the kick, is nonaddictive and does not produce tolerance as do many other drugs, which require ever higher dosages to obtain the same effect.

While it's beyond the scope of this book to argue the morality of limiting the penalties for the private use of marijuana, the crime lab problem is completely clear. One of the principal causes of the failure of crime labs to provide adequate service in other major crime cases can be charged to the epidemic of cases involving illegal drugs and the abuse of legal drugs. If the police were freed from the frenetic and often stupid pursuit of the moderate marijuana user by removing this victimless crime from the code books, the crime labs would automatically feel a relief in the case load.

Another important event which may be pegged approximately to the 1950s was the surging development of organic chemistry.

In the United States this was due partially to the German technology that became available to us with the winning of World War II, and partially to the increasing tempo within the scientific world.

One particularly significant development was the increasing ability to synthesize new drugs with unknown pharmaceutical potential. Rapid improvement in these skills matured as scientists improved their understanding of the basic building blocks of nature. Soon the organic chemists were not only able to predict what qualities might be possessed by newly conceived organic chemicals, but they were able to take desired properties from the drawing board and bring them to the marketplace.

This sort of chemical invention resulted in the production of literally thousands of man-made drugs, many of which would provide grist for the drug abusers' relentless and deadly search for new and easier kicks.

As the horrendous effects of the new drugs were discovered the hard way—with racked bodies, blank-faced, mindless young vegetables, and destroyed lives—each of the synthetics found to cause such problems was placed on the dangerous or illegal drug lists. But there was a lag between widespread use, abuse, and detection by authority. One or two years usually passed before a new drug was proved to be harmful and moved out of the over-the-counter market to the illegal list.

An earlier event which led to another peculiarly American cultural heritage is significant here. The Volstead Act and the prohibition of beverage alcohol was the springboard which thrust organized crime into the United States picture. With the grubstake from bootlegging, the various mobs increasingly moved into front activities.

By the 1950s, the underworld had its own fair share of scientists on their payrolls. As the police developed increasingly sophisticated scientific attacks, the scientific flunkies of organized crime developed their own batch of countermeasures.

Not that all the drug-involved chemists were in the pay of the mobs. Many were simply swayed by the attraction of a quick and legal buck. Without concern for their victims, these get-rich-quick artists studied the lists of organic chemicals and quickly slipped a cousin drug in place of those which were newly forbidden. The vicious cycle would then repeat itself as soon as authorities detected the harmful qualities of the substitute drug and removed it from the market. One such operation in San Francisco netted over one million dollars before the doors were closed on their legitimate enterprise by banning the legal drug. Undoubtedly, these criminal fringe chemists just did a quick shuffle and came up with still another legal drug to be abused.

Two additional groups of man-made drugs play a major role in our burgeoning drug problem. In hippy parlance, these are the uppers—the stimulants such as the amphetamine family—and the downers—represented by drugs of the barbiturate family. These are often used in tandem, an upper being taken to counteract the depressant effect of the downer, and vice versa.

All too often, a veritable potpourri of drugs will be used together. One deadly custom of the drug set is for each person to toss into a punchbowl assorted drugs, including prescription drugs liberated from the family medicine cabinet, and to indiscriminately combine a handful of the mixture of pills, capsules, and pellets, downing them in a single gulp, then to await the high. The phenomenon known as synergism—the combined effect being much greater than the additive effect—frequently offers such punchbowl participants a short cut to the morgue.

Punchbowling and mainlining amphetamines—the latter, shooting the drug directly into the veins—frequently leads to psychosis, often permanent. Countless flower children will spend the rest of their lives as vegetables as a result of such senseless practices.

Analysis of crime labs throughout the nation reveals increasingly choking streams of drug cases. Whereas other crimes may be solved without crime lab assistance, drug-related cases *must* be endorsed by the crime lab before any prosecution is possible. Who can say the felony of heroin possession has occurred until the lab technician identifies the confiscated material as heroin?

Consider a typical day in the special drug laboratory serving Santa Clara County, the nation's second most rapidly growing area. Some eighteen agencies bring evidence envelopes to the admission counter, where they must be received for processing with the necessary precautions to protect the vital chain of possession, without which no physical evidence may be entered in evidence in a trial.

In many of the cases, the officer is asked to wait while an immediate preliminary examination is performed to give him an investigative lead, or to form the probable cause basis for further action.

Like other cultural fads such as the hoola hoop and the skateboard, various drugs appear on the scene in waves of popularity. But in many cases, the criminalist is virtually certain as to just what potential drug he's dealing with from the physical appearance of the pill, capsule, powder, or plant. In the Santa Clara lab a short-cut procedure was developed by chemist Cecil Hider for swift detection—or elimination—of the unknown substances.

This time-saving technique can identify as high as ninety percent of the suspected drugs within fifteen minutes. The systematic scheme methodically programs a series of chemical tests with reagents which are specific for various drugs. A negative test on the first step calls for the next procedure. The testing continues until a positive reaction occurs (usually a color change) or the chart is exhausted.

Supplementary testing is then made to confirm the preliminary identification. This may include crystallography, the examination of the crystals produced by the organic compound, since the pattern of such crystals may be highly characteristic.

Frequently, the appearance of the pill or capsule will allow the examiner even speedier identification, since he can bypass preliminary reagents and proceed directly to testing with reagents specific for the suspected drug. All legitimate drugs are coded with color, shape, and marking identifications. When dealing with one of these, the criminalist can usually quickly pin it down by checking against reference pharmaceutical dictionaries.

After preliminary testing, addition cross-check tests are often undertaken, particularly if the identification is needed for prosecution. One technique frequently used for further corroborative check of the specific unknown drug is chromatography.

The framed needlepoint, hanging over the back bar of the beanery, advises; "Three-quarters of the earth's surface is covered with water. Therefore man should work one day and go fishing for the next three." Not a bad idea, if only to pay tribute to the enormous debt all life owes to the existence of water. Its peculiar liquidity range, as well as the particular temperatures which trigger its freezing and gaseous states are phenomena inseparably involved in the evolution of the earth and most of its life processes.

As with all liquids, water droplets have the interesting characteristic known as surface tension. This is a result of the simultaneous attraction of the surface molecules for each other and the downward pull of those beneath them. This produces the effect of a membrane covering the surface of the water, easily observable as water insects gaily gambol over the top of a pond. Unbelievably strong—equivalent to structural steel, weight for weight—this surface tension pulls the outside in in small droplets of water, giving them their roughly spherical shape. Remove the pressure of the atmosphere and the pull of gravity, and the droplet is indeed a perfect sphere, as demonstrated in space travel.

The attraction among the water molecules undergoes a sharp alteration in the presence of certain other substances. Glass, for example, causes the water to spread out, clinging to the surface and wetting it, as the nuclei of the hydrogen atoms shift their affection to the oxygen atoms belonging to the silicon dioxide of the glass.

Water's roving eye frequently involves it with the atoms of a host of materials, causing the water to resist its own surface tension and flatten itself against the desirable stranger. So great is the love affair—the water trying to embrace more and more of the other substance—that the water defies the force of gravity and climbs ever upward, seeking additional contact with yet more members of the new group. This phenomenon, called capillary action, is one we owe our lives to, since it makes all plant life possible.

This brings us to both paper and thin-layer chromatography, each of which depends on the capillary action of liquids as well as the assorted levels of affection of materials, each for the other.

Chapter 14

Paper chromatography, and TLC as we'll call the thin-layer version, add tremendously to the versatility of the crime lab, as well as supplying enormous assistance in medicine and industrial science. In the crime lab, the head-and-shoulders leader in the paper and thin-layer chromatography business is the family of abused drugs.

Each method is relatively inexpensive to practice, a matter of considerable moment to budget-strained operations. Principles involved are similar, but TLC is finding increasing favor for a variety of extra added services we'll consider shortly.

Both techniques are used to bring about physical separation of substances which are chemical neighbors, often needing considerable purification before further testing. Biological materials as well as organic and inorganic compounds all find possible involvement in these highly useful techniques.

One example is the ability of paper chromatography to detect semen. The technique is highly specific and can be used to identify the chemical remains of the millions of sperm cells months after they've expired and gone to their infertile death. This is a handy method for checking out a late report on a rape.

At the opposite extreme, in a sense, is the ability of TLC to detect pregnancy within a few days of conception. Conventional testing methods using rabbit immunologic procedures are useless until some twenty-one days after impregnation, and then rate only ninety-three to ninety-five percent accuracy. Thin-layer chromatography techniques confirm the condition as early as five days after conception, with a batting average any baseball player would love, of ninety-nine to a hundred percent.

Provocative as these examples are, the main tasks of TLC in the crime lab are two: the first, to identify an unknown; the second, to purify material so that further testing is possible.

Paper chromatography is practiced with filter paper of graded porosity which encourages capillary action of certain-sized particles, much as coffee grounds in certain coffee-makers are kept from the cup while the fragrant beverage filters through.

Standard technique for both paper and thin-layer chromatography is to spot the material to be tested along the lower edge of the paper, approximately one inch from the bottom, using a dispensing pipette or other method that insures spots of the same size. Both knowns and unknowns are spotted along the same horizontal line, and the paper is then hung by clips in the top of a glass container similar to a small aquarium, with the bottom edge of the paper just touching a small amount of solvent liquid. The glass container is then capped, and soon the constantly moving molecules of the solvent saturate the atmosphere above, as they perpetually fling themselves free of the liquid and alternately plunge back.

Now the upward race commences. The thirsty fibers drink up the solvent, which keeps well ahead of the spotted materials as they, in turn, charge higher, climbing the capillary system of the paper. A variety of conditions affect the rate of climb and ultimate altitude. They include polarity—relative electrical charge—of both solids and the solvent. As a rule, molecular weight limits elevation, just as a fat man usually cannot climb as well as his wiry companion. When exhaustion sets in for both climbing materials and the solvent front, it's report card time.

"Thin-layer chromatography is based on the principles of adsorption, partition, and ion exchange chromatography," reads the flyer for a manufacturer of TLC materials. "A combination of several mechanisms is usually involved, although adsorption is the most common. Adsorption can be defined as the attachment of molecules of gases and liquids (including dissolved substances) to the surfaces of solids."

After the materials have climbed as high as they'll rise, they are made visible by a number of methods. Many materials being tested for must be led into the visible spectrum by trick and device. One common method uses an ultraviolet viewing box where bombardment by the UV wavelengths of radiant energy excites the electrons of invisible substances into outer orbits, where they release visible photons on returning to their original orbits. The chromatograph may then be photographed, or the purified spot may be removed for still further testing.

Thin-layer chromatography is practiced with glass plates, usually of Pyrex, since techniques to bring the unknowns into the visible spectrum sometimes get mighty hot. The common coatings use silica gel about 0.2 to 0.5 of one millimeter thick. For comparison, an American dime is about 100 millimeters thick. Some crime labs prepare their own plates; others prefer to buy ready-prepared plates from commercial sources.

Once the silica gel slurry is mixed and squeegeed onto the glass plate, it is air-dried for about forty-five minutes, then placed in a 100-degree centigrade oven, (roughly 185 degrees in our kitchen ovens). After cooling, it is ready to be spotted in a fashion similar to that used in paper chromatography. Often the glass enclosure is lined with additional filter paper touching the solvent to provide a saturated atmosphere, and the glass TLC plate is hung inside just touching the solvent on the bottom. In short order the molecules are surging upward in the TLC version of a Klondike gold rush.

The resultant stain, or blot, of unknown material is then compared with the known spot for height, size, and characteristic shape. This sort of examination makes preliminary identification possible in many cases; with others, more definitive double checking is needed.

One fairly recent development is the commercial production of presoaked dots of known drugs. Both in clinical and in criminalistic use, a major problem exits in maintaining the enormous number of reference standards necessary to cover all possible drugs. This is particularly important for hospital use, since a patient in coma may depend on rapid identification of the toxic material before life-saving measures can be undertaken. These dot-spot references appear to be an inexpensive answer to this important problem, since they keep indefinitely and the appropriate dots can be slipped into the prepunched chromatography plates to quickly make whatever examination is necessary.

After refining by chromatography or some other method, the unknown can also be given a family screening with the twin-beam ultraviolet spectrophotometer. In this procedure, the beam of UV light is optically split with one portion channeled directly to a detector; and the other portion directed through a solution containing the unknown. Such a UV examination can determine, through characteristic curves, if a given drug family is involved, such as barbiturates.

With a positive UV read-out, a more specific determination can be made with a similar instrument, by infrared spectrophotometry. Material to be tested on the IR must be quite pure because of the enormous sensitivity of the instrument.

The unknown is ground to a fine powder in a marble mortar with spectro-quality potassium bromide, until the unknown is thoroughly dispersed throughout the mixture. The powder is then transferred to a tiny mold, where enormous pressure from a mechanical or hydraulic press compresses the powder mixture into a solid transparent pellet, usually in the shape of a lens.

This pellet is placed in the optical system so that one of the twin beams is transmitted through it. The infrared light source is then programmed through the desired portion of the IR spectrum. The amount of light emerging from the pellet is automatically compared, for each wavelength, with the full-strength twin beam, with the relative amplitude converted into a tracing on moving graph paper. Both the IR and the UV spectrophotometers operate on the absorption principle, in which the unknown material will absorb a portion of the light in a way characteristic of its molecular structure.

The amount of light which manages to make it through the pellet containing the unknown produces a tracing reminiscent of a stock market gone crazy. The hills and valleys of each of the many frequencies within the infrared band are highly specific for each organic compound; so much so that the IR graph of a pure material is said to have a fingerprint-level identification quality. The only rub is that organic compounds number in the tens of thousands, each with its own IR spectrogram. A laborious manual search through all of the possible graphs would create impossible delay, so a system of cataloguing has been developed which greatly shortens the search. Once located, the forensic scientist is able to make unqualified identification for any material for which there is an identical IR graph.

I recently observed an interesting application of TLC in the coroner's toxicology lab in San Diego County. Tox labs such as this are full partners in the criminalistic field, dealing as they often do with the ultimately undesirable byproduct of crime—a dead body.

This TLC usage screened urine samples taken from former heroin users now involved in the methadone maintenance program. It was also used to check out prospective candidates for the program.

Theoretically, methadone removes the desperate craving heroin addiction has instilled in its victims, although toxicologists close to these programs tell me the craving for the heroin fix is not removed; only the ability to get high on heroin. While the methadone maintenance patient may avoid crime and live a reasonably useful life, he must continue to coexist with his craving. While, theoretically, methadone is administered orally in the presence of the medical staff, there are many indications of loose handling in some locations, permitting abuse of the intent of the program. Methadone is itself highly addictive, and increasingly, methadone is being discovered on the illegal market. This new development is particularly chilling when one considers that heroin was initially developed as a drug to maintain morphine addicts.

Two ground rules control admission to the methadone program. First, the individual must be using heroin, since some societal drop-outs seek to be admitted to the program without any previous history of heroin addiction.

The second rule is that drug abuse must be abandoned when the patient is stabilized in the methadone program.

The TLC plates the San Diego toxicologist showed me were from a newly admitted patient whose heroin abuse needed scientific validation before he could be accepted as a methadone patient. This was a routine check for the toxicologist, such work comprising a large part of his work load.

Head of the class on this addict's TLC plate was a broad black line representing nicotine. The concentration was so strong I suspected his bodily fluids might be used directly as insecticide.

Next came not one but a host of drugs, proof that this sad creature was playing the punchbowl game, where great varieties of drugs are shot into veins, gulped, sniffed, even absorbed through the skin, disregarding the often fatal results of indiscriminate dosage and mixture of drugs. His TLC report card showed him to be using two stimulants in the amphetamine family, one barbiturate downer, and morphine. What a recipe for destruction!

The family fight is the meat and potatoes of the uniformed policeman's life. Next to the street drunk, such quarrels take more of his time than any other of the several hundred problems he's expected to solve with a combination of presence and wisdom. The answer to some of the questions raised would vex Solomon.

Actually, the difference between family fights and street drunks is usually only one of location—and of laws which permit the removal of the street drunk, but which severely curtail the police officer's ability to do much about battling relatives.

Fighting was the order of the day for Sam and Isabel, a middle-aged couple who lived in a trailer park. The low rumblings of the impending storm would first penetrate the adjacent coaches as ominous warning of the torrent to come. The shrill sounds were almost exclusively female, since Isabel had an unlimited capacity for berating her mate. His occasional rebuttals were drowned out by her increasingly virulent stream of invectives. Just before the coach exploded with female ferocity, the door would slam and the neighbors would observe old Sam lurching from the premises to seek asylum at the neighborhood bar until the storm passed—sometimes remaining until closing.

On Sam's departure, Isabel invariably reacted with banshee wailing, sometimes for hours, which set the neighborhood dogs to howling. This evening, Sam was scarcely out of sight before the next door lady felt uneasy. Something about this row was different from their usual fracas.

An hour or two passed before the neighbor suddenly tensed. *Now* she realized what was different. She hadn't heard the wild screaming which always followed Sam's retreat. At last she could stand the anxiety no longer. Late as it was, she went next door and knocked on Isabel's door. When there was no answer, she tried the handle and found it unlocked.

She entered the bedroom and recoiled as she found Isabel's still warm body. Heavy bruises mottled the woman's throat under each ear. While the neighbor lady had never seen Sam lay a hand on Isabel, it seemed clear that he'd finally broken under the strain of constant attack. Reluctantly, she called the police. In short order the law collared Sam and hauled him off to jail to face a charge of murdering his wife.

The postmortem examination of Isabel's body was concluded. Even though this was one of those sordid little dramas which play themselves out daily, the authorities were not jumping to conclusions as to the cause of death. In those locations where competent medical examiner-coroners routinely perform full autopsies, almost one-third of the cases show the physician's stated cause of death to be in error.

True, there were strangulation marks on the victim's neck. The preponderence of evidence gathered by investigators underscored the consistent pattern of their family quarrels. All that remained now, before sending Sam to trial for murder, was confirmation of the cause of death.

The forensic pathologist spoke to the toxicologist, who often attended such autopsies, seeking insight into further chemical analyses of the fluids and tissues from the body's vital organs. "Take a look here," the pathologist said. "The hyoid structure's not damaged. Maybe she wasn't strangled."

In most strangulation cases, the force is sufficient to crush the structure of the throat containing the voice box. The toxicologist examined the heavy bruises on the side of the neck. "Think the husband could have squeezed hard enough on the side of the neck to close off the trachea without harming the hyoid?" he asked.

The autopsy surgeon extended the incision. "Well, the trachea does show signs of pressure," he admitted. "But I don't think there's enough damage to have killed her. See what you can find in the lab."

Both paper and thin-layer chromatography provide quick preliminary routine screening for the illegal and over-the-counter drugs. Increasingly, coroner's cases are turning up evidence of overdose of common proprietary medicines which use antihistamines to induce sleep. "People *will* overdose," the toxicologist explains. "They just don't understand the danger of thinking that if a little is good, a lot will be better. Too many times, death is the penalty for not following medical instructions to the letter."

The paper chromatography test was quickly prepared, with separation of possible drugs into five distinct groups easily accomplished by extracting the tissue with organic solvents. The solvents were evaporated in air, picked up with alcohol, and carefully spotted on the paper for chromatographic analysis. The appropriate standards included nicotine, several amphetamines—speed in the abuser's lexicon—the opium family alkaloids such as morphine and heroin, and four of the barbiturates.

It's a little-known fact that barbiturate addiction is tremendously more dangerous than even that of heroin. One noted pathologist states he's never known death to result from heroin withdrawal—what addicts term going cold turkey. On the other hand, an equally prominent toxicologist states, "Show me a person who 'cold turkeys' a barbiturate habit and I'll show you a corpse." So violent is the withdrawal reaction to a barbituric acid addiction that physicians seldom reduce dosage more than one-eighth of one grain per day in slowly weaning the addict from his drug. How slight this quantity is comes in focus when one considers that an ordinary aspirin tablet contains five grains.

Among the barbiturates, the slow-acting phenobarbitol causes the least trouble. The medium-speed barbiturate, pentobarbitol, known under the trade name of Nembutol, is another matter. Tolerance is quickly gained for this drug, and addicts often operate from day to day at levels of the barbiturate which in a novice would produce a state of severe intoxication, if not coma. Secobarbitals, the reds of drug abuse, are quick-acting and addictive. Flirting with reds is issuing an invitation to death, because of the dangers that the supply can be taken away.

In a few minutes the toxicologist had the test ready, knowns and unknowns spotted side by side. Now the paper was placed in the tank, just touching the solvent, and the glass container covered. The toxicologist had no strong feelings pro or con about what he might find. It was his business to discover facts, not to root for an abused underdog charged with suspicion of murder. And his extensive experience had shown that one of the most common kinds of murder was between husband and wife, particularly where one of the couple was a shrew.

Still, he couldn't help hoping that the facts his test would develop could do something for the poor devil. But truth was truth. And if there was anything in Isabel's tissues which might exonerate Sam, he was going to do his level best to bring it out.

Chapter 15

When the test was completed and the chromatograph sprayed with appropriate reagents to make the climbing materials visible, the toxicologist did a double-take. Seldom had he seen a higher level of pentobarbital. A second extraction of the blood sample and subsequent ultraviolet spectrophotometric analysis provided a second parameter for identification. Clearly the cause of death was barbiturate overdose.

Subsequent investigation proved that Isabel was a card-carrying pentobarbital addict, her physician prescribing the pills a thousand at a time to keep up with her habit. Every day she walked around with enough of the drug in her system to sedate a strong man. Her only reaction was to worsen an already lousy disposition as she bitched her way through life in a continuing half-intoxicated condition.

Additional checks with more intimate friends revealed that when Sam stomped out, Isabel's favorite trick was to grab herself by the throat and try to choke herself to death, all the while screaming at the top of her lungs. "Never saw her without those do-it-yourself bruises," a friend commented.

Sam was released, all suspicion of murder removed. The toxicologist who shared this case with us remembers it well. "Not only did paper chromatography exonerate an innocent man," the toxicologist smiled wryly, "but Sam was the only man my work freed who bothered to come around later and thank me."

In February of 1972 the Midwest Research Institute announced their ability to detect marijuana in a user's urine. Until recently, detection of LSD in biological fluids was not possible either. The typical dosage of LSD is only one hundred micrograms, a microgram equalling one-millionth of a gram. The amount of LSD used for a typical trip is roughly equal in weight to three grains of table salt. Yet when this minuscule dosage is distributed throughout the six to eight quarts of blood in the body, the characteristic metabolates—byproducts of body chemistry—are detectable in an experimental program being developed by the Federal Bureau of Narcotics and Dangerous Drugs, using an immunological technique.

But much of the talent and time of skilled toxicologists is still occupied by the demands for drug identification, including those involving blood alcohol determinations. Most of the toxicologists we've interviewed feel examinations of this sort should be conducted by technicians who could monitor the instruments or conduct the routine chemical examinations under the supervision of their more highly trained associates. Such procedures would free the toxicologists for more extensive research into the exotic chemicals which are killing people, but escaping undetected.

Classifying fingerprints is child's play. Finding and raising latent prints at crime scenes is another matter. Techniques are simple enough: Objects possibly handled by the criminal must be found and checked out. Obvious sites abound, such as the painted sill where the burglar broke in, the murderer's cocktail glass, the cookie jar from which the money vanished—almost any shiny, smooth surface that might have been touched by the criminal and not by others. Some old-time policemen's reluctance to keep their hands off potential fingerprint evidence frequently brought despair to early criminalists.

Dusting with fingerprint powder of a color contrasting with that of the surface is standard technique. The powder clings to the moisture or waxlike material secreted by the pores of the fingers. Often the latent print can be seen by the unaided eye if lighted at an oblique angle, suggesting a flashlight as the fingerprint technician's friend. A burglary of a restaurant or butcher shop might produce beautiful fingerprints—in grease! Since ordinary fingerprint powder embraces grease like a bride greeting her husband, special phototechniques, using oblique lighting so that the fingerprint ridges cast heavy shadows, are called for. Sometimes the visible print will be left in blood, posing a special problem in preservation for possible court use. A criminalist is automatically suspicious of the print *too* easy to see, since all parts of the print—valleys as well as ridges—may attract the powder, creating an instant mess.

Once the print is raised, it is usually photographed in place with an identifying label. Then it can be lifted with transparent adhesive tape, which swoops up the print and is then transferred to a contrasting color card. Occasionally, prints will be raised black on black, as some operators dislike the light-colored dusting powders. In this situation the photos are taken of the print after transfer to the white card, since greatly enlarged photos are required for court exhibits.

Relatively little training is required to mess around with the nasty dusting powder. Given patience, tenacity, and a willingness to inadvertently perform in blackface, any intelligent technician can quickly master the art.

But latent print detection becomes sticky in the direct ratio to the smoothness and impermeability of the surface and the recentness of the impression. Some situations call for special measures, since the run-of-the-mill fingerprint is a fleeting thing, bedeviled by strong sunlight and undone by fog or dew. Such latents are usually forgotten unless the importance of the case calls for heroic measures.

Where ordinary dusting was difficult or impossible because of the nature of the surface and where photographic tricks availed little, a couple of last-ditch avenues remained. One was a special dusting powder which fluoresces under ultraviolet light; another was infrared photography.

A newer technique is the use of a dense metallic powder to be photographed with soft X rays. This is particularly valuable where there is a busy background which interferes with examination of the fingerprint pattern.

A still newer technique is mostly a twinkle in the eyes of workers at the University of California's Scripps Institution of Oceanography Visibility Laboratory. Basic to their concept is the strong possibility that in any given photographic negative, there's more to see than the human eye-brain combination is able to interpret. With the assistance of computer image processing programs, developed over many years, the laboratory has been able to do remarkable work in enhancing the quality of the intelligence obtainable from existing photos. The applications far transcend mere fingerprint photos, yet they have many possible applications in the fingerprint field. Forensic application is in its infancy, but these concepts offer much future promise.

Fingerprints sometimes turn up in the strangest places. I can recall almost hanging from a chandelier, trying to photograph a fingerprint left in the grease surrounding a high transom through which a burglar had gained entry to the restaurant. Often, it seems, prints can be located on surfaces and in positions which are difficult if not impossible to photograph *in situ*.

The fun has just begun with the lifted latent. The matching print may well be already in the local files, or certainly in the enormous files maintained at the state and national level; but this means nothing unless there is a known suspect, or a culprit so red hot that all ten of his digits grace a single-print file.

The Henry classification method is merely an orderly device for handling rolled impressions of all ten fingers—with escape hatches provided for amputations or other disfigurements. Properly classified, such prints can be matched with file cards in minutes. Since Mother Nature gets tricky at times, alternate classifications are checked where, for instance, there's doubt whether the prints contain an ulnar loop or a central pocket loop, to pitch the parlance. But before standard ten-print files are useful for latent print identification, the researcher must have a specific suspect in mind. Only then can his or her card be compared with evidence fingerprints.

Single-print files are something else. These are put together by cutting up standard ten-print cards into individual fingers, which are then classified in a more sophisticated fashion. Only the most wanted or the specialty criminals achieve honor position in these files. The beauty of single-print files, however, is that latents *can* be matched directly from the files without any idea of the suspect's identity. While local agencies who take the trouble to maintain single-print files get excellent payoff, the fact is that few such files exist anywhere. Practically, there's scarcely paper and files enough to accommodate everyone, nor are classification methods selective enough to handle enormous numbers.

This brings us to the disadvantage of practical fingerprint use in criminalistics. No magic device exists to locate a single latent print in voluminous files. The partnership between the investigator and the scientist is crucial. First comes the tentative identity of the suspect, then comes the fingerprint make.

Another commonly misunderstood aspect of fingerprint identification is the belief that the prints can be superimposed over each other to provide perfect fit. Flesh is flexible, so the overlay idea is out. What does matter is the positioning of each characteristic feature in exact relationship with all others.

Suppose the core of the print has two small ridges resembling the number 11. To the left of this central detail a ridge circles toward the tip of the finger, and shortly branches into a Y. The tips of this Y continue long enough to surround a dot, then reconverge into a single ridge. This kind of detail continues endlessly, with comparison made one feature at a time, until enough points of similarity are found to convince the expert he has a make.

The exact number of points of identification needed to achieve a make is hotly debated, since some characteristics are rarer than others and are given greater weight. Most experts agree that twelve simple features are enough. Many say they're satisfied with as few as six similarities, if they are unusual enough. There is general agreement, in common with other forensic areas, that the experience, judgment, and integrity of the expert counts more than the technique itself. In fingerprint matching, as in nearly every other facet of forensic science, more than simple technique is called for. Results depend on the skill with which the technique is administered.

While electronic wizardry is on the horizon, fingerprint search and identification is still a job for men, not machines. Even the two hundred million FBI prints are still searched manually.

The McDonnal-Douglas Corporation has developed a cunning mechanism which manages preliminary search, limiting the human examination to the last half-dozen possibilities. But before the intelligence can be taken out of the computer, it must first be fed in. Even though the system looks great, thus far there are no takers. Here again, science is a full step ahead of practice.

As hard as it is to get good prints and match them, though, it is always worse not having any prints or where impressions indicate that the criminal was professional enough to wear gloves.

Wallace Dillon is a fingerprint expert with the Long Beach, California, crime lab. The most unusual case in his twenty-five years of experience started when a burglary took place in a small commercial café. The cash register and vending machine had been forced open and the money taken. Dusting for fingerprints produced some completely clear impressions without any discernible friction ridges. The reason became clear when further inspection of the premises produced a single rubber glove of the type used by housewives to protect their hands while doing the dishes.

There was no chance for fingerprints, so Dillon packed up his fingerprint gear and prepared to return to the lab. As a matter of routine he preserved the glove, even though hundreds of thousands of such gloves were sold annually in the Los Angeles area. Outside of the gross hand size, the glove really offered no chance of physical evidence. Still, he thought it might be of some future help.

The glove lay there on Dillon's desk outside the instrument and wet chemistry section of the crime lab, almost mocking him as he wrote up the burglary report. The more he stared at the glove, the more of a personal challenge it became, since no other evidence had been found at the burglary scene. Long after he should have turned the glove in to the evidence locker, Dillon stared at it.

Suddenly a thought struck him. He'd never heard of such a thing, but could there possibly be a latent image *inside* that glove? With the greatest of care he turned the glove inside out and brought out his dusting kit.

Unbelievably, a latent image developed in the index finger area and in a portion of the palm. Palm and footprints can be as useful as the friction ridge pattern on the tips of fingers in suspect identification, although the search may take many times as long because of the size of the area to be checked.

What was needed now, of course, was a suspect to match with the latent—but that had to wait for the work of the investigators. It might be years before this burglar would slip and leave fingerprints to check for a match.

In the next few days, however, another element entered the case. Long Beach, like most progressive law enforcement agencies, keeps a record of all shakedowns—interrogations of individuals who are checked under seemingly suspicious circumstances. When such a stop is made and the individual not detained, a routine card is filed recording the incident and the identity of the suspect.

. 161 .

Before a week had passed, one of these cards came across Dillon's desk. When the shakedown card was checked against the file, it was found that the individual had been arrested in the past on suspicion of burglary. Dillon was still curious about the latent in the glove. Quickly, he took the fingerprint record from the files and secured the latent image taken from the inside of the glove.

It was a make! He was able to identify the right index finger of the suspect as that left in the glove from the burglary scene. An arrest was made the following day. When the larger palm prints were rolled, another match was made from that portion of the latent print.

The burglar pled guilty at the time of his preliminary hearing.

Certain crimes are so inexplicable and horrible to contemplate that the average person can scarcely bear to read about their details, let alone view pictures of the depths of degradation to which man can sink. The Tate and La Bianca cases were of this sort, senseless slaughter, where homes were broken into and unbelievable violence committed on total strangers.

Other bloody crimes, ranging from those of Jack the Ripper to the butcher murders of modern times, seem to be the product of demented minds who resolve sexual fantasy by wallowing in a victim's blood.

Equally chilling to the law-abiding is the thought of awakening to find a burglar at the bedside. The concept is even more terrifying when the burglar has forcible rape in mind—or worse.

A series of such burglary-rape attacks occurred in southern California during the early part of 1970. The victim would be aroused during the early morning hours by the criminal standing at the side of the bed. A sweater, with the sleeves cut off, was always pulled over his head, two slits cut into the material for eyeholes so the burglar could see without being seen. He invariably wore cloth gloves, eliminating the chance of leaving fingerprints. In some cases he carried a gun and enforced his demands with the threat of shooting the victim.

As soon as the victim was awake, the burglar pulled a pillow case over her head, making it impossible for her to observe details of his clothing. He then tied her up with materials improvised on the scene. If she were married, the husband was similarly packaged inside a pillow case and trussed so that he could not move.

Then the burglar would ransack the premises, taking the valuables to a vehicle outside. Finally, he always returned to the bedroom, untied the female, and forcibly raped her.

One burglary-rape case followed another, primarily in Long Beach and in the communities adjacent to the lovely home town of the *Queen Mary*. As with similar crime waves, terror clutched the hearts of many in the community. The nickname Phantom Rapist was applied by the press, and soon banner headlines greeted each new strike by the vicious criminal.

In spite of intensified activity by many police agencies in that portion of Los Angeles County, the rapist continued his attacks. In one instance where the modus operandi was similar, pillow case over the head and all, the victim had died.

And the evidence accumulated. Not fingerprints of course, but fibers were exchanged between the attacker and his victims during the sexual attacks. Soon, chief criminalist Martin Klein of the Long Beach crime lab knew that the rapist's concealing sweater-of-the-moment was made of wool, dyed a dark green. In several of the rapes, the severed ends of the sleeves and the area where the eye slits had been cut out had shed a fiber or two. Klein also knew that the gloves worn by the rapist had a brown cotton wristband, since, in two cases, threads of his material had been transferred to the rape scene.

The number of attacks was mounting; as was public pressure to stop them by catching the elusive criminal. By now the Long Beach investigators had developed the identity of a prime suspect. He lived in the nearby community of Lakewood, which is serviced by the Los Angeles sheriff's office under contract with the city. With the cooperation of the sheriff's detail, the Long Beach officers kept the suspect's house under constant surveillance, hoping to catch him in the act. Still, on occasion the suspect would be unaccountably absent for some period of time. And the burglary-rapes continued.

At last the police were able to develop one additional type of evidence. They raised a latent print on the point of forced entry of one of the burglary-rape cases. No ordinary latent, this print revealed the image of a cotton glove instead of human friction ridges. Apparently the glove had become increasingly dirty with the series of crimes, until it was leaving prints from the greasy residue remaining on the fabric. The burning question, now, was could the glove-prints be matched if the suspect were found with such a glove in his possession?

Detectives leading the investigation decided that the time had come to lower the boom. On the morning of March 20, 1970, they arrested Albert Raymond Savage, Jr. In his possession was found a sweater with sleeves cut off and with eye apertures cut in the front of the garment. In his pickup truck the investigators located a pair of cotton gloves. Wallace Dillon, veteran Long Beach identification technician, was given the job of trying to identify the seized gloves with the latent glove-print raised at the crime scene.

While gloves made from animal skins had been identified in previous cases, there was no known case of cotton glove identification made from latent prints. In the animal leathers, the random distribution of skin pores could supply considerable individuality; but mass-produced woven cotton gloves did not offer that opportunity for singularity.

Technician Dillon decided to treat the glove as he would a human hand to be checked for comparison prints. First, he inked the fingers of the glove with a rubber roller. Carefully, the glove was pressed against clean white cardboard. At first inspection, the inked print certainly resembled that of the crime scene latent. One particularly interesting feature was the pattern left by the little finger on the left hand. In ordinary gloves, the seam falls between the fingers. Evidently twisted from long usage, the seam of the left little finger of the glove had shifted around until it ran squarely down the middle of the impression left by the finger, making a long S pattern. Dillon took up the six-power magnifying glass used for fingerprint comparison. He hoped he would find enough unique characteristics to make positive identification.

After hours of work, he shook his head despondently. So far he'd made six points of similarity, unique points of a thread ending, a missed thread, or a break in the weave, which would not be a class characteristic and could not be accounted for by random distribution. But six comparison points simply weren't enough. There was no history, no precedent as to the number of points of similarity essential to positively identify a glove-print with its latent. Millions of fingerprint comparisons and thousands of tests in court had established the reliability of twelve or more points of similarity for fingerprints, so there was that to go on. But in a glove-print, six points seemed just too weak to use in testing a new type of identification—especially with charges as serious as burglary, rape, and commission of a felony while armed. This last charge was particularly serious and was based on the fact that the rapist had forced his will at gunpoint in five of the incidents and was a convicted felon.

So where should they turn now? Dillon conferred with chief criminalist Klein. Was there any route they might pursue which would strengthen the identification of the latent print left by the suspect's glove?

Long Beach chief criminalist Martin Klein had heard of the work of James L. Harris, Sr., associate director of the Scripps Visibility Laboratory. When Dillon announced that he could only find six matching points between the suspect's glove and the latent print, Klein wondered if the talents of the visibility laboratory might help.

As we mentioned before, visibility enhancement is based on the concept that there may be more intelligence in a photographic negative than the unaided human eye is prepared to interpret. A photo of the insignia on a commercial jet airplane, snapped during takeoff, may appear too fuzzy to read because the camera failed to stop the action. The visibility scientist first breaks down the negative image into many thousands of dots, which are stored in a computer's memory. Then, mathematically, he asks the computer how each smeared line of the airplane photo might look if it were squeezed back into a single dot. In their image-enhancement exploration, the Scripps scientists had developed computer programming to answer many dozens of such questions.

In the case of the Phantom Rapist, the critical question was whether image enhancement could provide enough additional matching points so that there could be no question that the cloth glove had left the print at the scene of the rape. A phone call later, and Dillon was on his way to see if electronic wizardry might bring greater clarity to the photographs of the glove and the latent print.

First, Harris used a tiny beam of light to copy the thirty-five-millimeter transparencies on which the evidence was recorded. The electronic scanner used more than sixty-five thousand dots of light to reproduce the values of the original photos. This information was then stored in the computer's memory, and the marvelous machinery went to work. Over the years the visibility laboratory had programmed several dozen types of processing, each of which was designed to extract meaning from images which needed some form of change in order for their message to come across. Selecting the appropriate prescheduled computer programs, the evidence images almost miraculously began to yield visual secrets which had been locked within the transparencies. Numerous details, previously hidden, sprang into focus almost like the developing image in conventional photography.

When the processing was complete, Harris was able to point out fourteen additional paired points on the evidence glove and the latent glove-print. Added to the original six matching points, no doubt remained that Savage's glove had left the latent print found at the scene of a rape and burglary a month and a half earlier.

The glove evidence was not alone. The matching fibers transferred during the attacks and the testimony of the victims were all part of the trial. After thirteen hours of deliberation, the jury convicted Albert Savage of all fifteen felonies, as charged.

The conviction was appealed on the grounds that there was no precedent for admitting evidence concerning the enhancement of glove impression evidence. As of this writing, decision from the appeal has not been rendered.

Much of what our society terms progress is owed to the ingenuity of a Chinese eunuch, Ts'ai Lun. A resident of the imperial palace of the Han dynasty in the Hunan province, Ts'ai Lun was by profession a sword-maker, noted for his skill in producing original weapons. He was disturbed by the problems encountered in recording official records on wood, bamboo slips, even silk; so his inventive mind pursued alternate methods less tedious than hacking wooden tablets. Like the medieval alchemists of a thousand years later, he concocted steaming potions of mulberry bark and old rags and fish nets. He boiled the mixture, attacked it with lime, then strained the resultant fibrous mass through a bamboo sieve. He spread it out and allowed it to dry. He had produced the first usable paper. The year was *A.D.* 105.

Ts'ai Lun's invention was enormously popular and its use spread rapidly. One manuscript, now preserved in the British Museum, goes back to *A.D.* 150, when it was placed in one of the ancient towers of the Great Wall of China.

The proliferation of Ts'ai Lun's creation meant immediate trouble. The universal use of paper inevitably led to producing documents of value. Venal men soon learned that what was done could be undone. Or *re*done, to increase the value of the document to the forger. Thus began the ongoing saga of questioned documents, their detection, and their exposure.

Many economists believe a simple index to the health of an economy is the total weight of the paper involved. No doubt we are a paper-oriented civilization, and criminalistics is involved with its fair share.

Check forgery, called uttering and passing in legalese, is the number one byproduct in the questioned document field. Fictitious documents relating to property ownership rank high also, forged ownership papers for stolen vehicles being a must in peddling hot cars. Among the most ingenious forgeries are alterations to wills or codicils which tamper with inheritance plans made by the deceased.

But tremendous obstacles have traditionally been encountered in prying prints from paper, with its voracious appetite for grease. In cases where criminals clearly handled paper, forged signatures, and altered wills and contracts, usable fingerprints have scarcely ever been used to link the criminal with his crime, because fingerprints on paper are difficult to retrieve.

Formerly, the technique for fingerprint development on paper relied on the chemical reaction between iodine fumes and the fatty residue of the fingerprints. A glass tube about five inches long was filled with iodine crystals retained with glass wool packing. Each end of the tube was stoppered with a rubber, perforated cork with thin glass tubes inserted in the cork openings. Warm breath was blown through the iodine crystals, and the apparatus directed the resulting brown fumes against the suspected fingerprint location on the paper. As soon as the first faint brown lines of the latent print appeared, a mighty puffing ensued, together with a race against time to capture the beauty on film before it took its bashful leave. Photography of prints on paper occurred so seldom, that outside of running short of breath or suffering occasional nausea from the toxic fumes, little actual fingerprint business took place.

Because of the unreliability of iodine fuming an alternate method was sought. In the newer technique the suspected area was swabbed with a silver nitrate solution. Silver ions will react with the sodium chloride, or salt, left by perspiration, forming silver chloride, a photographic chemical which can then be developed like a photographic print.

As with iodine fuming, in only a few cases was the silver nitrate treatment successful. However, for thirty years, it was fume or swab in vital searches for fingerprints on paper.

Then came Ninhydrin!

Chapter *16*

Consider if you will the number of times familiar objects are handled and have the opportunity to retain fingerprints. Subtract the number of prints which are smudged, imperfect, or layered one on top of the other. The remainder is the maximum number of fingerprints which might be developed by a technique effective even after three decades.

It's obvious that one of the greatest problems is a surfeit of fingerprints. We can only estimate just how many hands a forged check travels through from the time it is passed in a store until it is turned over to the check detail of the police department; so a good deal of luck is needed to minimize conflicting impressions.

The patented chemical, Ninhydrin, is usually first dissolved in methanol, or wood alcohol, and the methanol mixture is then shaken in a decanting flask with petroleum ether, permitting a minute amount of the Ninhydrin to diffuse into the other liquid. Because of the difference in specific gravity of the two immiscible liquids, they quickly separate, whereupon the petroleum ether is drawn off, ready to process a document that may contain fingerprints.

Several techniques are used in developing the latent images. The Ninhydrin reacts with the amino acids originally contained in the protein deposited with the fingerprint. Amino acids are the building blocks of nature, and the protein must be broken down by heating before the amino acids can react with the Ninhydrin. In the most common technique, a thin layer of solution is poured over the document in a shallow tray, much as a photographer develops the metallic silver image in a photograph print. The container is then placed in a humidity chamber, which is heated just under the boiling point of water, and the material left to develop slowly. When sufficient time—perhaps twenty-four hours—has passed, a faint pinkish image will begin to appear. When it has developed to maximum intensity, it can then be photographed and compared with exemplar fingerprints for identification. Some crime labs hasten the process by pressing the soaked document with a household iron until the image appears. Ninhydrin is widely used in today's crime labs with great success.

One of a successful check forger's greatest assets is the ability to remain undistinguished. Typically, he or she is difficult to remember, deliberately mousey, blending into the background. Even when confronted with eyewitnesses, there is a strong likelihood that the criminal will not be remembered.

The next step is usually handwriting identification, but this is always tough when comparing a single signature as compared with a more lengthy document.

With a Ninhydrin-developed fingerprint, however, all doubt is removed, and not only in check forgeries. In all types of questioned document cases, the ability to develop long dormant fingerprints can be of immense help to the examiner.

The Ninhydrin technique has application in a wide variety of other cases. On May 27, 1964, two men entered a bank in Richmond, Virginia, with the intention of robbing it. Convinced that a display of good faith would further their purpose, they went through the motions of obtaining a bank loan from the manager. The robbers then threatened the manager with a pistol and escaped with a $2,540 "loan."

Two customers saw one of the robbers light a cigarette, smoke part of it, and discard it in an ash tray in the bank. The cigarette butt was retrieved from the ash tray, being the only one found there, by an investigator and sent to the FBI's identification division for examination.

Using the chemical Ninhydrin for processing, a latent finger-print was developed on the short length of cigarette paper. A short time later, the manager of a surplus store identified a photograph as that of a customer who had purchased a revolver the day before the robbery. The man was found to have a criminal record. The latent print on the cigarette butt was identical with one of the prints of the man who purchased the revolver.

Several weeks later, the suspect was arrested on burglary charges in Oklahoma City, Oklahoma, and admitted having committed the Virginia bank robbery. He pled guilty and received a sentence of ten years to run concurrently with a three-year sentence on the burglary charge in Oklahoma City. His accomplice also was arrested and convicted of the Virginia bank robbery.

One of the major scourges in the expanding drug problem is the illicit laboratory. Not only are these home chemists manufacturing illegal materials; all too often they have no regard for basic cleanliness or purity standards, and may well be producing lethal mixtures.

Knowledge of one such operation was leaked to narcotics officers through their underground contacts. Since these illicit laboratories are somewhat similar to a floating crap game, one of the toughest enforcement aspects is to find where they're operating at the moment.

In this case, the suspect had evidently been feeling uneasy and had vacated the premises just ahead of the arresting officers. Clearly, this had been the underground drug laboratory, located in a filthy garage loaded with vats, distilling apparatus, and the other paraphernalia of the chemical bootlegger. Everything was coated with an accumulation of grime. The agents shuddered to think of the quality of the drugs such a laboratory might produce.

The most important piece of evidence—the operator—was missing. How close they'd come to catching him at work was indicated by the notebook he'd left behind. In it were his manufacturing formulae essential for the conversion of raw chemicals into such illegal drugs as LSD.

The raiding agents carefully preserved the notebook and brought it and the other evidence to the crime lab. They'd had a particular suspect in mind for some time whose fingerprints were on file from previous arrests. Could the lab bring up any latents on the paper on which these formulae were handwritten?

Twenty-four hours later, the criminalist peered hopefully into his Ninhydrin brew. Something was coming into view. He waited patiently as the image intensified, then took it out for examination. There was the bonanza they'd been hoping for, a strong latent print. Best of all, it was a perfect match with a print from the suspect's booking card. Thanks to Ninhydrin, another link in the infamous drug chain was cut.

The nephew who tilts Aunt Martha's intention to leave her all to the animal shelter by substituting a forged codicil (but without leaving fingerprints) may get away with the deed, unless someone recalls that on her deathbed Aunt Martha thanked the saints she'd resisted her ne'er-do-well nephew's importuning to alter her will. Such a recollection turns the spotlight on the codicil naming the nephew as beneficiary.

The writing looks a little strange and rather shaky. Remember, though, Aunt Martha was mighty trembly during her final months. So the questions is, did she or didn't she? Enter the questioned document section of the crime lab.

Such a case often hinges on two elements. First, is the document genuine? Second, where, when, how, and by whom was the document produced? Nearly all these inquiries are answerable by questioned document specialists, but some are tougher than others.

Handwriting, with its foibles, eccentricities, and changing character, is the chief product the Q.D. examiner deals with. The basic consideration is that handwriting is learned behavior which takes tens of thousands of repetitions before skill is mastered. By the time handwriting jells into the usual semiautomatic procedure it is for most people, the idiosyncrasies are well-established. The writing may vary slightly with speed, or the emotional or physical state of the individual; but for any given period, handwriting is remarkably consistent from sample to sample.

The most important element of handwriting identification involves movement in the line of script, such as in beginning strokes and relative heights of letters. Other aspects relate to particular habits in closing or not closing letters such as a or o, the angle and height at which the t is crossed or the i dotted, the relative size of commonly used letters, and similar slight variations characteristic to the individual. Obvious other elements include factors such as spelling, punctuation, and phraseology. The difference between freely flowing writing and the hesitant, slow, halting writing of all but the most skilled forgers is immediately detectable to the skilled criminalist.

While consistent during any one period in a person's lifetime, handwriting does change, particularly with aging. Since a basic principle in handwriting comparison is to match the questioned writing with that known to be genuine, it is most important to find exemplars known to be written at the same period as the questioned document. Such sources include correspondence, voting records, school and bank records, and others limited only by the investigator's resourcefulness.

As in the other areas of criminalistics, the partnership between scientist and investigator will determine the efficacy of the case handling. Since no two handwriting samples are ever precisely alike, it is most important to have an adequate number of samples for comparison purposes. When comparison standards are gathered from preexisting sources, conscientious examiners prefer at least twenty to twenty-five such samples.

The ball game is quite different when the samples are written after a suspect is in custody for the purpose of comparing his handwriting with that on a questioned document.

The investigator's skill in obtaining adequate, nondisguised samples is all-important. Techniques include obtaining samples in quantity, one after the other. Except for very simple exemplars, such as those used in comparing signatures, the accepted method calls for dictation by the investigator of the desired phrases and wording. Disguise of the thrust of the investigation often involves carefully planned statements containing key words and phrases from the questioned documents arranged innocuously, with no relationship to their order in the questioned document.

As each statement is dictated to the suspect, the exemplar is removed and the same exercise repeated then or at a later time. Concealment of normal writing practice becomes difficult when these techniques are employed.

In the Juan Corona mass-murder trial, the prosecution tried to violate this procedure by demanding that Corona copy the language of the evidence documents, including mistakes of spelling and grammar. On advice of counsel, Corona refused to play this highly prejudicial game, even though it cost his attorney time in jail for contempt. In my opinion, however, the order was an abuse of ethical questioned document technique.

Evidence ground rules must be scrupulously observed in all phases of interrogative procedure, including the obtaining of handwriting exemplars. Foremost is the genuineness of the exemplar used to tie the forger to the questioned document.

Witnesses must be available to testify that the suspect wrote the material used as exemplar. The court may hold that the sample writing used for comparative purposes did not have relevance to the case at hand. This aspect is becoming less of a problem as courts lean toward admission of handwriting exemplars, regardless of subject relevance, as long as they were undeniably written by the suspect. In a few instances, the genuineness of the comparison writing may be established by a witness who can convince the judge or jury of his familiarity with the handwriting of the accused.

In situations of this sort the difficulties may be overcome by showing the accused the documents the investigator desires to introduce, and gaining his admission that he authored the writing in question.

In the case of samples written by the suspect, it is most important that they be accompanied by a statement, generally written on the first page of the exemplar, that the sample was given voluntarily.

Most of these precautions are the responsibility of the investigator, prior to the review of questioned documents and exemplars by the crime lab, since if all legal niceties are not met, the Q.D. conclusions may be inadmissible in court.

Much has happened to the art of paper manufacturing since the days of Ts'ai Lun, with mammoth machines now spewing forth paper at the rate of literally a mile a minute. Production techniques in vogue during any given historical period assist the examiner when genuineness hinges upon inherent paper qualities. Modern bond paper is a thin sheet of matted or felted vegetable fiber with a filler such as clay and sizing such as starch, casein, or rosin. In very recent years, manufacturers have added fluorocarbon sizing, which responds to the ultraviolet wavelengths of light present in most illuminating sources, converting them to the visible range. All this makes the paper appear whiter than when seen without UV light.

This one characteristic is particularly helpful when erasures are made, mechanically or chemically, since the fluorocarbon content is often affected at the erased spot. Where the unassisted eye might detect no sign of the alteration, the camera responding to the UV light source will single out the forgery.

At the other end of the visible light spectrum, the longer infrared rays frequently see where man's built-in visual limitations make it impossible. A Toronto case recently involved the theft of a number of government checks by an employee. The normal check-writing technique used by this agency was to print several asterisks, followed by the figures for the amount of the check. In this case, the check was originally written for forty dollars, preceded by four asterisks. The forger erased the asterisk in front of the number 4 and substituted the number 2, which increased the amount by two hundred dollars. The forgery was done skilfully, with no question asked in the banks that cashed the altered checks.

Under the infrared eye, however, the added 2 was glaringly apparent. At ten magnifications, the evidence photo sent the forger to a deserved stretch in prison.

Check forgeries, such as the one just described, occupy enormous amounts of investigative effort and form the bulk of questioned document work in most jurisdictions. Like heroin addiction, the virus of check forgery seems to addict its victims incurably. Virtually all the clever check swindlers ultimately fall afoul of the law and end up in the bucket. While serving time, most of these people swap experiences with other check forgers and are scarcely able to wait until release and another go at forgery, sure that this time they will escape punishment.

A large-scale gang operation relied on the combination of stolen checks, stolen check-writers, and the gullibility of individuals selling their own automobiles. Armed with forged credentials and checks, members of the gang answered advertisements and bought cars from people so surprised at the easy sale that they failed to take rudimentary steps as to the determination of the identity of the buyer.

These cars were quickly altered to disguise the original identity, shipped hundreds of miles, and resold in another part of the country. The larcenous feature which seemed to clinch these deals was the certified impression on the checks, suggesting they were good as gold. This feature was achieved by a fairly crude substitution, on a portion of a genuine rubber stamp, of the term *Certified,* which was pasted in place.

The substitution left faint irregular marks on each of the

checks, giving the questioned document examiner his version of the jigsaw fit. In short order, the hundred-thousand-dollar scheme was traded for extensive time in prison, where, no doubt, other ingenious schemes would be hatched by this incurably optimistic breed.

The historical development of inks is well-known, to the sorrow of forgers of ancient manuscripts. In the days before the ballpoint revolution, permanent inks were preferred for important documents. Document age could be estimated with some reliability, since record ink, containing iron gallotanate, undergoes an orderly series of color changes. First, the ink darkens under the influence of light and oxygen. Then, within a few months at the most, the fading process commences, imperceptibly weakening the image over the years until, half a century or more later, only a rust-colored deposit remains.

Until the forties, when large-scale manufacture of ballpoint pens in Argentina created popular use of the 1880 invention, some fairly accurate estimates of permanent-ink age were attempted on the basis of chloride migration. In theory, the invisible chlorides of permanent ink start shuffling away from the parent line before the ink is fully dry. This process continues at a predictable rate. After bleaching and other chemical processing, the chloride migration can be compared with similar migration in specimens of known age. This is a useful technique when the specific age of the writing is in question, as with Aunt Martha's codicil, which may prove to have been written after her demise.

Regrettably, economic pressures have forced ink manufacturers to substitute cheaper sulfates for the chlorides, and there are no known tests for their age. Scratch one formerly usable technique.

Another age dating device is hidden literally just below the surface of the paper. Pressed into the paper during manufacture by the romantically titled dandy roll, the watermark offers yeoman service in dating a particular piece of paper. Design of watermarks change, with the period relatively easy to establish from records most paper companies maintain. Recently, paper producers have introduced inconspicuous coding marks to date production even more closely. Add to that the wear and tear on the dandy roll, with production samples regularly placed in files, and paper dating may be relatively simple.

In one case of income tax evasion the defendant was charged with fudging on some hundred thousand dollars of taxes. He introduced into evidence a work sheet allegedly used to prepare his 1962 income tax form.

The FBI's examination of this work sheet revealed a watermark containing a vertical code marking under the second O in COTTON, a portion of the watermark. To the defendant's sorrow, this marking was used to date paper manufactured in 1971. Exit one tax evader.

Dating ballpoint writing is something else, and ballpoints comprise more than eighty percent of today's Q.D. cases. Ballpoint ink, unfortunately, consists of organic dyes and organic vehicles which, thus far, have resisted any dating methods.

As if to compensate for this lack, recent techniques were developed to identify a specific ballpoint pen with its writing, based on the excellent likelihood that in spite of the millions of such pens produced, many will possess unique flaws which the persistent Q.D. examiner may use to mate a document to its pen.

Examined under high magnification, writing strokes from ballpoint pens often are discovered to be striped, both vertically and horizontally. Representing areas on the minuscule ball which are failing to retain ink, certain of the stripes running in the direction of the stroke are class characteristics found in most such pens. Others luckily turn out to be highly individualistic, due, in all probability, to a microscopic burr or imperfection on either the ball or encapsulating mechanism. It is thus possible—if only occasionally—to specifically match such writing with its source. The rub is that only one-eighth of the ball is involved in any given stroke; so, statistically, another seven samples must be traced before the matching imperfection will return to view. Practically, the examiner might need a hundred strokes, or a thousand, before the payoff.

Occasionally the would-be forger, recognizing the danger of writing a document by hand, will think he can beat the game by using a typewriter. Alas for the felon, typewriters have peculiarities quite as useful for Q.D. purposes as those of handwriting.

First task for the Q.D. examiner is locating the make of

typewriter involved. The enormous files of the FBI are available for this purpose. Many of their typewriter standards show dates when styles of type were first introduced as well as those dates when periodic modifications were made. Style variations are easily discernible. The files, which are constantly updated, cover virtually every typing instrument manufactured in modern times. Add to that the immense experience of their Q.D. examiners and the resulting information on make and model facilitates the next vital phase of the investigation—locating the particular machine which produced the evidence. Here's where investigative skill must match that of the crime lab.

Once located, the typewriter is a veritable tattletale. Should the questioned document have been written on a new ribbon, the ribbon itself may retain the whole of the message. This is especially true of carbon ribbons.

In a 1970 case handled by the FBI, a bank in Pine Bluff, Arkansas, was robbed of over seven thousand dollars by a bandit who left his handwritten note demanding the money on the bank counter as he fled with the loot. A possible suspect was identified and was arrested a few months later on suspicion of bank robbery.

Meanwhile, a gent named Ronald Leroy Long had written to a Pine Bluff pawnshop, requesting that a ring and two watches he had pawned be sent to him. When the pawnshop owner received word that a man of the same name was being questioned by the FBI on the bank robbery, he turned over his letter from Long requesting the return of the pawned items.

Laboratory examination of the demand note and the pawnshop correspondence developed the almost incredible intelligence that the note written before the bank robbery which demanded the loot had been on top of the pawnshop letter when it was written. The impression of the robbery note was clearly indented in the other paper. No doubt Long will hesitate before writing another felonious note on top of a letter to be sent elsewhere. His conviction and six-year sentence should give him plenty of time to decide on the error of that way.

Second-sheet impressions or those on fresh carbon paper may identify the source of a questioned document. Who among us has not seen the sleuth on the late movie who scrutinizes the blank tablet alongside the missing girl's telephone, and deciphers the imprint of the message indented on the blank sheet below? The same potential exists for the back-up typing sheet.

Under certain circumstances, the typewriter offers mute testimony dating the age of the questioned document far more accurately than is possible with inks. Consider the situation in a busy office where a hard-working typewriter is subject to continuous day-in-day-out service. From time to time anxious fingers jumble the type, leaving minute traces of the collision between type bars. Such encounters may elevate, twist, or depress typeface alignment, as may other wear-and-tear action. So as the work grinds out, the aging record of the machine remains in the dated office files, to one day help establish the approximate date when the same machine typed the questioned document.

The typewriter's proclivity for snitching often saves the day, as in the FBI case where a will dated December 14, 1925, proved to have been typed on a Remington typewriter using Pica No. 1 type—a style not designed until 1926 nor used in production models until 1927.

Even though the careful comparison of the typewriter's eccentricities with those of the questioned document may produce machine identification as reliable as that of the fingerprint, there still remains the task of proving who operated the typewriter.

A number of legal no-nos lie in wait for the careless Q.D. examiner. He must be exquisitely careful not to add or detract from the evidence he's examining. Circled combinations of letters or other overwriting with which he celebrates discovery of identifiable characteristics may toss him out of the box when the case arrives in court. Marks from staples or pins may offer cause for rejection of the evidence, since the document obviously "ain't quite what it used to be." But staples can be useful too.

Chapter 17

The man was acting strangely, the witnesses remembered. In spite of the warm day, one of the three men took a poncho out of the trunk of the parked car and draped it over his head and shoulders. He took something else out of the trunk which the witnesses couldn't see and thrust it out of sight up under the poncho. Then he and one companion sauntered in the direction of the bank a couple of blocks away. In a few minutes the driver pulled from the curb and drove in the direction of the bank.

About that time two stocking-masked gunmen entered the bank, one threatening with a sawed-off shotgun, the other with a hand gun. They obtained some seven thousand dollars in loot, including a hundred-dollar bundle of marked money. Warning the bank employees not to call for help, the robbers escaped in the waiting car.

Half an hour later the suspect car was stopped in a neighboring community. The car was registered in the driver's name, an item which lessened suspicion since no self-respecting bank robber would commit such a *faux pas*. The driver did, however, have about twenty-one hundred dollars in cash in his possession, which he stated he was taking to another city to pay some overdue bills. He accounted for the money by saying it was part of a forty-five hundred dollar court judgment he'd received a few months earlier. Investigation showed that he was telling the truth about the judgment.

The suspect wasn't exactly off the hook though, because the bank teller stated she recognized several of the bills in the suspect's possession. One bill, in particular, had the number 17 written on it with a felt-tipped pen. This number stuck in her memory as having been there when she'd counted her money just before the robbery. In addition she recalled counting several one-dollar bills that had been torn apart and repaired by stapling the halves together. Four such bills were in the twenty-one hundred dollars in the suspect's possession when he was stopped.

First step in the criminalistic examination was checking the bills for fingerprints of the bank employees. Even Ninhydrin failed to come up with any identifiable prints, so that avenue had to be abandoned.

True, there was the cashier's memory of the number 17 on one bill. This alone would add weight to a case. But more was needed—much more. If only some other way could be found to prove those bills had come from that bank.

The staples! Was it possible that the action of the stapler might leave marks which could mate a particular staple to the stapler which had driven it home?

The marks made by staplers are pitifully small when compared with toolmarks left by crowbars, chisels, and even the punches used to knock out safe knobs, but three types of stapler markings are possible. First come those made by the ram, which strikes the top of the staple and drives it through the material being stapled. Next come markings made by the anvil at the base of the stapler, which closes the prongs of the staple, or in some cases spreads them out. Finally, there may be characteristic scratches made by flaws or burrs within the shaft through which the staple slides when struck by the ram.

Fifteen staplers were brought in from the bank. Experimentation showed that identifiable marks were made only when a stapler was struck with considerable force. Still, the original examination of the staples securing the four evidence bills showed they did have markings left by the stapler. So the criminalist continued testing the exemplars being produced with heavy blows.

One by one, the staplers were eliminated, until only two were left. Here the criminalist struck pay dirt. One of the staplers produced marks from the ram which exactly matched one of the stapled evidence bills, even to scratches on the side of the staple. Now, the district attorney had strong associative evidence to tie in the money in the suspect's possession to that robbed from the bank.

The skilled Q.D. examiner can detect illegal tampering with sealed envelopes, including invasion by steaming. Scanned under the UV and IR lights, the most skilful erasure may reveal its presence. Displaced edges or added glue disclose the tamperer. Occasionally, the examiner may even discover a jigsaw fit in glue.

While the seriousness of any particular offense may be open to debate, the depredations of shoplifters exceed four billion dollars annually in the United States. One out of eight customers steals, according to one study. Others believe the figure more likely to be one in four. Women predominate, with a sixteen-to-one ratio to male pilferers. Furthermore, there are strong indications that their shoplifting is due less to desire for the merchandise than to psychosexual motivations in those who feel themselves to be underloved.

One case, however, featured a man who was observed picking up two pairs of socks in a Canadian department store. He ripped off the labels, tossing them aside, and sauntered out of the store without the formality of paying for the goods. He was followed by police, but denied entering the sock department of the store. He unashamedly explained the two pairs of socks, which bulged his pockets, by saying he'd purchased them elsewhere, several days before.

Socks and labels were presented to the Toronto, Ontario, Centre of Forensic Sciences where a curious Q.D. examiner puzzled on the possibilities of proving that the labels originally clung to these particular socks.

Examination under ultraviolet radiation revealed some faint irregular patterns on the socks and on the labels where some of the label glue adhered to the fabric of the socks. Photography of the irregularities was further improved with filters and high-contrast film. When compared, alignment of the patterns was unquestionable. Thanks to science, the Great Sock Robbery was thwarted. When confronted with the evidence, the scoundrel confessed all.

Lest we seem unappreciative of the Canadian concern with the application of forensics, even in a two-bit case like this, may we point out that across the border in the United States, some two million burglaries annually receive no attention whatever from forensic scientists.

Some of the uneasiest people in the world ought to be those who work for armored delivery services such as the Brink's Company. Countless plots are machinated to separate them from the heavy bundles of coin and currency they circulate during their daily rounds. They are fair game for any freak with a Saturday night special (cheap hand gun) who wants to try for the big time.

On occasion, the would-be felons are on the inside of the cumbersome coin carriers. While most people who deal with money as a commodity tend to develop total indifference to the long green during working hours, the thought that it would be nice to share this wealth can scarcely have failed to occur to most of them. Since such persons are the first to be scrutinized when the loot disappears, they usually put the idea out of mind. Besides, the near certainty of detection and punishment makes it easier to be honest. So when the Brink's driver was found trussed in the back seat of a car in the aircraft company's parking lot, the first concern of the police was how badly he was hurt. He was taken to the nearest hospital where his scratches were swabbed and bandaged. Then he was asked to tell just what had happened.

He hardly remembered. He'd just left the truck to take the payroll into the cashier's office of the aircraft plant when something heavy struck him from behind. He came to to find he was tied up and being carried over the parking lot like a pig to the slaughter. The robbers thrust him in the back of a nearby parked car and warned him they'd be watching for the next half-hour, and if he cried for help he was a dead man. He was so frightened over what they were going to do to him, he couldn't even remember how their voices sounded, or just how many of them there seemed to be. All he knew for sure was the ferocity in their voices when they warned him to be silent on penalty of death.

The amount robbed from him was not hard to calculate. When all other money was accounted for, the sum of forty-four thousand dollars was missing.

Police investigators are not noted for their naïveté, and they were just rude enough to check back with the doctor who had examined the victim. Were the injuries sufficient to have caused loss of consciousness?

"Not unless the man blacked out from fear," the doctor responded. "The scratches on his head would have hardly bothered him."

"Could the wounds have been self-inflicted?" the detective asked. The doctor nodded.

One item the investigators hadn't counted on was the scurrying action of the Brink's driver the moment he left the hospital. Within minutes he had returned to the scene of the robbery. In a few seconds he'd recovered a hidden bag and was on his way to a nearby town less than a half-hour away.

By the time the investigators had finished checking back with the doctor, the driver had arrived at a bowling alley he'd been casing during the past weeks. In another five minutes he had signed up for a locker and stashed the bag inside. He was home and in bed in another twenty-five minutes; and was even able to answer the telephone sleepily and tell the investigator he had a terrible headache, but he thought he'd be okay in a couple of days. Sure, he'd be available to listen to voices in case they caught any suspects. He'd sure like to help put away those goons who clobbered him over the head.

Like any avid reader of crime fiction, he knew that the worst thing he could do was give the appearance of sudden wealth. He did not plan to even visit the bowling locker for several months. He'd paid the rent for a year in advance. With forty-four thousand sitting there waiting, he would take his own sweet time. That money wasn't going to go anywhere. Or so he thought.

It just so happens that people who haunt bowling alleys are sometimes a trifle loose-fingered. From time to time a bowling ball, a pair of rented bowling shoes, or something else of value disappears. The management does not exactly announce the extra service to locker renters, but about once a month a couple of their people check out every locker in the house. Sometimes they make trouble for the sticky-fingered clients who are storing stolen property in their lockers. More often, they just keep a closer watch on them when they come to bowl.

Fred and Charley grumbled quite a bit when the manager told them it was about time for them to perform their locker duties this month. They preferred to bowl a few frames, one of the fringe benefits when things were quiet, or to relax with a beer or two. They continued to grouse as they inspected locker after locker, moving the sometimes heavy contents, even working up a little sweat in the process. Real work was not what they enjoyed most. Their tune changed when they came to the locker so trustingly rented by the Brink's driver. They could scarcely believe their eyes when the stacks of bills tumbled out of the paper sack. Transferring the loot to a locker of their own, Fred and Charley finished their locker inspection in the best of spirits. They even surprised the manager by suggesting he join them for a cool one after the inspection job was finished.

Nothing was quite good enough for Fred and Charley for the next few months. Meanwhile, the patient Brink's driver was still relaxing under the hawklike attention of the law. He wasn't about to lead the detectives to his guaranteed future.

It's a pity that the lower classes can hardly stand to see anyone enjoy himself. Given the likes of Fred and Charley who suddenly come into a fortune, there's always some envious stoolpigeon who'll rat on them to the detective who is allowing him to stay out of jail temporarily. But that's the way it is in detective work. Most phases of detective work could not exist without informants. The informants are inevitably criminals with records as bad as or worse than those they rat on. Sometimes their motive is simply to maintain their freedom, since the agent continually dangles their most recent crime over their head. In addition, the agent is authorized to pay rewards for suitable information leading to the arrest of major criminals. So the informer is a relatively fat cat as long as his connection with the arrests remains unknown. In the interests of his health, the informant usually disappears into the woodwork after fingering a couple of suspects.

So a stoolie sent Fred and Charley firmly into the arms of the law. By now most of the forty-four thousand had been blown, but just enough remained that when Fred and Charley confessed to stealing from the locker the investigators were quick to recall the robbery of the Brink's driver.

The driver's mistake had been in signing for the locker. A single signature isn't usually easy to identify in questioned document work. Nor was this one. But after he'd worked with it for a while, the examiner was certain. The signature on the bowling alley contract was positively that of the Brink's driver. Besides, the bowling alley manager remembered the bandages on the driver's head as he signed the locker contract. Fred and Charley already had given statements which established that the forty-four thousand dollars had been found in the locker shortly after the fake robbery. All that remained to close the case was to sentence the Brink's driver to a long term in the penitentiary.

The Chinese topped their invention of paper in *A.D.* 105 with their discovery, about the ninth century, of gunpowder. Until then, harsh words between people or nations might lead to sticks and stones, even to slings and arrows. Since military success depends on supremacy in weapons, the dagger yielded to the sword, the mace to the lance. Horsepower overran manpower.

All that ended with the invention of explosives. Now a physically superior enemy could be felled with a pea-sized projectile. Yet no sooner was the pea-pellet successful, than someone was working on one the size of an olive, then of an orange. With each successive innovation, the capability to kill and maim increased. Each conqueror was overthrown by the first warrior to develop superior hardware.

Usually, these nuisances were perpetrated with relatively slight involvement of the civilian population. However, when not fighting a war, a soldier becomes a civilian. And if during his military training he has been taught how to make things go bang, the temptation to direct his new skills toward civilian pursuits sometimes becomes irresistible.

Enter a new ingredient in modern policework—the bomb.

Bombs which already have exploded are one sort of problem. There's the mess to clean up, the surviving victims (if any) to treat, and the bomber to be found. The unexploded bomb—real or alleged—is something else. In the infancy of criminalistics, one sick joke in police circles was that a bomb expert practiced his art until he encountered a genuine bomb. Then the department got a new bomb expert.

Until well after World War II, bomb incidents, real or threatened, occurred so seldom that there was little need of a bomb specialist within police agencies. If a bomb threat took place every three or four years, the nearest military ordinance installation was called to examine and disarm the infernal device.

Then came Vietnam. What greater way to instill terror into the hearts of civilians and military alike than to plant explosives in totally unexpected places?

Guided by an evil genius, Viet Cong Major Zen Lanh, the Cong planted explosives in motor cars which were driven to strategic locations, then abandoned to detonate and destroy innocent bystanders as well as military objectives.

The bombs were ingeniously concealed in every imaginable spot—in bicycles whose tubing fragmented into shrapnel, in old gasoline cans, in water tanks, in vegetables, inside special bricks, in ladies' handbags, even in coffins. Over thirty-three thousand deaths, primarily of civilians, resulted. The Saigon police detected a great many more devices that never went off. The concealed explosives they intercepted were sufficient to have destroyed every single American installation.

In the late sixties, the terrorist methods were increasingly adopted on the other side of the Pacific. Some sources believe the bombing bug found its way to the United States haphazardly, without plan or direction. Others believe the epidemic was plotted and executed by Maoist Chinese. Whatever the genesis, use of explosives grew by leaps and bounds. By June of 1971 no less than 1,858 bombing incidents involving 2,352 devices were reported to the National Bomb Data Center, established by the Law Enforcement Assistance Administration.

Reflecting the times, the leading motive assigned to those incidents where intention was known or suspected was racial protest. Juvenile vandalism was second, trailed slightly by political protest and revenge. Harassment of public safety officials and labor disputes wrap up the list of leading causes.

Once started, the terrorist game is like the snowball rolling downhill. The immediate reaction to the 1970 insurrection in Jordan was an acceleration of terrorist excursions, often with totally innocent people becoming the victims. The ongoing struggle between Israeli and Arab interests continues the use of explosive devices. Subsequent to the kidnapping and slaughter of the 1972 Israeli athletes at the Munich Olympic Games, a world-wide onslaught commenced against prominent Jewish citizens and diplomats, using the bombs-by-letter method.

To reach intended targets, letter bombs must be capable of withstanding the considerable jostling of postal processing without premature detonation. The explosive must be flat rather than round and bulky, and the triggering device must anticipate the variety of ways in which letters are opened. These requirements are met by strips of plastic explosive, with a detonating device which is triggered in much the same fashion as the practical joker's mousetrap cap exploder, which is placed between the pages of a book with a provocative title, to explode when the book cover is lifted. In letter bombs the separation of the folded pages of the letter allows a similar release, triggering the explosion.

Fortunately, the use of portable X-ray equipment greatly assisted in the examination of suspected mailings, which often betray their purpose because they must be heavier than average mail in order to accommodate enough explosive to be lethal. But in spite of the best countermeasures, some of the bombs inevitably reached their targets undetected. Others, as in the case of the intended victim who had moved, maimed and killed innocent postal employees or others who inadvertently triggered the infernal devices.

The crime lab can be enormously effective in pinning the explosive-using criminal to his murderous act. The cases divide themselves into two categories: those in which the bombs explode, and those in which they don't.

Because of the mushrooming number of bombing cases, the National Institute of Law Enforcement and Criminal Justice has been providing important assistance in training police to recognize commercially manufactured explosive devices, including ordinance from the principal countries of the world. In addition, the NILECJ handbooks give explicit instructions concerning the kinds of devices manufactured in backroom laboratories. For many years, underground revolutionaries have been distributing directions on making bombs and incendiary devices from readily obtained materials. Ordinary granular sugar is one-half of a simple formula which, when mixed with another common ingredient and confined within a pipe bomb, has 40 percent of the explosive effectiveness of dynamite. Many ordinary materials—sulfur, powdered aluminum, Coke bottles, match heads, toy caps, tacks, nuts, bolts, and BB pellets—are used in makeshift bombs. In spite of their crude preparation, these bombs can kill and maim almost as effectively as military grenades.

In addition, there is the whole arsenal of materials to be found in any gun store, where the alleged gun enthusiast may secure stockpiles of explosive materials under the guise of obtaining supplies for reloading target-shooting ammunition.

A series of bombings in one of the most exclusive residential areas in the country had the entire community terrorized. Most of the bombs were manufactured from lengths of pipe stuffed with an assortment of gunpowders and lit by fuses. The nature of the targets indicated political motivation for the most part, with suspicion falling on radical organizations such as the Minutemen.

Some of the bombs failed to explode and were disarmed and brought to the crime lab for analysis. In other instances, portions of the homemade bombs were collected at the bombing scenes and preserved as physical evidence.

As the number of cases increased, the criminalists carefully examined and analyzed the contents of the unexploded devices. Under magnification, specific types of powders were identified. Exploded fragments were analyzed by several methods including infrared spectrophotometry, gas chromatography, and paper and thin-layer chromatography.

With the increasing data, it became necessary to maintain a large chart showing the locations of each bombing incident and the kinds and proportions of ingredients involved. For their part, the crime lab had more evidence than it could use. What was needed now were suspects.

In the meantime, police investigators had managed to infiltrate an ultra-right-wing radical group suspected of the bombings and in time were reasonably certain of the methods and location where the bombs were being manufactured. (Interestingly, one member of the group had a Federal explosives license to resell ammunition and gunpowder, so their source of supply was assured.)

The intelligence also revealed that this group was in possession of a number of illegal weapons including submachine guns, and that any raid attempt might well be met with enormous firepower. It was vital therefore to plan such a raid with total secrecy, making sure that even the members of the raiding party were not aware of details that could jeopardize the success of the mission by permitting an innocent remark to be heard by the wrong ears.

H-hour was finally at hand. The well-coordinated raiding party assembled in the briefing room. Included in the party was the criminalist whose evidence stood ready to convict if only it could be matched with equivalent physical evidence from the illicit bomb manufacturing site.

The planning was successful. The raiding party swooped on the suspected site, search warrant in hand, and captured the occupants without firing a single shot.

Inside was a veritable criminalistic treasure. During the course of manufacture of dozens of bombs, there had been a mixture of explosive materials which never could have been accidentally duplicated elsewhere. The type and quantity of the seized gunpowders showed exact duplication with some of the unexploded bombs. Only one item puzzled the criminalist: Stored with the effective explosives was a supply of black powder, which is a treacherous material, particularly when fired from handguns, since it tends to explode rather than burn rapidly as do most gunpowders used to propel a bullet. Anyone reloading hand-gun ammunition with this powder was inviting suicide.

The answer was ironically simple. One of the goals of this militantly rightist organization was elimination of the radical left. Knowing full well that they were peddling death, this group had sold the unpredictable black powder to the Black Panthers.

So all the answers were provided by the expertly mounted raid. Now the crime lab could match the seized evidence with that remaining at the scene of each of the bombing incidents. The combination of skilful police work and forensic science resulted in the removal from society of an entire group of bombing terrorists.

One hundred thousand times last year, a trigger was pulled, a shell exploded, and a lead- or copper-clad bullet penetrated human flesh. Eight thousand victims paid with their lives when they were deliberately murdered by firearms. These totals exclude many thousands of additional shootings that were accidental or occurred during suicide attempts.

In spite of the national concern following the shootings of President John Kennedy, Dr. Martin Luther King, Senator Robert Kennedy, and Governor George Wallace, the Congress of the United States has not seen fit to enact laws which would adequately limit possession and use of firearms. Moreover, the realities of the political world being what they are, there appears little likelihood that this country will see even limited hand-gun restriction in this century. This, in spite of the fact that murder-by-gun has doubled since 1964.

The gun is here to stay, as is the disaster its misuse brings to humanity, with a predictable hundred thousand plus victims rung up each year; many of whom will end up as cases being analyzed by the crime lab.

Chapter 18

Frequently there will be no mystery as to the identity of the person firing the gun. In the overwhelming majority of shootings, the victim and the person who did the shooting are either blood relatives or are known to each other. In 1970, killings within the family made up one-fourth of all murders, with one-half of these incidents charged to spouse killing spouse.

When a hand gun or a rifle is fired, the bullet may be scratched in a characteristic fashion by the unique machine-tool marks made in manufacturing the weapon. While these characteristics may change slightly with wear, there are usually enough unique markings to mate a bullet with its barrel if the bullet is not damaged too badly after leaving the gun.

Some small-caliber, short-barreled guns produce so much heat that the lead bullet is close to melting on the surface and may retain little characteristic detail. Where the weapon has been fired extensively, wear and tear may alter the scratch marks made on later bullets. Under either of these circumstances, the failure of match does not necessarily exclude the weapon from consideration.

Other ballistic markings are produced on the cartridge case by the firing pin, with additional markings on the case as the explosion drives the cartridge backward against the breech. More markings may be made by the extraction and ejection mechanisms.

Not every bullet makes a good candidate for firearms identification. The bullet may have collected too many scratches from external sources, or be so distorted by impact that comparison is impossible. Or the bullet may be bald. In very worn guns there may not be sufficient identifying detail to make comparison possible. Nevertheless, in a great many cases there will be sufficient detail to insure positive identification.

In the early days of ballistics, the exemplar bullets were produced by firing the gun into a container of soft fibrous waste of the type used in machine shops to wipe excess oil from machine tools. While soft, the collecting material made some markings of its own and wiped off some of the delicate detail made by the gun barrel in slowing down the bullet. In most crime labs today, the bullets are recovered from vertical or horizontal containers full of water which allows the bullet to safely dissipate its energy without accumulating markings or losing those it has.

Preliminary examination by eye or with a hand magnifier often allows rejection of an exemplar bullet without further testing. An obvious example would be bullets of different calibers or with rifling marks which angled in opposite directions, *e.g.*, a lefthand twist as compared with a righthand twist.

If preliminary examination suggests a closer look, the bullets to be compared are mounted in the holding device of the comparison microscope. This clever mechanism permits the bullets to be precisely aligned so that comparable features of evidence and exemplar bullets can be evaluated at the same time, with one bullet under the scrutiny of the left eyepiece, the other viewed by the right. The two fields of view butt against each other, forming an optical junction, or margin. With bullets which match, the examiner scratches his mark indicating the point of beginning. Then he slowly rotates the bullets, noting the number of marks which exactly coincide, excluding the marks left by the lands and grooves of the rifling, which are class characteristics similar in all guns of the same model.

As in fingerprint comparison, certain markings carry greater weight than others. A series of identical striations, for instance, carries great weight in convincing the ballistics expert he has found a true match. There is no arbitrary number of points of similarity before match is certain, but there must be sufficient number to subjectively convince the examiner the bullets came from the same source. Certainly, he would never be convinced by two or three points of similarity, as happened in several murder cases we have had an opportunity to examine, with class characteristics included in these small numbers. This sort of bullet identification would raise grave doubts as to the abilities or integrity of the ballistic expert.

When match is certain, sound practice calls for preserving the evidence with photomicrographs, both to show a jury and so that other experts can verify the basis on which the examiner concluded that evidence and exemplar were fired from the same gun.

Similar comparisons can be made of the markings left on the cartridge when a gun is fired. While less area is involved, there may well be sufficient characteristic detail to mate the shell to the gun that fired it. This can be particularly helpful if no bullets have been recovered, as often happens, or if they are so damaged as to be useless for identification.

Shell cases are frequently recovered at crime scenes, particularly where automatic weapons are used which eject the case as soon as the weapon is fired.

To be admissible in court proceedings, certain precautions must be taken with ballistic evidence by both the finder and the ballistics examiner. Foremost is the careful record identifying each piece of evidence as to where it was found, the circumstances, the chain of custody, and the specific ballistic analysis. These goals are achieved by identifying the evidence with markings, label, or marked containers, together with notes and reports that are completely specific for each separate bullet or cartridge, whether evidence or exemplar. There must be no confusion as to which individual bullet matched with which exemplar.

The specifics must be completely clear, and this becomes much easier when photographs have been made to reenforce the expert's testimony. Notes and formal reports should be made at the time of examination. This is particularly true in a crime lab having a high volume of activity. Without such reports to refresh memory, it is virtually impossible to remember accurately the minutiae of dozens of separate cases.

The detective was known privately as the worst shot on the police department. Range practice was beneath his dignity, even though monthly shoots were required of all sworn officers. The pistol range was located in a mountain canyon. On those rare occasions when Detective Bob deigned to practice his shooting, it was alleged he not only missed the target, but that he couldn't hit the mountain behind it.

Most policemen do not really look forward to a shoot-out and are usually unpleasantly surprised when one is called for. Many policemen spend their entire careers without ever firing their weapons in real action.

No one doubted Detective Bob's guts, however, so when the bank called to say that the bandit who had held them up a couple of weeks before was seen lurking in the area, Bob was the first to arrive. Gun drawn, he confronted the suspect and when the bandit drew his gun, Detective Bob let blaze. The street echoed with the exchange of gunfire. When it stilled, the bandit lay dead on the street, a single shot through his head.

"Great shooting, Bob!" the chief of detectives praised the hero. The papers carried banner headlines, and Bob was a big man in his neighborhood and in the department. It just showed that when the chips were down, ol' Bob could come through with flying colors.

The celebration was short-lived. Even though half a dozen witnesses saw Bob's sharpshooting marksmanship, the criminalist quietly obtained the fatal bullet from the autopsy surgeon and made exemplars from the guns involved in the shoot-out.

The news was less than welcome when the criminalist interrupted the celebration in the office of the chief of detectives. The criminalist held out the still-dripping photo-micrographs of the bullets involved. "Bandit killed himself," he said dourly. Luckily, sharpshooter Bob hadn't mowed down some of the witnesses who certified that Bob had outdrawn the bandit in the shoot-out.

Many criminalists feel that the crime laboratory should serve at the local level, since most crimes are committed by people residing within the local area. As Anthony Longhetti, laboratory director of the San Bernardino County crime laboratory puts it: "Only a local laboratory can provide the response time and service to investigating agencies on a routine basis.

"A local laboratory should serve and have the cooperation of all law enforcement agencies within the area. It will then be able to correlate physical evidence from crimes in different jurisdictions and have a sufficiently broad base to develop the experience, reference materials, and case load to justify sophisticated equipment and properly qualified personnel.

"Routine test firing of all guns seized by law enforcement agencies should be carried out. This would allow the laboratory to determine if they were in fact used in some unsolved crime and to build a reference collection for study and comparison."

Let's examine a case in which the practice of this philosophy paid substantial dividends.

The murder took place on the night of July 21, 1959, in the city of Redlands, California. The victim had stopped to assist a young couple who had run out of gas on a rural road. He took the couple to pick up gasoline and returned them to their car. After letting the couple out, the good Samaritan, sitting in the driver's seat, was approached from the right by two men who had apparently been waiting in an orange grove and attempted to rob him. The victim stepped on the gas in an attempt to flee and was shot twice with a .45 automatic pistol. One shot entered his upper left leg, and one entered his right side. Both bullets penetrated the body and were recovered from the vehicle. The victim lost control of the car about a hundred yards down the road and crashed into a telephone pole. He died from loss of blood and with over nine thousand dollars in his possession. Two cartridge cases were recovered from the side of the road, one during an extensive search after burning off the weeds.

Both recovered cartridge cases had similar and unusual indentations on the sides at an angle, as well as the usual firing pin, breechblock, extractor, and ejector marks. The unusual markings on the side of both cases suggested a consistent characteristic from the suspect gun which was not normally present in the United States Army .45 pistol, from which the bullets appeared to have been fired. Test shots from fourteen .45 auto pistols confirmed the absence of this unusual marking.

On September 12, 1960, almost fourteen months after the shooting, a Colt .45 auto pistol, Commander model, was submitted to the laboratory on a routine basis along with other guns that had been seized by the San Bernardino county sheriff's office in a major burglary ring investigation. On collecting the casings from the laboratory test firing of this gun, indentations on the sides were noted and their significance was recalled.

The test cartridge cases were immediately compared with the fatal casing from the scene of the murder. A classical match of breechblock markings was observed. The extractor marks were also found to match; however, the firing pin impression did not.

Furthermore, the test bullets fired from this gun did not match the fatal bullets! The conclusion reached was that the fatal casings had been fired from this gun (at least from the slide of the gun), but that the firing pin had subsequently been modified or replaced. The only reasonable explanation for the fatal bullets not matching were that this barrel had been changed or the gun had been very extensively fired in the interim.

Subsequent interrogation of the burglary suspects and additional investigation showed that the gun had been lent to Arthur Jones on the night of the murder by the owner of a restaurant and bar. On return of the gun, the barrel had been removed and replaced with another one. Melted candle wax had been poured in the original barrel, and it had been dropped down into a stud wall.

The hidden barrel was recovered and submitted to the laboratory on September 21, 1960. The wax was removed, and the barrel was cleaned and oiled. Test bullets fired from this barrel were then compared with the fatal bullets, with the result that the reassembled gun was identified as the one used in the homocide.

Arthur Jones and James Bushbaum were subsequently convicted of the murder and sentenced to life imprisonment. They escaped from San Quentin state prison eight years later. Jones died about a year after the escape under unusual circumstances. Manhattan Beach, California, police officers investigating a series of robberies were contacting possible witnesses at a motel in that city. Jones apparently thought they were coming to take him into custody and attempted to hold them off with dynamite. He was killed when the dynamite exploded. Bushbaum is still at large as a fugitive.

Another laboratory which routinely screens recovered firearms is the Toronto Centre of Forensic Sciences.

On July 4, 1971, the police were called on a shooting in northern Ontario where a man had shot and killed his wife in a motel room. Before turning himself in he managed to dispose of the weapon. Examination of the bullet retrieved from the bed clothing under the victim indicated that it had been fired from a .32 caliber firearm, rifled six grooves, righthand twist. The rifling specifications were the same as the Winchester model 94, .32 special rifle. The cartridge case found at the scene was designed for use in a lever-action-type rifle, such as the Winchester or Marlin, both of which use this .32 special ammunition.

A month and a half later a badly rusted Winchester model 94, .32 special was found in the trunk of a car. The markings left on the cartridge case at the July 4th murder scene was identified as having been made by this rifle.

The policy of routinely checking all firearms coming to the centre's attention paid off in December of the same year. A routine check of a Toronto auto revealed a .22 caliber semiautomatic pistol on the floor of the driver's side. The pistol was checked against two fired cartridge cases recovered at the scene of an armed robbery earlier in the year. These cases were identified as having been fired from this pistol. As a result, three persons were charged and convicted of armed robbery.

Sometimes the crime lab is called on to perform bizarre deductions. Following a midnight holdup of a car wash, the police were given the description of the robber. Shortly thereafter, a young man answering the description was halted for interrogation, and a shoot-out occurred in which the suspect was killed. The officer claimed that as he approached the suspect he noticed a sawed-off rifle in his hands. The officer twice ordered the suspect to drop the weapon. On the second warning, the suspect raised the gun and pointed it at the officer, who fired. The sawed-off rifle flew from the hands of the suspect.

The crime lab examined the sawed-off weapon and some wooden fragments which had been removed from the left thumb of the slain suspect. Inspection of the splinters proved them to be chips of black walnut, identical to that of the rifle. A groove in the wood of the front portion of the rifle stock corroborated the officer's story that the weapon had been pointed in his direction when he fired.

Concerned police training officers emphasize to their rookies that they are more interested in having their own men safe than in attempting heroic arrests. In major departments, any time a police weapon is fired, regardless of the outcome, a full and complete report is filed, and an investigation follows. Particular emphasis is made in training new policemen that every contact with the public, whether a shakedown of a prowler, a stop for a traffic offense, or the capture of a fleeing robber may turn into a situation in which the individual involved may attempt to kill the officer. The little old lady appearing to ask directions may have a passionate mad-on for the law and a bolo knife concealed in her chemise. Most important, the violator of vehicle laws may be an armed and deadly felon attempting to escape. Axiomatic in traffic enforcement is that the traffic officers making the most stops are the ones who apprehend the greatest number of felony offenders.

In spite of every precaution, the traffic officer is at a disadvantage every time he checks out a motorist for a traffic violation. The policeman ordinarily has no forewarning of evil intentions of the fleeing criminal. Such incidents are interspersed with hundreds of routine stops. And even though the policeman maintains complete vigilance, he can scarcely stop each traffic offender with drawn gun and the order to "come out with your hands up!"

The sun burned down on the Mojave Desert on the road leading to Las Vegas. The highway patrol officer started out in pursuit of the speeding car. Sweat dripped in his eyes as his speedometer needle climbed to almost the 100 MPH mark.

Finally the speeder pulled over to the shoulder of the road at the demanding wail of the police siren. The highway patrolman picked up his pinchbook from the car seat and slid out on the driver's side, ready to write another speeding ticket. He had no knowledge that in another two minutes his radio would shriek a warning that the car he was stopping had just been reported stolen.

He was never to find out. As he approached the car, the driver leaned out and fired a shot through the highway patrolman's heart. As the policeman fell to the ground, the murderer fired a second shot through the patrolman's head, at contact distance. In another few seconds tires screamed as they hit the macadam roadway, tearing away.

The investigative work was first-rate, and a week later the dragnet closed in on the suspect, who was apprehended in a Shell Beach motel. He made full confession of the shooting and agreed to participate in a pioneering effort by Inspector Percy Sellas of the San Bernardino sheriff's office in making a sound and color movie reenactment of the shooting.

The case appeared to be in the bag. Here, for the first time anywhere, the murderer had walked through his crime at the actual crime scene, freely reenacting his role in a senseless murder. Most jurisdictions would have congratulated themselves on the innovative motion pictures and left the case as it stood without bothering about further evidence.

Which would have been a mistake; because, by the time the case went to jury trial, there was a whole new version of the movie invented by the defense. Surely the jury could see the sound motion pictures were just a police trick. Clearly his client had been duped into placing himself in front of the camera and following the directions of the investigators, doing what they said without really knowing just why they had him out there in the desert.

As good as the reenactment movies were, they needed the back-up of corroborating evidence.

The investigators were not idle during the period between the arrest of the suspect and his preliminary court hearing, when he was certified for superior court trial on probable cause of committing murder. Not that what they found was too encouraging. As nearly as they could determine, the murder gun had been dismantled and the individual parts widely scattered along desert highways, piece by piece. So if no gun could be found, where were the exemplars to come from?

Considering the immensity of the Mojave Desert, search for the needle in a haystack was child's play compared with the chance of finding the actual murder weapon. Discouraged but tenacious, the investigators dug deeper, seeking to find some way to develop physical evidence which might tie this murderer to his crime.

After running down a number of fruitless leads, the detectives finally turned up an investigative avenue that held a whisper of promise. The murderer, they found, had been keeping company with a local beauty queen, one Miss Bloomington. Possibly she might have some knowledge that could prove helpful.

The girl was more than cooperative. Why, yes, she recalled, her boyfriend liked to target shoot. In fact she'd gone with him one time, somewhere out there in the Mojave Desert, where the boyfriend fired at the Joshua trees. There was a remote possibility she might remember the location where the target shooting had occurred. The spot was somewhere past Baker, the California town nestled at the foot of the four-thousand-foot climb into the mountains which surround Las Vegas, another hundred miles further east.

Chapter 19

A team of homicide detectives, an I.D. photographer, and a criminalist accompanied Miss Bloomington over the burning road through the dusty desert. After driving beyond Baker, Miss Bloomington searched the thinly scattered growth of the monotonous desert. The car climbed the steep road leading into the foothills, where the cooler air of the higher altitude permitted the stunted shrubbery to grow as high as a man's knee. Here and there a few misshapen Joshua trees began to appear. Perhaps they were entering the country where the suspect had practiced shooting his gun. Twice the group pulled into turn-outs that Miss Bloomington thought might have located the scene of the target shooting only to find no familiar landmarks.

Almost twenty miles past Baker, Miss Bloomington called for the car to stop. "This looks like the place," she said. The weary party disembarked to permit a closer inspection. Finally she nodded, "I'm sure this is it. Here's where he fired the gun."

The investigative team spent more than two hours searching the burning sands for some evidence. They were about to give up when the criminalist spotted a live cartridge at the side of the clearing.

Miss Bloomington came over and said that she was certain this was the exact spot the suspect had stood as he had shot at various objects in the desert. "I think that's the tree he was aiming at," she said, pointing at a Joshua tree about twenty-five feet away.

Examination of the tree revealed several bullet holes, but no embedded bullets. They had either gone clear through the tree or ricocheted to some unknown location in the desert.

While they had virtually nothing to show for their wearing search, the photographer set up his tripod to photograph the bullet holes in the tree. As he was placing one of the legs in underbrush, he saw a spent bullet, partially covered by blown sand, in the bottom portion of a broken bottle. The hot and weary crew came to life.

The bullet was quite well-preserved, sufficiently undeformed to exhibit considerable ballistic detail. It could be matched to the bullets taken from the body of the slain highway patrolman.

Thanks to this evidence and the testimony of Miss Bloomington, the shooting could be reconstructed, in spite of the missing gun. Following conviction and the automatic appeal to the California Supreme Court, the murderer paid his price in the gas chamber at San Quentin.

According to Sam, the evening started innocently enough. First he combed his hair and slicked up for the evening on the town. He'd halfway promised a couple of older ladies he knew, Sally and Belle, that he'd drop around. They weren't bad ol' gals, full of fun, liked to drink a little whisky with a man, perhaps shoot a friendly game of craps.

Sally and Belle welcomed Sam's arrival and his short half-pint of whisky, but pointed out that the evening was young and they both felt a powerful thirst coming on. So after Sam's bottle had been passed around until dry, he headed out to replenish the liquid larder.

By the time Sam returned, a slick chick and a guy named Big Bill had joined the party, and the chick was really something! After a few drinks she told Sam that Big Bill meant nothing to her. She really went for the line of sweet talk Sam dished out.

The party got better. With more whisky sloshing, some dancing, and finally a good ol' crap game on the floor between the living room and the bathroom hall. Best of all, the slick chick was all over Sam as she watched the crap game. Only Big Bill refused to join the fun, getting more and more irritated, and finally demanding that Sam get his hands off the girl.

Sam responded by saying he had as much right to handle the girl as Big Bill. And if Big Bill didn't like it, he knew what he could do.

Big Bill rebutted by pulling a gun and started shooting. This not only broke up the crap game. It seemed like the two ol' gals got a little messed up as Sam sprinted for the door. Next thing he knew Sam arrived at his pappy's home, and his sister pointed out that there was a mess of blood on Sam's topcoat and other clothing. She suggested that Sam go to the police and tell them his story.

That was Sam's version, one he'd had a couple of hours to work up, according to investigators who checked out the time elements of the interesting tale.

The investigation revealed a somewhat different version. It was Christmas evening and their first knowledge of the twin murders occurred when Sam arrived at the police station to make his report. When they found the bloody mess in Sally and Belle's house, the detectives felt a strong need for criminalistic back-up. The first thing that struck them was the odd pose of the victims, Sally and Belle. Both had their arms outstretched and their ankles crossed in a crucifixion pose. A quick glance at the bloodstains showed the bodies to have been moved to this unnatural position. Moreover, Belle had her panties off, suggesting the possibility of a rape as well as murder.

It was almost midnight when criminalist Jerry Chisum arrived. A quick glance at the scene, which included numerous religious pictures and the crucifixion pose of the victims, suggested strong potential for physical evidence to assist in reconstructing the events as they had really happened.

After the scene had been recorded, the evidence gathered, the bodies removed, and the house sealed, it was time to analyze the physical evidence. Chisum began with Sam's topcoat. First, there was the peculiar distribution of bloodstains. Two separate powder burns were six inches apart, with the larger powder burn surrounding a figure-8-shaped hole in the left chest. A few inches below this was a mottled-appearing triangular bloodstain, with the apex pointing toward the hole. Close by the hole and again on the left sleeve were facial powder and lipstick marks.

Chisum scrutinized telling marks, which clearly plotted the sequence of events to his trained eye. He explained his logic to the investigators: "See these two powder burns? The one near the hole is from the muzzle, the other one from the cylinder of a revolver with a six-inch barrel. These other stains show that Sam grabbed Sally by the head and shot her with the gun close to his chest. The coat was pinched between her head and the muzzle. That's why the figure-8 hole. I'll make you a bet we won't find any powder marks on her skin. But we will find that it was a contact shot." He smiled at the amazement on the detective's face. "Better have someone get over to the morgue right away to get samples of Sally's lipstick and powder. We'll want them to match with the marks on the coat."

The pathologist's autopsy of the victims produced verification of the lack of powder burns on Sally's body. It also discovered a thread inside her skull which later could be found exactly similar to the fibers making up Sam's topcoat.

Belle's autopsy provided additional pieces of the puzzle. She had been shot three times, once in the neck, once between the eyes, and once in the jaw. The pathologist discovered a bruise on the head too, so severe he wondered why it hadn't fractured her skull. Further examination showed him why. Belle's was the thickest skull he'd ever encountered in forty years of conducting autopsies.

The examination of the victims introduced a new problem area, which the reconstruction needed to resolve. Even though Belle had been found without her panties, neither of the women had been sexually molested.

Added to the equation was the lack of blood on the cuffs of the raincoat as contrasted with the blood on Sam's shirt cuffs. This presented a pattern that could only be achieved by dipping the fabric in pooled blood. There was also blood on the bottom of Sam's shoes; and a baseball bat in the bathroom with a couple of hairs clinging to it.

As Chisum reconstructed the affair from all of the bits and pieces of physical evidence, it was clear that Sam had visited the women's home all right, but if others were there, they left before the shootings. Someone had taken a bath—probably Belle, as she wasn't completely dressed. Sam had grabbed the baseball bat and struck Belle with it, knocking her to the floor of the bathroom. Thinking her unconscious, he then grabbed Sally, who was in the doorway, and forced her head under his left arm. He pulled his gun from his belt, a Smith and Wesson, model 1917, .45 Colt revolver loaded with .45 auto-rim ammunition, stuck it against Sally's head, and fired. A moment later Belle ran past, panties in hand, trying to escape. Sam dropped the lifeless Sally and grabbed Belle. She pleaded for mercy, but to no avail. His three shots guaranteed there would be no witness.

Now, Sam surveyed the scene. It was warm and he took off his topcoat. He rearranged the bodies in the crucifixion pose. Then he returned to the bathroom to relieve himself and wash his hands. He put his overcoat back on and went back into the night.

He then got rid of the gun, returned home after making up a good story, and then went to the police.

The final blow to Sam's fairytale occurred on the day before the trial. The gun, which had never been found, but which had been identified as to make and model by ballistic examination, was finally reported stolen. Before visiting Sally and Belle, Sam had been at a Christmas party at which a gun had been displayed. The owner said the gun was a six-inch Smith and Wesson, model 1917, .45 Colt revolver loaded with five rounds of .45 auto-rim ammunition. Immediately after Sam had left, the owner started to show off his Christmas-present gun to some late arrivals and found it missing. Sam was the only one present at the original showing who had left the party.

In the face of the evidence, Sam pled guilty to both homicides.

As we've already indicated, the unprecedented plethora of scientific instrumentation spawned by the space age is the bright side of a forensic picture. On the other hand, in the two most notable crimes of this century, the assassinations of President John F. Kennedy in 1963 and of Senator Robert F. Kennedy in 1968, considerable doubt has been raised regarding the management of the forensic science.

The Warren Commission notwithstanding, there remains substantial doubt that Lee Harvey Oswald was the lone killer who struck down President Kennedy in his prime. As related by Marshall Houts in *Where Death Delights* (Coward-McCann, 1967), the autopsy of the last president's body was incredibly mismanaged. One would think that the profession of forensic pathologist was totally unknown to those who selected the surgeons to conduct this vitally important investigation into the causes of death of an assassinated American president.

Houts quotes Dr. Milton Helpern, a man of vast experience and undoubtedly one of the foremost forensic pathologist, concerning the fact that Mrs. Kennedy was asked to name the site for the autopsy. He comments:

> It shows that we are still laboring under the
> delusion that an autopsy is a computerized, mathe-
> matical type of procedure, and that *any* doctor

is capable of performing it, especially if he is a
pathologist. If he can run a correct urinalysis,
ergo, this automatically qualifies him as an expert
on bullet wounds in the body.

Dr. Helpern quarrels with many of the presumptions made by
the inexperienced autopsy surgeons in President Kennedy's case,
such as the testimony that a full-jacketed bullet, without
deformation, passing through the skin would leave a similar
wound for both entrance and exit—a pivotal matter in determining the existence of a second marksman. He considered it
unlikely that a single bullet could pass through President
Kennedy's neck and wound Governor Connally, shattering his
fifth rib, fracturing a bone in the wrist, and finally going on to
slash his thigh. Helpern bases his objection to the Warren report
conclusions on the fact that the bullet alleged to have performed
these multiple damages had an unfired weight of 160 or 161
grains and lost only 1.4 to 2.4 grains of its initial weight in the
course of its violent trip.

As Dr. Helpern puts it: "The Commission has asked too much
from this bullet. . . . I cannot believe either that this bullet is
going to emerge miraculously unscathed, without any deformity,
and with its lands and grooves intact." (The lands are the raised
portions between the grooves in a gun's barrel rifling.)

Perhaps the most poignant note is contributed by Dr.
Helpern's plaintive comment: "The tragic, tragic thing is that a
relatively simple case was horribly snarled up from the very
beginning, and then the errors were compounded along the way.
Here is an historic event that will be discussed and written about
for the next century, and gnawing doubts will remain in many
minds. . . ."

Let's move now to the assassination of Senator Robert
Kennedy on June 5, 1968, in the Ambassador Hotel in Los
Angeles on the eve of the senator's sweeping victory in the
presidential primary.

In some police circles, Los Angeles shines as one of the finest
law enforcement agencies in the United States. No one can
quarrel with their tough selection standards and outstanding
training programs. Certainly if there is a fully professional local
law enforcement operation anywhere in this country, it is to be
found in the Los Angeles police department.

But how about their forensics?

Critics claim that it is scarcely possible to imagine a case which was so botched in the physical evidence collection, preservation, analysis, and testimony as was the crime lab work in Bobby Kennedy's killing.

While Sirhan Sirhan has been convicted and apparently lost his last hope of appeal, there is, at this moment, a very real doubt that all the facts are known—or possibly ever will be. The doubts include such startling possibilities as the fact of a second gun—and obviously a second assassin—who was in fact Senator Kennedy's actual killer.

At no time during the Sirhan trial did the judge, court attachés, three prosecution lawyers, or three defense lawyers ever notice that the bullets identified by expert testimony as being shot from the Sirhan gun were, in fact, taken from an envelope labeled with the serial number of a completely different gun, a gun which was subsequently destroyed by the Los Angeles police department.

To this day, authorities refuse to permit testing of the weapon, which clearly was carried by Sirhan Sirhan, and which unquestionably he fired with the full intent of killing Senator Kennedy.

The possibilities still exist that he missed Senator Kennedy and that a completely different weapon in fact delivered the fatal bullet.

Let us quote from the sworn statement of William W. Harper, an independent consulting criminalist, whom I have known for many years:

> An analysis of the physical circumstances at the scene of the assassination discloses that Senator Kennedy was fired upon from two distinct firing positions while he was walking through the kitchen pantry at the Ambassador Hotel. FIRING POSITION A, the position of Sirhan, was located directly in front of the Senator, with Sirhan face-to-face with the Senator. This position is well established by more than a dozen eyewitnesses. A second firing position, FIRING POSITION B, is clearly established by the autopsy report. It was located in close proximity to the Senator, immediately to his right and rear. It was from this position that 4 (four) shots were fired, three of which entered the Senator's

body. One of these three shots made a fatal penetration of the Senator's brain. A fourth shot passed
through the right shoulder pad of the Senator's
coat. These four shots from FIRING POSITION B all
produced powder residue patterns, indicating they
were fired from a distance of only a few inches.
They were closely grouped within a 12-inch circle.

In marked contrast, the shots from FIRING
POSITION A produced no powder residue patterns on the
bodies or clothing of any of the surviving victims,
all of whom were walking behind the Senator. These
shots were widely dispersed.

Senator Kennedy received no frontal wounds. The
three wounds suffered by him were fired from behind
and he had entrance wounds in the posterior portions
of his body.

The affidavit continues:

It is evident that a strong conflict exists
between the eyewitness accounts and the autopsy
findings. This conflict is totally irreconcilable
with the hypothesis that only Sirhan's gun was
involved in the assassination. The conflict can be
eliminated if we consider that a second gun was
being fired from FIRING POSITION B concurrently
with the firing of the Sirhan gun from FIRING
POSITION A. It is self-evident that within the brief
period of the shooting (roughly 15 seconds) Sirhan
could not have been in both firing positions at the
same time. No eyewitnesses saw Sirhan at any
position other than FIRING POSITION A, where he
was quickly restrained by citizens present at that
time and place.

Harper adds that serious doubt exists that test bullets from the
weapon taken from Sirhan were ever entered in evidence in the
Sirhan trial, since this exhibit (#55) was labeled with the serial
number of gun No. H18602, while Sirhan's gun bore serial No.
H53725. As of this writing, authorities have chosen not to permit
further firing of test bullets from the Sirhan gun, hence
comparison was only possible with a bullet removed from
William Weisel, who was standing roughly twenty feet behind
Senator Kennedy. The affidavit continues:

From the general circumstances of the shooting,
the only reasonable assumption is that the
bullet removed from victim Weisel was in fact
fired from the Sirhan gun. This bullet is in
near perfect condition. I have, therefore,
chosen it as a "test" bullet from the Sirhan gun
and compared it with the bullet removed from
the Senator's neck. The bullet removed
from the Senator's neck, Exhibit 47, was one
of those fired from FIRING POSITION B, while
the bullet removed from Weisel, Exhibit 54,
was one of those fired from FIRING POSITION
A, the position of Sirhan. My examination
disclosed no individual characteristics
establishing that Exhibit 47 and Exhibit 54
had been fired by the same gun. In fact, my
examinations disclosed that bullet Exhibit 47
has a rifling angle approximately 23 minutes
(14%) greater than the rifling angle of bullet
Exhibit 54. It is, therefore, my opinion that
bullets 47 and 54 could not have been fired
from the same gun.

On May 28, 1971, Los Angeles attorney Barbara Warner Blehr
filed charges with the Civil Service Commission alleging the
following deficiencies in the handling of the physical evidence in
the assassination of Senator Robert Kennedy:

1. A statement by the LAPD [Los Angeles police
department] criminalist that he "mis-labeled"
court exhibit 55 in the trial of Sirhan B. Sirhan.
2. Permitted test gun H18602 to be destroyed.
3. Lost or destroyed spectrogram films in the
Sirhan case.
4. Lost or destroyed part of Senator Kennedy's
clothing.
5. Failed to mark or record which of the test
bullets in the Sirhan case he had used for making
his identification.
6. Failed to make any comparison photomicrographs
of his bullet identification in the Sirhan case.
7. Failed to make any kind of laboratory report
regarding his spectrographic analysis of the
bullets in the Sirhan case.
8. Failed to count the number of identifying
points on the test bullets in the Sirhan case.

The charges of forensic inadequecy were hotly denied by the chief of police of Los Angeles, and a substantial civil suit was filed against Mrs. Blehr and a number of John Does. The controversy continues as of this writing, including new attempts by Sirhan Sirhan's attorneys to reopen his case. No adjudication has occurred as yet as to the alleged mishandling of the forensics in Senator Robert Kennedy's assassination. Meanwhile, additional charges of mishandling of physical evidence have been raised in yet another sensational murder case. It will take clear and firm judgments in civil and criminal courts to erase the doubts raised in the minds of many about the competence of the Los Angeles police department's forensics.

But if doubts are raised in the handling of these two most sensational assassinations, consider what may be going on in crimes of lesser importance.

An incident that gained world-wide attention was the police raid upon the Black Panther Chicago headquarters in December of 1969. Not even an hallucinating mind could conceive of the evidence travesty, bias, malfeasance, and probable deliberate distortion that was practiced by the Chicago police department and their crime lab. Because of charges and countercharges, a Federal grand jury was impaneled. Following are some excerpts from its report, published June, 1970. The opening statement from the introduction sets the scene:

> At 4:45 A.M., December 4, 1969, fourteen Chicago police officers assigned to the Cook County State's Attorney's Office, executed a search warrant for illegal weapons at 2337 West Monroe in a flat rented by members of the Black Panther Party. Nine people were in the apartment. Two were killed in the gun-fire which broke out: Fred Hampton, the militant and controversial Chairman of the Black Panther Party of Illinois, and Mark Clark, a Panther official from Peoria. Four other occupants were wounded, but survived. Two police officers sustained minor injuries.
>
> Public reaction was prompt and polarized. The State's Attorney's Office reported sketchily and then in detail that the officers were fired upon as they sought entry, and that they returned the fire and secured the premises after an intense gun battle with the occupants.

> By noon Black Panther spokesmen claimed that Hampton and Clark were victims of a Chicago-style political assassination pursuant to an alleged official national policy of genocide. . . . *Panther guides claimed the physical evidence proved the police did all the shooting.* [emphasis added]

The physical evidence was destined to be the real star of the show. Let's take a look at the techniques used to gather this all-important element of this controversial case.

Chapter *20*

After the shoot-out, the raiding police gathered assorted evidence, in random fashion, dumping it in a pile in a box in the livingroom, failing to identify it by markings or to record the discovery site of any of the evidence potpourri, which included ejected shells fired from police weapons.

A few minutes after the conclusion of the fracas, a roving evidence technician arrived at the scene to assist in gathering evidence. The grand jury report continues:

> As the technician approached the door of the flat, another officer whom he knew requested that he get his camera and go inside to begin taking pictures. Inside, he found the place very crowded. As the technician was assembling his equipment, he was approached by a plainclothes officer . . . who told him, "They shot through the back door and we want a picture of the hole in the back door." He was shown to the back door which was slightly open with a sheet hanging over the inside and directed to take a picture of the hole in the sheet as it was draped over the door. He did not move the sheet nor examine or photograph the covered portion of the door.

Fred Hampton's body was lying on the floor. Witnesses are confused as to just what happened then. The evidence technician says the body was moved before he had a chance to photograph it. The sergeant who led the raid said he instructed the technician to take photos and was later told by the crime lab that the photos did not turn out.

The report discusses at some length the evidence gathered by the original assault team. It then considers the evidence gathered by the mobile evidence technician in the original search, which lasted less than ninety minutes, and in a second visit two weeks later which took two days to complete. The second search, obviously, was the result of the enormous heat generated meanwhile by the case.

During searches by the Black Panthers' attorney the day of the shooting and several following days, additional evidence was found which had been missed during the first cursory inspections. This evidence became the basis for the Black Panthers' claim that all the shooting was done by the police.

The grand jury's following comment is of special import:

> One of the significant impressions the Grand Jury obtained from parts of the investigation conducted by the survivor's attorneys—and, indeed, from parts of the official investigation as well—was the extent to which the predisposition of the individuals conducting the investigations affected the results. Any investigation that is designed to prove a theory rather than to establish the facts has to be thoughtfully scrutinized and should not be accepted as objective without such scrutiny.

In the meantime, the Chicago crime lab managed to identify two fired shotgun shells as belonging to the Black Panthers and as having been fired from their weapons. This resulted in indictment of the survivors of the shoot-out.

Subsequently, the FBI was called into the case and found that these two shells had in fact been fired by the police, and had been mistakenly identified by the ballistics technician in the Chicago crime lab. The unsupportable rebuttal of the technician was that all the weapons involved in the shoot-out had not been available to him—utter nonsense on the face of it, since such ballistic evidence is routinely mated to its gun on the basis of unique impressions left by breechplate, firing pin, extractor, and ejector mechanisms, and such impressions are either present with sufficient comparison points or are not.

Not that the Black Panthers were purely innocent bystanders. The grand jury deplored the stockpiling of ammunition and weapons. Further, there was little doubt that the Panthers had fired at least one time with a deer load in a shotgun. Whether this firing was in response to police attack or preceded the attack will probably never be known, since the police proved highly unreliable in their accounts of the occurrence.

The report comments:

> The major concern of this Grand Jury has been the
> irreconcilable disparity between the detailed
> accounts given by the officers and the physical
> facts and evidence examined and reported by the
> FBI. . . . As noted previously, before the officers
> were permitted to testify before this Grand Jury,
> they were advised of the fact that a thorough
> examination of the bullet holes, ballistic exhibits
> and trajectories could confirm but one shot having
> been fired by all the seized Panther weapons.

Interestingly, even though advised that the grand jury knew
the truth, the officers testified much as they had before the
coroner's inquest, attributing the bulk of the firing to the Black
Panthers.

The box score relating to the evidence collected is as follows:

Agency	Dates	Items Recovered
State's attorney police	12-4-69	62
Crime lab unit	12-4-69	7
Survivors' attorney	12-4 to 12-17-69	43
Crime lab unit	12-17 and 12-18-69	8
FBI	12-22, 23	
	12-29 to 31-69	
	1-5 to 1-21-70	
	2-9, 2-13-70	
	3-8-70	30
Other	2-70	1
TOTAL		151

The report notes that no fingerprints were taken from the
seized weapons at the time they were obtained, and because of
repeated handling none were subsequently available.

Finally, the grand jury comments about the Chicago crime lab:

> The operation of this agency in this case indicated
> a serious lack of professionalism and objectivity.
> The whole purpose of a crime laboratory is to gather
> and analyze physical evidence. A scientific
> approach, in the Grand Jury's view, is necessarily
> objective and unbiased. It is inconceivable how the
> activities of the Mobile Crime Lab team can be

justified in light of this standard. The team
recovered but seven items and left behind at least
eighty projectiles and casings and at least as many
other items of physical evidence. The testimony of
the team leader that the team's only purpose was to
gather evidence supporting the officer's stories
makes it clear that there simply was not thorough
professional examination made of the premises.
Regardless of the directions allegedly received
from the State's Attorney's Police on the scene,
the Chicago Police Crime Lab should have insisted
on such an examination if for no other reason than
to guarantee the integrity of its own report.

Similarly, the work done by the lab after it
received the limited amount of evidence submitted
displays questionable professionalism. While any
firearms examiner can be excused a mistake—even one
with serious consequences—there was more involved
here. Not only did the State's Attorney's Police
fail to turn in their weapons for testing; the
Crime Laboratory did not even request them to do
so until after a mistaken report was prepared and
indictments based on it and after this Grand Jury
investigation was initiated. Had the Crime Lab
refused to conduct an analysis of any recovered
bullets and casings without having all the weapons
present in the apartment, there is every possibility
that the mistake would never have occurred and been
submitted as fact to the Cook County Grand Jury.

In short, the Crime Lab was responsible, in part
at least, for a totally inadequate search and for
a grossly insufficient analysis. The testimony of
the firearms examiner that he could not have refused
to sign what he believed was an inadequate and
preliminary report on pain of potential discharge
is highly alarming. If true, it could undermine
public confidence in all scientific analysis
performed by this agency.

The Grand Jury recommends that an immediate
evaluation of the operating rules and procedures
of the Crime Lab should be undertaken by the Chicago
Police Department. Recommendations should be
developed which would require the absolute
independence of that agency and which would insure
that the capable staff there will be free to pursue
their work with absolute scientific detachment
free from pressure or interference by anyone.

> Virtually all physical evidence is gathered by
> someone other than the criminalist, so the system
> goal rests upon an interdependent relationship seldom
> equalled in other areas of human endeavor.

Processed evidence is no better than the investigative work which produces it. In all but the most compelling cases, the forensic scientist is the helpless captive of the evidence investigator. Most crime labs spend some of their effort in discovering leads for further investigative work, with the balance used to develop evidence to convict. So unless the investigator collects the proper evidence, regardless of the skill of the criminalists or the excellence of his scientific instrumentation, neither desirable leads nor court evidence will be available.

Here is the great problem area. Crime labs are found only in the largest political subdivisions and at the state level, and then only in a few states. Proven techniques are ignored on a wholesale basis until it is only the exceptional crime which receives even the most meager attention from the crime lab technicians. Physical evidence collection is at an all-time low ebb, with incompetent investigators overlooking all but the most obvious items.

Phoenix, Arizona, for example, has some thirty thousand major crimes per year. By simple math this works out to nearly three thousand per month. Yet when I visited their crime lab toward the end of a spring month, personnel from the laboratory of criminalistics were personally involved in collecting evidence at the crime scene in exactly seven cases. This sort of situation seems to be the general rule rather than a rare exception. For every major crime which is solved with the tools of science, there are undoubtedly a dozen which go as undetected as were the foul deeds of the early arsenic poisoners.

This monstrous situation stems from inadequately trained police, who inherit the duty if not the ability to search crime scenes properly for physical evidence. Only thirty-one of the fifty states offer any guidance and programs of police training. Not until the last decade did most police agencies seriously concern themselves with training divisions. A majority still lack all but the most primitive training capability.

The Federal Law Enforcement Assistance Administration recently reviewed the crime lab situation in cities of over a hundred thousand population. They found only forty labs in all, with 111 cities having no locally operated criminalistic ability. Some 459 civilians in the labs possess B.A. degrees or better. Only a fraction of the sworn personnel—full-time policemen who are assigned to these jobs—hold such educational qualifications, though the lack of such degrees by no means disqualifies them, if they are properly trained by adequate in-house methods.

A built-in problem in those few agencies where physical evidence training is given to evidence collectors is that excellence produces promotion. Just about the time experience plus field training from the criminalist produces a first-class crime scene searcher, we have a new sergeant or lieutenant and the whole dreary process must begin anew. The obvious answer is ongoing training, with the system developing a continuing supply of back-up men to carry on when the first-line troops move upward.

Attrition of the police pupils trained in zone schools by the Federal Bureau of Investigation illustrates the hopeless magnitude of the problem. For years only the FBI concerned itself with the inadequacies of local training. Special agents, themselves highly skilled and excellent communicators, offered regional courses, usually one or two weeks long. This instruction attempted mastery of the most important of the over two thousand skills needed by the journeyman policeman. Typically, such a course was taught for twenty rookies from three or four neighboring departments. In about eighteen months the same police chiefs would request a repeat of the course, because all of the trainees had abandoned ship. When one considers that even today the average small-city policeman earns less than four hundred dollars per month, the turnover is understandable.

Even in reasonably adequate training situations, physical evidence collection is usually limited to a fun-day break in the serious regimen of absorbing court demeanor, rules of evidence, or how to handle the nontoilet-trained drunk. The training consists of a mock crime scene carefully devised like a party game. The rookie is exposed to a planned series of planted clues, leading, ultimately, to the puzzlelike solution of the guilty party. This charade is totally unrealistic, since in police service the patrolman will probably never be allowed to handle a major crime scene.

While such training high jinks are better than the all too common practice of hiring a man off the street, handing him a badge and gun, and declaring him a police officer, they add little to successful location and collection of crime scene physical evidence. The mock crime scenes invariably feature murder, and the average policeman will deal with no more than two or three nonfamily homicides in his entire career. In other felony cases such as burglary, aggravated assault, rape, and robbery, the police department's traditional policy usually limits its physical evidence search, if any, to the collection of fingerprints.

Even in sophisticated states like California with a well-organized, amply financed state police training agency, the recruit curriculum is in the order of only 250 hours, compared with the minimum fifteen hundred hours needed. In only a few exceptional agencies is any real concern given to the training in evidence potential of the rank-and-file policeman.

Nor is the situation much better in those hallowed detective halls, since the dicks were originally patrolmen, with little or no training in the beginning and no specialized physical evidence training given when promoted to investigator. By virtue of sheer experience, the older dicks have some exposure to physical evidence, usually through being embarrassed by their blunders. In the detective bureau there are at least a few slightly experienced halt to lead the newly appointed blind, however imperfectly.

Indifference, ignorance, and inefficiency interweave in the general failure to use forensic tools in major crime. Even in agencies enjoying criminalistic service, the old dogs' reaction to the new tricks is usually apathy. I vividly recall a brutal robbery that took place in 1947. The victim operated two butcher shops in town, each of them heavily patronized. This Friday evening the owner had gathered the week's receipts from his first place of business, wrapped them in clean butcher paper, and driven to the second butcher shop, which was already closed, to put the money in the floor safe.

As he opened the door, the robbers seized him from behind. They then snatched the wrapped money from his pocket, dragged him to the floor safe, and sadistically pistol-whipped him as he tried to open the safe at their demand. When the loot was in their possession, they slapped him around, threatened to emasculate him with one of his own butcher knives, and finally slashed at his throat with the knife, missing by a fraction of an inch and cutting off his tie at the neck.

Next, after binding his wrists behind him and gagging him cruelly, they forced the terrified merchant into the enormous freezer in the back of the store. Hurling him to the sawdust-covered floor, they slammed the soundproof door of the freezer and snapped the outside padlock in the hasp. No one would enter the store until Monday morning, two days away. The temperature was well below freezing in the refrigerator. The butcher was as good as dead.

With enormous determination, the dazed victim moved a large galvanized container to the central post of the freezer. Spindly cross-boards had been nailed to the post, as a ladder, starting about six feet above the ground. Ordinarily, an agile youth had difficulty making the climb. Somehow, the butcher managed to mount the galvanized can and strain his way upward with his back to the climbing post, his bound wrists almost completely immobilizing his hands.

Exhausted, he finally reached the top, where the overhead coils of the refrigerator were located. He wriggled, snakelike, along the narrow beam which led to a punch-out opening through which the coils could be replaced. Threatening to plunge to the concrete floor below as he teetered on the beam, he drove both feet against the pluglike opening. Nothing happened. Then another try, and yet another. After seeming hours the plug moved imperceptibly. His frantic efforts were weakening. Could he kick one more time? The urge to sleep, to give up was overpowering. Yet he forced himself for one last try.

The crash of the plug door on the outside floor dimly reached his ears. Somehow he found new strength to wriggle through the opening and fling himself to the floor below.

The newly created I unit officer was the first to respond to the dazed man found wandering a block from the store, still bound and gagged. Round the clock, these special evidence units patroled the streets, available to apply their physical evidence gathering expertise in all major crimes. Carefully, the identification technician cut the bonds from the victim's purple wrists, making sure not to harm the knots which might be linked to whoever had tied them. Next, he removed the gag and gently eased the victim onto the stretcher of the ambulance he had summoned.

The butcher could scarcely speak, but enough of his story came clear that the I man radioed the detectives to join them at the hospital.

Slightly revived by the doctors, the victim told his story. Soon the detectives and the evidence technician sped back to the scene, ready to gain entry with the owner's keys.

The detectives sloshed around in the sawdust, eliminating any possibility of gaining footprint intelligence, which might have helped the investigation. They clearly resented the whippersnapper of an evidence technician. For more than thirty years each of them had plied his trade without young squirts suggesting that things be left alone until examined for physical evidence.

The evidence *coup de grâce* was delivered by the more portly of the detective pair. "Found this," he proudly announced, tossing over the butcher paper in which the money had been wrapped. It was the only object with a potential for fingerprints, since butcher shops' traditional coating of grease defeats normal dusting methods.

"Here, young feller," the detective again picked up the wrapping paper and moved it a few inches closer to the evidence technician. "See what you can do with this." The smile on the fat detective's face seemed to say that he too could locate evidence with the best of them.

Too late, the technician lifted the paper with tweezers and preserved it in a cellophane bag. Later the police chemist would find prints all right—the detective's—squarely on top of the only fingerprint that might have placed the criminal at the scene.

The worst part of this thirty-year-old story is the likelihood that it would be repeated in most American cities if a similar crime were to occur tonight.

The postwar period produced another crime that received international attention. It started when the calm of the peaceful yacht anchorage at Balboa, California, on the blue Pacific, was disrupted by a sudden explosion. As spectators rushed to render aid, the *Mary H* gurgled horribly, sucking in the bay waters through the gaping hole in her bottom and plunged to the muck on the floor of the bay. Divers attempted a rescue in the shallow waters, but soon reported the hopelessness of the two victims stretched alongside the yacht's motor covering.

Not until the boat was raised and taken to drydock was suspicion aroused. Gasoline in the bilge of a yacht can be explosive, but this had been no gasoline explosion. The splintered planking had been burst asunder by a far greater force, such as dynamite.

The investigation soon focused on the victims' only daughter and her handsome boyfriend. Rumor recalled violent quarrels between the daughter and her parents as they tried to break up the torrid romance between the dowdy girl and her suave suitor.

Then investigators discovered that the boyfriend had recently purchased several sticks of dynamite. Preliminary search of the area near the explosion produced the remains of a wire curiously twisted, as though it might have been wrapped around just the number of dynamite sticks bought by the boy. The wire was tied with a sophisticated knot usually known only to seamen and Boy Scouts, and the boyfriend had risen high in the Boy Scout organization. The final touch was the discovery that the mirror on the boyfriend's jalopy had been wired in place with wire identical to that found in the sunken yacht. Moreover, it was fastened with the same sort of unusual knot.

Confronted with the evidence the suspect smiled and answered easily, that he'd bought the dynamite for dear old Dad, who sometimes tired of the hook-and-line routine and liked to blast the fish out of the water. So what if it wasn't quite sporting! Evidently the blast had been a trifle premature this time, catching Dad and Mom by surprise. What a shame!

It had to be determined whether the dead couple had been alive at the time of the explosion or whether they'd been bludgeoned (as seemed likely from marks on their heads) and then blown up. The key element was the position of the bodies. If evidence could be found to reconstruct the situation at the moment of explosion, the real events might be known. Much of the clothing was missing from the battered bodies. The investigators searched the engine deck, but little could be found in the area where the bodies had been found, which ended with a narrow passageway leading under the outside rear deck, and obviously the clothing had been blown to smithereens. How sad, because it appeared that the boy's defense would be difficult to counter without the missing clothing.

The worst fears of the police were realized as the trial progressed. The prosecutor had to admit that the demure heiress and the scrubbed Eagle Scout certainly didn't appear capable of such a heinous murder.

Chapter 21

The trial progressed with the defense freely admitting the youth's purchase of dynamite. The focus and blame were shifted to Poppa and his newly exposed fondness for harvesting crops of pressure-killed fish. Daddy, the defense emphasized, had simply miscalculated in preparing the explosive.

The blows on the victims' heads might be somewhat harder to account for, but the defense was cheerful about them. Everyone knows that explosions toss things about a bit. Certainly it was plain that much of the victims' clothing had been blasted away. Much too late in the game, the prosecuting authorities requested qualified criminalists to search the yacht for additional evidence.

Proper examination of the bilges produced the bulk of the missing clothing fragments. The fact that they'd been blown through the narrow opening between the engine deck and the slightly elevated outside deck was clear proof that the bodies had been lying on the lower deck at the time of the explosion. Had the victims been standing, only the lower portion of the man's trousers would have cleared the upper deck partition to blast into the bilges. The rest of the clothing would have bounced off the bulkhead and rebounded into the engine room.

Regrettably, the discovery came too late to be effective. The jury apparently had already swallowed the grim defense picture of the overbearing father and his unscrupulous fishing methods. The arrival in the case of the evidence clothing could not overshadow the impressions already formed about the demure heiress and her clean-cut escort. The couple was acquitted.

Before the not guilty verdict reached a shocked public, the county supervisors were taking steps to upgrade their forensic capability. Never again would Orange County expose itself to charges of forensic incompetence. Thanks to the notoriety of this case, a crime lab was created which has since become internationally famous for its excellence.

Criticism of the investigative techniques used in determining whether the explosion was accidental is as simple as most

Monday-morning-quarterback analyses. Considering that only a sprinkling of criminalists were practicing in the entire country, the failure to seek expert forensic help at the beginning of the investigation is forgivable.

Such an oversight would be less excusable now, yet this very drama would likely repeat itself most places if it occurred tomorrow.

In one study reported in *Medicine, Science and the Law*, an evaluation by the San Francisco coroner's office of some five hundred consecutive autopsies showed the clinical diagnosis to be wrong 45 percent of the time. In some four hundred additional cases, eight deaths were found to be from unnatural causes. The reverse of this coin was that 30 percent of the cases thought to have died from unnatural causes proved to be natural deaths.

How about other parts of the world? A London study showed that of some five thousand deaths thought to be natural, some 263 were found to be unnatural, about 5 percent of the total.

The clear conclusion is that in the most grievous crime of all—murder—a substantial number are unpunished if for no other reason than that they are undetected. One answer is 100 percent autopsy in all coroner's cases, with forensic pathologists conducting the examination. In addition, a reasonable percentage of noncoroner's cases should be randomly autopsied to detect those perfect crimes.

While murders by poisoning persist in some portions of the world, using the old standbys such as arsenic, they are virtually a thing of the past in the United States, except for a few unenlightened areas in the South.

The threat of murder by poison, however, is far from removed. At this moment there at least half a dozen highly toxic chemicals readily available to the chemically informed murderer. Since these substances are never routinely tested for in toxicological examinations, it would take a high level of investigative suspicion and a more than competent toxicologist for a murder by these substances to become detected. And even if the cause of death were to be blamed on one of them, a number of logical ways exist for a victim to have fatal exposure. (For obvious reasons, we're deliberately not naming the substances nor the ways in which they can be introduced into the victim.) Undoubtedly dozens of murderers are secure in the knowledge that they have gotten away with the perfect crime. Perhaps they number in the thousands.

In one case in our experience, a woman was found in her garage with a garden hose attached to the exhaust of her car and leading into the barely open window on the driver's side of the otherwise tightly closed car. The woman's husband was prominent in the community. Equally well-known was the fact that he was having an affair with another woman.

An empty prescription bottle of phenobarbital was found on the kitchen sink. The old-school detective, whose pear-shaped figure reflected the unending supply of free meals he gouged from restaurants, picked up the bottle to read its label. He presumed that the woman had simply wanted to guarantee her suicide. No attempt was made to check the bottle for fingerprints, nor was an autopsy performed. The case was written off as a suicide, even though it might well have been a murder, discoverable with adequate examination for physical evidence.

Then there was the scene at the vehicle-maintenance shop of a large laundry. The police were called because one of the mechanics had been found dead, lying on the floor alongside his workbench. When the detective arrived, he found the victim's complexion was blue-black, a medical condition called cyanotic. Alongside the dead man a whisky bottle stood upright on the concrete floor. Without worry about fingerprints or just how the bottle had managed to land upright on the concrete floor without breaking, the detective gingerly picked up the bottle with his bare hands, opened it, and cautiously sniffed the contents. "Cyanide," he announced authoritatively, arbitrarily assigning the mechanic's death to a dosage of cyanide mixed with the presumed whisky in the bottle.

No attempt was made to determine the circumstances of the victim's life, or where he—or someone else—might have obtained the cyanide. The whisky bottle was never examined for fingerprints, not even those of the detective. Chemical analysis of the contents of the bottle was not attempted, and again no autopsy was performed. The entire investigation took a little over twenty minutes, from the detective's arrival until his declaration of suicide. And all this in a city with crime lab facilities.

Some understanding of the magnitude of the problem of

detecting certain chemical agents of murder can be gained from a case of murder by insulin, cracked by the Los Angeles sheriff's office in 1967. Reminiscent of the early arsenic murderers who had to kill several persons before there was suspicion of wrongdoing, this case began as an inquiry into six suspicious deaths over a period of twenty years, starting in 1947. Over four hundred witnesses had to be located and interviewed before the successful conclusion of the case and the conviction of one William Dale Archerd on three counts of first-degree murder.

In the Archerd case, the suspect left a trail of mysterious deaths in his wake sufficient to arouse the suspicions of a three-year-old. His actions were so blatant that he virtually begged for detection. Yet six persons were to die before overwhelming investigation of the case finally pinned him to his murderous deeds.

While we thoroughly applaud the tenacity of the Los Angeles sheriff's investigators and their ability and willingness to mount a major investigation into the case, we can only wonder how many discreet one-time killers have successfully achieved their objectives.

Little wonder then that tens of thousands of major crimes escape physical evidence attention. Add to those, equal or larger numbers of very real crimes which are never reported, from fear or lack of confidence in the police, or which are buried by the police in their deliberate attempts to make the records seem better, and the picture becomes more appalling.

Not thirty days before this was written, my secretary was held at gunpoint in her own backyard by a probably drug-crazed youth, whose conversation indicated his firm intention to rape her. Such detention constitutes kidnapping in the legal sense. Possession of the weapon and its concealment before and after the girl's restraint is another felony, as was the probable drug use. Only her husband's unexpected arrival home prevented a tragedy. Yet the San Francisco police not only refused to respond to the call, with the great likelihood of capturing the criminal—they refused to even accept a report.

Of all the states, California has the largest number of crime labs, staffed with highly respected criminalists, striving avidly to upgrade their professional competence. Yet a report by the

California Council on Criminal Justice states that less than 1 percent of the known major crimes ever receives the attention of a trained criminalist. Even in those few cases where forensic know-how is applied in some degree, not one in a hundred gains the personal attention at the crime scene of the trained scientist who ultimately must discover, analyze, interpret, and testify concerning the vital evidence.

In a recent review of evidence-gathering practices in all cities of over a hundred thousand population across the United States, the California Traffic Safety Foundation discovered that the minuscule portion of cases receiving criminalistic action in California is high compared with that in the balance of the country. All too few agencies report special evidence-gathering facilities or technicians. An unbelievable number are simply unable to even estimate the percentage of crimes receiving no physical evidence search, even for fingerprints.

In 1968 the Berkeley, California, police department cooperated in a noble experiment. Trained criminalists from the University of California's School of Criminalistics accompanied police investigators to all major crimes for a period of three months. The police were instructed to gather evidence as usual, while the civilian criminalist observed the evidence actually gathered and the potential evidence overlooked. As might have been predicted, the misses far exceeded the hits.

Even though the observers averaged less than fifteen minutes per case, they found collectable evidence in 1,397 of the 1,601 Part I offenses (which include burglary, auto theft, theft—petty and over fifty dollars—robbery, rape, assault, and murder). The study's conservative conclusion was that in at least nine out of ten major crimes, physical evidence is there for the finding. In most cases there's more than one type of evidence, such as soils, fibers, glass fragments, and bloodstains. The average of evidence types for this study ranged from robbery with but one type, burglary with three, and murder with six.

Of the 8,203 cases reported, 489 resulted in evidence being transmitted to the crime lab. The current drug crisis accounted for 452 of the 489. In the remaining 37 cases, only four produced physical evidence to be sent to the crime lab from the major crime categories.

Berkeley is considered a progressive community, with a good police department. Their willingness to examine themselves and the fact that their reported crimes are twice the nation's average clearly indicate that they are trying to sweep nothing under the rug.

Yet only four cases produced pieces of physical evidence sent to the crime lab out of 1,397. What, then, is the scorecard likely to show for the rest of the nation?

Which brings us head-on with one of the saddest facts of life in the whole of forensic science: In the average burglary in the United States, no attempt whatsoever is made to gather some of the most plentiful kinds of evidence.

Statistics kept by the FBI show major crimes per hundred thousand population for the period of one year as follows:

Type	Number per 100,000
Murder	7.8
Forcible rape	18.3
Aggravated Assault	162.4
Robbery	171.5
Auto theft	453.5
Larceny (over $50)	859.4
Burglary	1,067.7

Obviously, burglary is the big one. Yet even in large cities such as Atlanta, Indianapolis, Lansing, Los Angeles, and Omaha, to name but a few, only a small percentage of the breaking-and-entering cases receive evidence-gathering attention for more than fingerprints, if that. The extent of simple failure to search is chilling when one considers the missed potential.

Burglaries constitute 75 percent of all major crimes in the United States. Six times more frequent than robbery, the nearest competitor, burglaries suffer from massive police indifference. Scarcely any other crime is less likely to result in gathered physical evidence.

Typically, most large cities ignore the vast majority of burglaries, all the while charging after the drug abuser—the very person who is responsible for an enormous portion of the burglaries. This seems all the stranger when we consider that a hundred-dollar-a-day narcotics habit demands something close to a five-hundred-dollars-a-day attack upon society, fences being notably disinclined to buy hot merchandise at retail rates.

Even more peculiar, burglaries as a class offer one of the best opportunities for findings that point to the criminal. Yet in nearly every city boasting crime lab capability, the response to a reported burglary varies from the suggestion the victim bring down a list of his stolen property to an outright refusal to take action. This is particularly true if the dollar value of the loss is not excessive by current police standards, say, only a thousand dollars. In some locations the beat officer will be dispatched, grudgingly, to accept a report at the scene of the loss. He is totally unprepared to inspect the scene for physical evidence, nor is he interested in doing so.

If the loss or the victim is important enough, a token investigation may occur. Common treatment of major burglary involves fingerprint search only. Conceivably, a photo technician will shoot a picture or two in the unlikely event that some additional recordable evidence is discovered by the fingerprint man. Neither of these worthies pays attention to the manifold possibilities of tire tracks and footprints, soil samples, glass chips (which abound in forced entries), paint exchanges at entry point, fibers, or toolmarks.

In all fairness, a few hopeful places in the nation have mobile evidence vans, which do respond to as many crime scenes as possible. Also, most victims have only a slight idea of their losses in extensive burglaries, having kept no inventory of property, identifying marks, or serial numbers. Lacking this information, the chances of property recovery are nil.

Certain burglary categories, however, seem to receive more police attention than others, safe burglary claiming top billing. Mess with a safe, and police passions are inordinately aroused. Such fulmination is understandable since the safe burglar, almost by definition, is a practicing professional, while the run-of-the-mill house burglar is more likely to be the boy next door. Let one safe burglary occur, and the police bristle. A dozen, and vacations and days off are cancelled. Shock troops search round-the-clock for the heinous perpetrators. All the while, traffic accidents on the streets adjacent to the safe burglary location cause loss in death, injury, and property a thousand times the magnitude of the safe depredations. Even the over-looked house and apartment burglaries undoubtedly total in excess of safe losses, but there's no glamor to these burglaries. They're simply unable to compete for police attention with the haulers, blowers, and peelers of the safe trade.

The blow boys are the big-time of the safe professionals, a highly specialized field where amateurs end up as splattered casualties. Explosive residuals provide excellent evidence for spectroscopy, and a number of crime lab techniques have found application as countermeasures against the blowers, even though their depredations are relatively few. In addition to the criminalistic aspects, the very uniqueness of attacks by explosion provides two kinds of programs for police action.

First comes the use of the *modus operandi* file. The idiosyncrasies of this ilk tend to identify the individual who practices his trade in a characteristic and individualistic manner. Burglars who use explosives are somewhat like master forgers—there are so few in the business the likelihood of being identified is fairly great.

Less glamorous in the safe burglar hierarchy are the peelers. The penny-ante peeler may apply his stripping techniques to assorted coin boxes ranging from street newspaper vending machines to the elaborate and expensive machinery which dispenses an enormous assortment of merchandise in thousands of public and semipublic locations.

But whether the peeler is stripping a telephone coin box, invading a beverage dispenser, or stripping off the outer layers of a safe, the evidence potential is much the same. His tools need to be tough enough to puncture metal and to have some method of gaining enough mechanical advantage to force the case-hardened tool bit through the shell of the container guarding the coins.

The tools the peelers use frequently look familiar. One such device, on exhibit in the museum of the New York State crime lab, was made by welding a huge cutting end to an enormous prybar. Except for scale, it looks for all the world like the can opener found in any kitchen, only this opener was used to rip into a building roof to gain entry and then to neatly peel open the safe.

Peeling or stripping is the most popular way to open a safe. Brute force, mechanically enhanced, is used to rip off the outer coverings concealing the goodies. This category includes the torch specialists, who burn their way into safe interiors with cutting blowtorch, and the punch men, who use sledge hammers and punches to drive out the locking mechanism. All of these metal-tormenting methods offer particular opportunity for the criminalist to establish positive toolmark identification. This evidence is often as good as fingerprints, if the tool can be found in the criminal's possession.

The haulers, a third group, kidnap the safe to some isolated spot far from the madding crowd. There they attack it with equal parts of sheer strength and ingenuity, occasionally leavened with a generous portion of stupidity.

The muscle men sometimes demonstrate physical power of the carnival strongman class, carting a safe up a hillside to some high lookout point. Like the sea bird that carries a clam to soaring heights, then smashes it open on the rocks below, they fling the safe to the mercies of gravity. Regrettably for the members of the safe-cracking fraternity, the result usually is one banged-up intact safe, with doors and locking mechanism permanently jammed.

The haulers are about the most helpful in leaving a string of clues for the criminalist. The lonely site they seek for uninterrupted exploration of the safe's innards may retain perfect tire marks from the vehicle employed. Unique flora may be transferred to the person or vehicle used. Where the burglars enjoy any degree of success, a whole new dimension of evidence is added—the safe lining.

The safe manufacturing process is uniquely messy when it comes to the insulation materials stuffed between the safe's inner and outer shells. The manufacturer may dump as much as fifty tons of insulation in his storeyard, indiscriminately mixing diatomaceous earth, plaster, asbestos, and other fire-resistant materials. As the pile grows low, from time to time a new batch will be added, all contributing to the individuality of the mix in any particular safe. If, during its life, the safe receives any patching—say, from an earlier burglary—still more strange junk is added.

This procedure enables the criminalist to discover a physical or spectroscopic match between material found at the crime scene and that discovered on the suspect or in his vehicle. A small problem arises with the busy burglar who may have traces from several safe jobs littering his trunk. But if the uncontaminated lining can be located, then there's a fair chance of convincing a jury that the two safe linings came from the same source. Even the microscopic creatures whose skeletons constitute diatomaceous earth may differ in appearance, depending on which location and geological eon produced them.

Finally, there is the class of burglar whose sole specialty seems to be stupidity. He ignores signs which declare the safe door to be unlocked with nothing negotiable inside, whaling, pounding, stripping, or peeling to get inside when he only had to open the door. One result of this moronity is jamming of the mechanism so that the safe is ruined or takes expert and expensive treatment before the documents stored only for fire protection can be released. One such clownish practitioner stands out in my memory.

This gent concealed himself somewhere in the recesses of a theater while the movie was showing, outwaiting the tired crew, who could scarcely wait to leave for home after the final reel ground out.

After coming out of hiding, the burglar first assaulted the vending machines, smashing the small glass windows, scattering paint, leaving scraped jimmy marks in a dozen places. A veritable shower of evidence littered the carpeted lobby, including half a dozen candy bars, which apparently escaped from the burglar's bulging pockets.

Next, he attacked the large glass window of the theater office, through which the safe could be seen, depositing a little of his own blood in his zeal to crawl inside before the window opening was quite large enough. Ignoring his dripping wound, he flailed away at the safe with his jimmy.

He earned an A for pure attacksmanship, considering the extent of his destruction, but his small jimmy was not in the safe-cracking league. All he gained by this sortie was cut flesh, sore hands, and a few more identifiable toolmarks.

Exhausted with his futile attempt, he started to leave the

theater, then discovered a new problem. Most break-and-enter artists have to get in first. If the break-in doesn't work, at least they are still on the legal side of the wall. This burglar must have had a few troubled moments when the stout outside glass doors failed to yield to the maneuverings of his junior-sized jimmy.

Momentarily thwarted, he retreated to the lobby, where he discovered a fire ax and liberated it from its cabinet. The ax was heavy enough to shatter the glass exit door. (It was actually stout enough to have penetrated the safe if he'd thought of it.)

As he wriggled out of the front door opening, he lost his wallet on the carpet, complete with his name and correct address.

The detectives were waiting for him when he arrived home, the loot still in his possession. Even the candy bars matched the selection in the theater's vending machine. He might at least have eaten up that evidence.

Chapter *22*

Sadly, not all criminals exhibit such cranial incapacity that the police are waiting for them when they get home. This is particularly true of nonresidential burglaries, which cost business and industry millions annually. Fully professional thieves sometimes are a full step ahead of security specialists in utilizing science. Plant security surveillance techniques utilize ultrasonic sound, vision intensifiers, photoelectric eyes, closed circuit TV, and sound monitors to replace the superannuated guard walking his lonely rounds and punching his timeclock. At the same time, at least some of the people on the wrong side of the law have developed electronic countermeasures that allow them to intercept or bypass properties smug in the presumed security of their modern protective devices.

Criminals seem to respond as rapidly as society's habits change. The national bike boom has produced a bicycle theft crime wave in proportion. California alone suffers more than a million-dollar loss annually in bike ripoffs, with a minuscule proportion being recovered. The city of Davis, one northern California campus of the University of California, had a loss of a hundred thousand dollars last year from bike thefts, approximately one-fifth its entire property loss to thieves. On this campus one commonly sees the incongruous sight of a several-hundred-dollar, ten-speed bike weighing only 19½ pounds protected by a battleship-type chain weighing several pounds. But as love laughs at locks, so do bicycle thieves. Massive chains are snipped like so much butter with four-foot-long bolt-cutters or sliced through with tiny torches. Laboratory science is even applied by the criminal who pours liquid nitrogen over the chain. The minus 195 degrees of the liquid gas creates a brittleness in the crystalline structure of the metal so that it fractures with a tap from a hammer, liberating the bicycle.

As yet criminalistic ingenuity has not been able to develop an innovative countermeasure to the bicycle theft problem. However, one of the most promising police playthings is the remarkable development of the Sylvania Corporation, called Digicom.

The Digicom console is mounted on the dashboard of a police car. It has a small cathode-ray tube about the size of a teacup, alongside a map-holder about the size of a piece of typing paper. Underneath are a series of pushbutton control keys and a compact keyboard like that of a small calculator.

Some eighty maps can be inserted in the map-holder. To indicate his location, the officer needs only to touch his pinkie to the map. Instantly this intelligence is carried, via the car radio beam, to the dispatcher where it is translated into a spot of light on a master map indicating the exact location and number of the police unit.

The pushbuttons and keyboard have direct access to one of four computers. The policeman types in a vehicle license number (or the name and driver's license number of a motorist), punches the appropriate control key, and the system does the rest. It will check the warrant file in the local nine-county computer or switch to the warrant file for the entire state. It bounces directly to the state capital to the highway patrol computer, which gives status information on the vehicle within seconds, telling whether it was stolen, wanted for involvement in another crime, or repossessed, as well as information about the owner. The fourth computer contains the total driving records of some twelve million individuals, including stops on their license renewal because of existing warrants or revocation or suspension of their driving privilege.

Any information possessed by any of the computers returns directly to the mobile police car in the form of a visual display on the cathode-ray tube. While there are a few bugs to be worked out (the signals are transmitted on voice channels and must await their turn when vocal traffic is heavy), this marvelous system promises tremendous improvement in dispatching police units, maintaining deployment control, and in giving front-line police-men vitally needed information.

But what about the crime lab situation in the same city?

The present competent staff are so overworked they lack time for the basic niceties of making photomicrographs in ballistics cases. Some years ago the police agency moved into a sparkling new building with an excellently laid-out crime lab, complete with over fifty thousand dollars in new equipment of the most modern sort.

Today, this equipment has been gathering dust for five years, almost totally unused. "It takes more time to keep it on line than we can possibly afford," the chief criminalist remarks resignedly. "If I tried to keep the apparatus functional and accurate, I'd have to skip the SOS cases." He shrugged his shoulders, "I have only a few years to retirement. Every year I beg for help to get this lab out of the Stone Age. Guess we're lucky topside lets us keep what we have."

This, in a town having one of the worst burglary records in the country. This, in a town enjoying the experimental use of the space-age Digicom!

In the midst of the crime lab's scientific cornucopia, we discover an anomaly which often defies explanation: With rare exceptions, as technical expertise expands, practical use decreases! Not everywhere, not all the time. But as more potential crime-busters emerge from the kingdom of science, science is increasingly overlooked in the solving of major crimes. Even the old standbys, so effective in the past, fall into disuse. Crimes which two decades ago brought speedy response by the police and reasonably effective use of forensics (considering the state of the art) are literally kissed off in all too many jurisdictions today.

A random review of the evidence-gathering potential of Buffalo, Cleveland, Omaha, and Honolulu showed not more than two available evidence technicians on any given shift, even though these jurisdictions deal with major crimes in the tens of thousands per year. In the California Traffic Safety Foundation study, Honolulu reported that only 10 percent of such crimes are even processed for fingerprints, a total by no means atypical.

In communities not having the benefit of specialized evidence units, the officers who might gather physical evidence have little or no scientific background, a paltry number of training hours in the forgotten recruit days, and dimly remembered knowledge of the basic principles and potential of physical evidence collection. The wonder of the inadequate system is that any crimes get solved with the aid of forensics.

As much as we might wish that crime would go away, all indications point to the continuing acceleration of lawlessness and violence in our midst. The FBI reports a 156 percent increase in violent crimes in the decade of the sixties, with a 180 percent increase in attacks against property. Reported major crimes from the areas representing only 84 percent of the United States population run in excess of seven million annually, with increases expected with each passing year.

Because of the steady yearly increase in major crime, the Federal government recently commissioned the Stanford Research Institute to take a hard look at the American criminal justice system's inability to reverse this alarming trend. The government's particular interest was in the possibility of plowing more Federal funds into crime labs, particularly to assist them in taking advantage of new technologies.

Stanford Research Institute soon found that there were no studies of the cost-benefits of the use of criminalistics in crime solution. One great difficulty is the problem of whether to put a price-tag on solved crimes or on ones which are never commited because of the deterrent effect of swift and effective justice.

Early in their investigations they discovered the inundation of drug cases, which are preempting crime lab time at the expense of more traditional crimes calling for forensic treatment.

The role of criminalistics in the United States is clearly antithetical. On the one hand space-age technology promises unlimited horizons. On the other, crime laboratories in no sense control their own destinies. With the crime lab improperly located in bureaucratic structures, the criminalist has virtually no control over input, case loads, or the use of the crime lab services.

The crime lab is overworked, swamped under the increasing deluge of drug cases, which in turn causes neglect of major crime evidence. Because of manpower shortages, virtually every crime lab in the nation is unable to fill its manning table. And the production of new criminalists, even in the three universities still graduating them, has fallen to a mere trickle. The situation which the study uncovered was so bad that Brian Parker and Vonnie Gurgin, who conducted the analysis, concluded their report with the statement: "It is highly questionable whether the current social basis, in terms of which the examination of physical evidence has been found to be valuable, is worthy of additional investment."

The temptation in an open-and-shut investigation is to let well enough alone and accept the obvious facts, including a confession of guilt. For this reason, many cases never see the inside of a crime lab, but cry for a search for truth. Regardless of how many witnesses observed an event, the existence of overpowering motive, the full and free confession of the assassin, the physical evidence ought to receive the same attention as if the murderer were unknown.

The most notorious example is the assassination of Senator Robert Kennedy and the complete thrust to confirm the eyewitness testimony that he was shot by Sirhan Sirhan.

Following any notorious murder there is an outpouring of confessions by troubled individuals who had nothing to do with the killing. Just as every highway fatality should be regarded as murder until proven not to be, so should every confession be considered spurious until corroborated by other evidence.

In New York, a fight occurred in a bar, following which one of the men involved in the altercation left and returned with a rifle which he fired, killing an innocent bystander, and then fled. When apprehended, he freely confessed and turned over the alleged murder weapon to the arresting officers.

Before the weapon was processed and examined ballistically by the crime lab, the man was brought to a speedy trial, pleaded guilty, and was sentenced to the penitentiary.

When ballistics tests were made on the rifle they proved it was not the weapon that had fired the fatal bullets. Interestingly, the criminalists involved are trying to get this case reopened, but have had no success thus far. Possibly the charged man was indeed the killer, and the wrong gun was somehow turned over to authorities. In any event, the man is still in prison when the evidence presently in hand would have exonerated him had he pled not guilty and gone to trial.

The chief goal of criminalistics is to pin the criminal to the scene of his crime—if guilty—or to exonerate him if innocent.

Ideally, the forensic scientist, above all else, should seek truth. He should have no interest in making someone—an individual or a department—look good by adjusting evidence findings to conform with the case.

One of the most neglected aspects of forensics in the United States is the availability in crime labs of adequate physical evidence analysis for the defendant. While most labs give lip service to defense as well as working in the public interest, the actual number of such services offered each year could be counted on the fingers of one hand. Not that the criminalist does not protect the rights of wrongly accused individuals. This happens automatically with proper laboratory findings. What does not occur is *both* the defense request and acceptance by the crime lab of evidence evaluation for the accused.

Most criminalists, however, are permitted to accept private consultation—and do. Inevitably, this produces head-on clashes with friends in the business. Adversary proceedings often produce bitterness and rancor. When scientists find themselves on opposite sides of the evidence fence, the loser is likely to feel that his opponent of the day has subverted the truth to fit the needs of his client.

Many types of scientific evidence take considerable explanation and selling to juries. The trip through the fingerprint labyrinth obviously demands a tour guide pointing out each of the pattern similarities in the blown-up photographs. Fatal bullet photomicrographs inevitably reveal numerous scratch marks, conspicuous by their absence on the test bullets, since bouncing off sinew, bone, plaster and woodwork inevitably leaves marks on fatal bullets not found on the gently recovered exemplars. Thus, with most forensic evidence, the expert criminalist is a must for reasonable understanding.

In the face of the often diametrically opposed testimony of prosecution and defense experts, juries are bound to be confused. Ordinary witnesses may only testify about facts personally known to them as witnesses. Experts, on the other hand, are permitted to express opinions, frequently fuzzing a juror's understanding of a so-called fact under discussion.

In those rare locations where a genuine effort is exerted to discover physical evidence, the favorite type of evidence is the jigsaw fit. The most inexperienced juror can observe for himself that the paint chip from the entry window slips exactly into place. If the testimony proves this chip was discovered clinging to the clothing of the suspect, the burglar is nailed to the scene of his crime.

Take a chunk broken from the outside rear-view mirror,

severed by the pedestrian's body as the hit-and-run car slammed it to the pavement. Mate the chunk to the mirror still attached to the suspect's car, and the jury will hasten to convict.

Sometimes they are even too hasty. A cast of a footprint left by a tennis shoe in the soft dirt under the entry window may gain instant acceptance when compared with the shoe removed from a gentleman captured jogging two blocks from the crime scene. The fact that ten thousand copies of this tennis shoe were cast from the same mold may never enter into the case, unless the integrity of the criminalist prevents *his* adoption of class characteristics. The lack of unique identifying marks such as blemishes, cuts, lodged twigs, or pebbles may simply not arise in minds that do not differentiate between extraordinary factors and those shared in common. If the People's representatives rely on such flimsy evidence, a false conviction may well jail the ignorant, or those with cultural or language barriers.

Like the old saw about figures lying and liars figuring, physical evidence must be reviewed in an objective atmosphere seeking only truth. Perhaps the greatest sin in the field of criminalistics is trying to make the evidence fit the suspect, instead of the facts. This is the primary argument for separating the crime lab entirely from any law enforcement or prosecution agency.

In a police-operated crime lab, the criminalist becomes well-acquainted and friendly with the investigators who gather evidence and develop the cases. This fraternity may well develop to the point where the criminalist accepts the investigator's comments at face value without subjecting them to rigid scrutiny.

"Here's a cast of the footprint," the policeman might offer. "I checked with the shoe we got off Joe Hernandez. It's the one, all right."

Fine and good if it is, but suppose it isn't.

Except for screening and eliminating evidence from consideration, class characteristics should not be used in developing matching points. Theoretically, the wear and tear of use develops differences, if only microscopic, in all manufactured items. While the criminalist must be extremely cautious in blindly applying this concept for production-like items, the basic tenet is that all objects have detectable differences. The key factor in identifying a jimmy as the specific tool which pried open *this* safe and left

. 241 .

this mark is the number of uncommon points-in-common. Human freedom is too precious to make light judgments which will be accepted as gospel by prosecutors, judges, and juries, A recent poll taken of public defenders—attorneys assigned by the courts to defend the penniless accused—indicated that a possible 10 percent or more of current felony arrests are in error. With the proven fallibility of eyewitnesses, correct interpretation of physical evidence becomes even more vital.

How many similar points make a *make*? Obviously, the more, the merrier. Start with twelve points of similarity between the footprint in the soft dirt and the suspect's shoe. Add to this the fingerprint on the sill with six points of similarity. Take additional dollops of evidence—the eyewitness's identification, the loot found in the pocket. Now we have a dandy circumstantial case. Add a confession of guilt, and no one need search his conscience as to whether an innocent man is being convicted.

Given something less, say only six points in the shoe print, how does the criminalist make a decision? Here we must rely heavily on the value of experience—qualified experience, since the processing of a large number of cases matters less than a full understanding of the principles involved. All these factors being equal, it is one thing to have examined five hundred bits of impression evidence, another to have worked on only five cases of this sort. In matters of competence it is relatively easy to slip from the known to the unknown. Success in one field too frequently invites testimony slightly beyond true competence, which, in turn, leads to expounding in fields completely over the so-called expert's head. It is imperative for the criminalist to bend over backwards to make certain that another's belief in the guilt of the suspect does not get translated into faulty testimony concerning the physical evidence.

Though relatively rare, such abuse of professional privilege occurs for a variety of reasons, mostly with individuals who are not truly qualified in the field into which they have strayed.

Chapter 23

Some forensic matters are relatively uncomplicated. With a few days' formal training and perhaps a year of on-the-job supervision, any reasonably intelligent individual can testify on fingerprint comparison. No two fingerprints are ever precisely alike, even those rolled in two successive tries from the same finger.

The relative arrangement of significant detail within the fingerprints, however, is clearly apparent, even to lay persons, in proper photographic enlargements with comparable features pointed out by numbered lines.

Tire and heel or shoe patterns left on dusty surfaces or in soils are likewise easily identifiable, when unique similarities are found. As we've stressed before, these do not include class characteristics, such as common tennis shoe design or a maker's logo moulded into the rubber sole. The qualities which matter are those that have developed with wear and damage—the small cut, the broken line, the wedged pebble. Little training is needed to observe and testify adequately about these factors.

The wicket grows stickier when the witness moves away from his field of expertise into an area in which he has little qualification, such as that of mathematical probabilities.

In the early days of criminalistics, many practitioners who were less then knowledgeable in mathematics introduced the questionable practice of applying mathematical probabilities to the various facets of the evidence.

Like a weed in a flower garden, this mathematical flower bloomed inordinately, enjoying a period of faddish popularity. The probabilities practitioner blindly ascribed mathematical likelihood to a host of random occurrences for which no valid data existed. With oversimplistic enthusiasm, basically nonapplicable mathematical techniques were used to convince juries of the uniqueness of particular evidence.

As an exaggerated example, suppose a button is found clutched in the fist of a murder victim, and a button is missing from the suspect's coat. The out-of-his-depth expert might testify:

"The coat had four buttons. One was missing. Odds against this situation are at least one out of four. The button was dark brown, one of twenty-six standard button colors. It measured half an inch in diameter, one of seven common button sizes. It was sewn on with a no. 40 thread, one of five available thread gauges. It was linen, one of four common thread materials. The odds against chance occurrence of these circumstances are 4 X 26 X 7 X 5 X 4, which equals odds of 14,560 to 1."

These odds are large enough to convince most juries that the button came from the suspect's coat, who then must be the murderer.

Perhaps he was. But ascribing probabilities in this fashion abuses the true mathematical laws of probabilities. Some authorities believe there is no place whatsoever for the use of mathematical probabilities in most forensic areas. Yet just such probabilities are used every day in very real cases affecting the freedom of individuals charged with criminal offenses.

The heart of the problem is the lack of baseline data from which to derive supportable probability tables. Partial data do exist in a limited number of evidence types. Blood typing, for example, has been carried out with sufficiently large numbers of the population to establish supportable presumptions. Type AB is found in no more than 3 to 5 percent of the population. The assumption is justifiable, therefore, that a suspect with type AB blood has no more than a one-in-twenty chance of matching the AB bloodstain left at the crime scene. However, with a population of two hundred million in the United States, these odds are scarcely sufficient for conviction on this basis alone: there are at least six million individuals with type AB.

Ample background data have been collected for a few other evidence types. With almost two hundred million fingerprint cards in the FBI files—no two of which have ever been found identical for different individuals—an expert may reasonably state there is little possibility that a print with twelve or more points of similarity belongs to anyone but the defendant.

Several other evidence types deserve nearly as much credence as fingerprint identification. Spectrograms with all lines identical in location and density should carry great weight. Striations left by the uneven edges of a tool are often detected in safe burglaries. Matched line for line with a tool found in a burglar's possession, such comparisons provide virtually positive identification, the only real question being the ownership of the tool. Glass fractures with the random fracture patterns matched in three-dimensional jigsaw fit can be completely convincing without handicapping the evidence with made-up mathematical probability calculations.

One use of mathematical probability is inescapable. This is the semiautomatic calculation performed by the marvelous computers we call brains. Any time we make a judgment, our brains assess not only the immediate factors, but a lifetime of stored information, bringing far more intelligence to bear in the decision-making process than ordinarily comes to conscious attention.

Whatever we label it, this experience is of inestimable value in forensics. The fact that Dr. Milton Helpern has participated in over seventy thousand autopsies, including several thousand each from burning, drowning, or gunshot wounds, lends a weight to his findings that far exceeds those of surgeons whose experience includes only a few such cases.

No scientist objects to the examination of his findings by a scientist of equal competence. The true scientist has no desire to railroad his judgments in blind pursuit of some tenuous goal. He knows that scientific decisions must truly be objective and repeatable. Yet many eminent criminalists feel that making ballistic microphotographs, which permits such evaluation, is a waste of time. This may be supportable if the original evidence is available to reputable scientists on the opposing side, which often is not—particularly long after the case, as in the matter of Sirhan Sirhan.

In a few cases, the enthusiastic but misguided criminalist strays into territory so unfamiliar that his testimony becomes sheer malpractice. Such sworn testimony denigrates the entire field and leaves the perpetrator wallowing in a morass which ultimately engulfs him. This is particularly true of the criminalist, possibly competent in several fields, who strays into a totally different discipline such as forensic pathology.

Few criminalists would consider testifying that a single hair can be so personalized that it positively identifies a particular individual. Yet for years, one notorious individual testified as the mood struck him, sending possibly innocent people to jail on such incredible evidence as a single human hair.

Hair technology is constantly improving with increasing likelihood that in the future hair factors will be sufficiently personalized to make such identifications. But it is not possible today, and it was not during the years this magpie prostituted the truth to the needs of the prosecution.

In another matter, this same man readily identified a shotgun as the weapon in a murder case. With a man's life at stake, he testified under oath that a particular twelve-gauge shotgun, owned by the defendant, had killed the victim. While so-called deer slug shotgun loads may possibly be mated to the firing weapon, no possibility exists in doing likewise with the pellets of shotgun loads. Yet this so-called expert based his conclusion on the examination of the wadding removed from the victim's belly. It was twelve-gauge, the suspect's gun was twelve gauge—Q.E.D., the defendant killed the victim. In actuality, the murder weapon was only sixteen-gauge, a full size smaller. The wadding recovered from the victim was simply swollen with body fluids.

Whether the perpetrator of these evidentiary disasters was totally dishonest—for sale to the highest bidder—remains an open question. No doubt of his woeful ignorance. To be charitable, his fault may have been his blind determination to match the named suspect to the limited evidence, a failing even good men sometimes yield to.

Until his recent death, this man testified, often completely on the wrong side of the facts, for over three decades. Surely he should have been disqualified, even jailed for perjury, yet one of his last acts in a long and dishonorable career was to identify the alleged handwriting of Howard Hughes in the power struggle over control of the elusive billionaire's enormous Nevada holdings. In the Hughes affair, his testimony was believed by the courts and his handwriting judgment accepted. We'll probably never know just where the truth lies in that matter.

Little wonder that criminalists of integrity, the vast over-whelming majority, cry as this sort of phony expert continues to operate with immunity.

Abuses of this sort have caused a concerned spokesman for forensic integrity to privately deplore the pseudoexpert who "casts objectivity to the winds and violates every basic tenet of forensic science and proof by becoming a crusading advocate. This is rationalized as being entirely legitimate since the accused is guilty anyway which makes the social objective worthy of the means required to obtain it. . . ."

Dr. Milton Helpern puts it this way: "I have always considered the giving of evidence under oath one of the most serious and important responsibilities of the forensic pathologist, and that evidence describing and explaining postmortem changes and findings in the human body should not be given by an unqualified person working in a related but entirely different field of investigation, such as a non-medical, non-pathologist member of a police department also involved in some aspects of the overall investigation of a suspicious violent death."

In the above statement, Dr. Helpern is referring to the transcript of evidence given in a murder trial in which the pivotal defense element hinged on the suspect's alibi. The victim had been found lying on his stomach alongside a bed. Examination of the body showed signs of permanent postmortem lividity on the victim's back. Permanent postmortem lividity does not occur until at least four hours after death, and the defendant had a watertight alibi placing him roughly 150 miles from the murder scene within an hour of the death. Permanent postmortem lividity, furthermore, is found only on the portion of the body that has been subject to the downward pull of gravity. When the body was found, the postmortem lividity was uppermost on the prone body. Unless some mechanism could be found to account for the movement of the body from the position in which it took four hours at least for the lividity marks to become established to the position in which it was found, there would be reasonable doubt as to the suspect's guilt.

The explanation devised by the police expert was childishly simple. After death, the liquids of the body settled into the legs of the victim hanging off the bed (the defense said only the feet were hanging over the bed), changing the center of gravity so that, when enough of these waters were lower than the body remaining on the bed, the weight toppled the body over into the prone position it was found.

Webster defines *center of gravity* thus: "That point in a body about which all the parts of the body exactly balance each other." The next voices you hear will be the defense counsel questioning this police "expert" who propounded the waters shift theory to account for the body's movement:

Q. By the way, when [the victim] was lying on that bed on his side, where was his center of gravity?

A. Where was his center of gravity? What part of the body are we talking about?

Q. That's what I'm talking about, the body, the whole body; where was his center of gravity?

A. In several different places.

Q. All right. Tell me where.

A. Well, we have the feet, to begin with. We had the feet hanging over the bed. I mean, we have got so many points of center of gravity, we are going to be here all day.

Q. Was there a time he was lying on his side when his whole body was on the bed? . . .

A. No.

Q. In your opinion, his feet were off the bed at the time he was shot?

A. I reenacted it yesterday, and his feet were off the bed at all times.

Q. Over the end of the bed; is that right?

A. That's correct.

Q. Assume the feet over the end of the bed and everything else on the bed, where is the center of gravity?

A. Well, sir, the center of gravity is not located in any one part. With parts hanging over the bed, you would have to take the part hanging over the bed and establish the center of gravity to those parts in the center of the abdomen.

Q. Somewhere in the center of the abdomen?

A. No, I didn't say that.

Q. Where is it?

A. I said it would be in several locations.

Q. Tell us.

A. You have to first take the hanging feet over the bed. The center of gravity at that point would be at one position. And we would have to take the whole body and make a study of the entire body, and I don't think that in the case of parts

hanging over the bed you could ever establish the
center of gravity at one point."

But let's move further into the testimony about the fluids
which settle, and, according to this witness, caused the victim's
body to topple from the bed.

Q. Oh, By the way, you talk about fluids settling.
What fluids settle that change the center of
gravity?

A. What fluids settle?

Q. Yes, sir.

A. All of the body fluids would settle. There
would be no question about that.

Q. First, let's name some. Blood would settle
first; is that right?

A. I don't think that blood would before any of
the others.

Q. We are talking numerically, so I can start
somewhere.

A. I would just rather talk generally, rather
than numerically, because next you will be telling
us it was first.

Q. Well, is blood one of them?

A. Blood is one of them.

Q. How much weight change is there, in your
opinion, in the settling of blood, assuming no
less for the moment?

A. How much weight change?

Q. How much are we talking about settling?

A. I don't think there is anyone in this room
that could calculate the weight change, if you're
talking of the settling of blood in a specific
gravitational area. We know that it is there. We
know the direction of pulls, but I'm certainly not
going to establish any weight change.

Q. I'm talking about how much blood is going to
change location, how much in weight?

A. How much blood is going to change location?
Why don't we have a medical doctor tell us that?

Q. All right. Then what other fluids are there
that will change location in order to affect the
center of gravity.

A. Any of the body fluids.

Q. Name some.

. 249 .

A. If you would like me to name specific fluids,
there would be all kinds of intercellular waters:
We would have blood, we would have even
materials in the lymph glands themselves separated out
of the blood; lymph; we would have kidney waters; we
would have stomach waters; we would have stomach
fluids of all types, so we could keep going.

Q. And all of these changed location after death;
is that right?

A. They certainly would be affected by gravity and
would be changed, some of them more than by others.

Q. All of them would change location after death; is
that right?

A. They would have to, yes.

Q. And they would tend to settle downwards; is
that right?

A. They would be affected by gravity and pulled
down; that's correct.

There's more, much more, in the same vein. Concerning this
and other related testimony, Dr. Helpern concludes:

> There is not only ignorance of the mechanism of
> postmortem changes but of what structures in the
> body are involved. . . .
> It is very clear from the answers that the witness
> does not know how the processes take place. As a
> non-medical police officer he is not required to
> know how or why such phenomena occur. Such
> expertise is not part of his responsibility as a
> police officer or criminalist. His replies
> represent gratuitous ignorance of a human
> biological process and the misinformation can
> be misinterpreted by the court and jury.

The star of the following drama deserves a niche in the
criminalistic hall of fame for his development of pioneering work
in the field, and we'll deliberately not mention his name since his
contributions far outshadow his occasional lapses. Ego is a
powerful motivator, and this great man displayed far more than
his share of conceit, temperament, and blindness to his mistakes.

With full acknowledgment of his many admitted talents, no
one would accuse him of ever quite mastering photomicrography.
While soft effects were flattering to aging faces in portrait
photography, the out-of-focus photo is anathema in the ballistic

business. The laws of optics limit the depth of field according to the focal length of the lens and the size of the diaphragm opening. Photography of bullets under the comparison microscope brings the built-in problem of a very shallow depth of field. The greater the magnification, the shorter the depth of field.

The murder case hinged on the comparison of the fatal bullet with an exemplar from the defendant's gun. In virtually every ballistics case, much damage can be observed on the fatal bullet which is missing in the exemplar, for reasons we have already discussed. Yet in this case the photos were overly bountiful in common detail. True, the focus was slightly fuzzy, but the match of the scratches on both sides of the dividing line between the right and left sides of the photo was beautiful. Every line on the lefthand image—without exception—was aligned with a similar line on the righthand image. Bonanza! Not one bullet comparison in a million is this perfect. The defendant was duly convicted of the murder on the basis of the evidence and the expert's opinion that the fatal bullet had been fired from the defendant's gun.

For some time forensic rumor mills had been grinding out little tidbits concerning this noted expert's occasional trifling with the truth. His supporters blamed the gossip on jealousy of other criminalists and their reaction to taking their lumps in court when testifying on the opposite side from this man.

Still, even in the most bitter confrontations of forensic personalities, the lie is seldom hurled. Perjury is much too serious a charge to be mouthed lightly, and few criminalists will pursue their advocacy so blindly as to subject themselves to a possible prison sentence.

Therefore, it wasn't until much later that another disinterested ballistic expert had occasion to examine the evidence photo. He merely furrowed his forehead and whipped out the pocket magnifier most criminalists carry constantly. First, he closely examined the matching details on either side of the mating of the two photomicrographs, the so-called optical margin. Never in his experience had he viewed a fatal bullet and exemplar which matched so perfectly.

Then he gave closer inspection to the junction of the two photos. Stunned at his apparent discovery, he flipped another lens in place in the Hastings triplet magnifier, thereby increasing the magnification. Under the greater power, he scrutinized the entire length of the junction.

He was shocked to find that the optical margin was, in fact, a black line drawn on the photo in India ink. In this professional's judgment, the right and left optical fields under the comparison microscope had been superimposed! Instead of butting up against each other so that continuity of scratch marks could be demonstrated between the two different bullets, the pictures had been overlayed so that the view of each eyepiece in the microscope contained the details of the other. With such abuse of the comparison microscope, the pictures were bound to match exactly, since they were, in essence, two versions of the same picture. This tactic, of course, could not produce an optical margin. But why worry, when pen and ink were handy to provide the missing junction point?

Defenders of this man claim this assumption isn't true, that the fuzziness of the photo simply confused his judgment. But even they cannot seek to justify the drawn-in substitute for an optical margin. It is terrible to contemplate that a man was found guilty of murder on the basis of this evidence.

Several solutions are possible to instances like these. Unfortunately, the highly respected American Academy of Forensic Sciences decided in its early days not to become involved in the matter of qualification and certification of the competence of individuals in the practice of forensic science. They felt this would be an usurpation of judicial authority. The academy does, however, have a procedure for reviewing any complaints of unethical practice on the part of its members. They feel their role in complaints about nonmembers should be limited to recommending two experts in specific fields who could be available to counter fraudulent testimony in the courtroom.

Another suggestion is the creation of a criminalistics review board consisting of men of unquestioned ability and integrity. Any question arising in the field of criminalistics could be referred to this board with confidence in the accuracy and integrity of their judgments.

No such structure exists anywhere within the United States. The creation of some device to achieve these objectives is long overdue.

Before criminalistics can find its rightful role in the criminal justice system, changes must be made which are tantamount to tearing down the present system and completely rebuilding. There are a dozen facets necessary for restructuring the forensic architecture, all of them complicated, most of them enormously difficult.

Among the most important components is readjustment of the position of the criminalistics function in the governmental structure. Virtually every crime lab today is the creature of a law enforcement agency or a district attorney's office. In addition to occasional improper pressure, the prime argument against such a system is the criminalists' inability to apply their attention in the directions and toward the priorities which their own scientific training uniquely fits them to do.

Several comments extracted from the larger and much more detailed Stanford Research Institute evaluation suggest the nature of several of the problems facing adequate use of criminalistics in the criminal justice system. The first is: "Criminalistics is confined to the examination of physical evidence only in those cases which are politically important and those cases in which the presentation of an examination is legally required. . . ."

The report goes on to say:

> For all practical purposes, it is reasonable to view criminalistics in its current status as an atrophied appendage of the administration of the law. As such, it is bureaucratically controlled by purposes which do not represent the potential professional capabilities of the activity of criminalists.
> Criminalistics has become an office in a bureaucratic arrangement in which the materialization of professional purpose must be viewed against the background of institutional objects that often subvert, compromise, or reconstitute the various purposes

. 253 .

that the bureaucratically controlled professionals hold.

While there is no general agreement as to where crime labs should be located administratively, the important principle is that the scientists should control their own sphere of operation. Not only should they have a major say in the collection of evidence; they should also make the decisions as to the meaning of the evidence and the presentation of the evidence in matters before the court.

Several administrative channels could be used to accomplish these objectives. One would be the establishment of the criminalistics function at the department level of government, with workers reporting directly to the chief administrative officer. Another might be its structuring within the court administration. Still another would be to remove local control, such as occurs in adequate state-wide systems. Since the search for truth is the prime purpose of the courts, this particular choice seems to be the administrative structuring most consistent with achieving an operational search for truth as the overriding function of the crime laboratory. Another benefit would be the provision of criminalistic services to defendants, such assistance being virtually unused, if not unavailable, under the present situation.

The above considerations are purely theoretical at the moment. They have not been explored in any political subdivision in the United States, and would require a major effort, probably including the passage of legislation, before these kinds of administrative change could be undertaken.

An alternate method which *is* being tried and which is undergoing rapid development with the support of the Law Enforcement Assistance Administration is the development of regional crime labs and networks of such laboratories.

California, for example, is in the process of establishing a series of regional laboratories offering reasonably complete coverage for the entire state. These will be staffed with sufficient criminalists, and backed up with equipment comparable to that found in the better crime labs presently servicing populous metropolitan areas. An even greater number of satellite laboratories are scheduled to be located strategically throughout the state, primarily to handle alcohol and other drug examinations as well as a limited quantity of other relatively simple criminalistic procedures.

In addition, two major core laboratories are to be established, one in the San Francisco Bay area, the other somewhere in the Los Angeles-Orange County concentration of urban population.

Parallel crime lab organizations are arising throughout the nation to the extent that the Stanford Research Institute staff believe an entire network of regional crime labs will be operational within a few years.

While encouraging on the face of it, such a proliferation of laboratories poses many difficulties. For one thing, personnel development in criminalistics is presently so inadequate that such new laboratories can be staffed only at the expense of existing crime labs. If the California situation is any indicator, the new crime labs may create as many problems as they resolve. At this writing, one first-class local crime lab lost five key men within two weeks to the competition of the developing state system and others.

It remains to be seen if such regional laboratories will have any effect on the present system of collecting and processing physical evidence through the criminal justice procedures. As the SRI report puts it: "The potential of a criminalistic service is poorly defined and largely unfilled as a consequence of its lack of control of the initiation of its service." They comment further in reference to the Santa Clara Laboratory of Criminalistics, which was the prime agency evaluated in-depth. One of the reasons this crime lab was studied was its excellent reputation in the field. "Of those cases submitted to the Santa Clara County laboratory," the report continues, "over 50 percent produced a useful output to the investigator. Yet, requests for criminalistics service in Index Crime categories (major crimes) fell from over 20 percent in 1960 to less than 10 percent at present."

So the mere expansion of available laboratory services is no guarantee of improved criminalistic quality, if the criminalists do not have the major role in the collection and use of physical evidence.

The satellite drug-processing aspects of the California master plan, however, seem to offer tremendous promise. With the alcohol and drug load off their backs, the criminalists may have an opportunity to do a better job with the evidence which does arrive at their door. But if major improvement is to be made, ways must still be found to insure greater involvement of the criminalist with the evidence collection process.

Improvement of the system by the slow and painful upgrading of each of the elements may well occupy the balance of this century. Yet one relatively simple answer could produce enormous improvement in criminalistics use in a short time. This would consist of the thoughtful creation of legal responsibility and authority for the criminalist, which would be the equivalent of those of the modern medical examiner-coroner.

With a legal mandate, the authority to require notification of the commission of crimes, and the ability to supervise the quality of evidence collection, a whole new era would begin. Not that the mere passage of such a law would provide a criminalistic utopia. A number of the steps would have to occur in orderly fashion. The principal difference would be some assurance that the changes would occur and the greater likelihood that they would be developed properly.

Foremost among these is the need for enormously improved training for the police, at every level. In the most progressive local law enforcement agencies in the nation, there is little or no guarantee that the police investigating a crime scene will have any competence to detect and preserve physical evidence. Two separate approaches may be made in rectifying this situation.

One philosophy is aimed at developing the capability of every patrolman to handle any crime from discovery to conclusion. Except for frequent crimes such as check forgery, which justify full-time specialists, this concept virtually eliminates the traditional detective function. The officer may work in uniform or in plain clothes, depending on the particular type of crime he is involved in solving.

Built into such a concept is an enormous foundation of training. Some of this may be obtained by educational prerequisites before employment, supplemented with testing and retraining in any areas the candidate proves weak in. In leading jurisdictions at present, the police officer recruit receives little more than two or three hundred hours of training. The goal of the universally capable policeman probably requires initial training at least ten times that long.

Furthermore, there must be a regimen of continual in-service training, particularly for first-line supervisors, who would have the continuing duty of checking the performance of the patrolman in each of his many activities. All those who are in a position to collect and preserve physical evidence should periodically and systematically be reviewed. One indication of the need for this is the fact that few aggravated assaults result in gathered physical evidence, while most murder cases do. In each instance there has been a violent attack on a person, equally capable of producing discoverable physical evidence. Yet where the victim survives, the investigator rarely if ever even attempts to verify the facts of the crime with physical evidence.

Even more important is the need for ongoing training for top-level management. Executive training for the decision-makers in law enforcement can bring them up to date on the potential of criminalistics.

The enormous problems inherent in achieving the all-purpose police officer suggest a less strenuous alternative—the specialized physical evidence collection unit. Assignment to such duty should carry at least one higher rank than patrolman. Men should be promoted to such specialized units only on completion of intensive training. There should be sufficient units on duty at all times that they can respond in all known felonies and in the appropriate misdemeanor cases.

Most important, such officers should be considered an adjunct of the crime lab, trained and supervised in evidence collecting by the criminalists. The criminalists should spend considerable time in the field with such collection teams to continue improvement in the quality of evidence being collected and as in-service training for the police investigators.

Under present conditions, this last objective can be achieved only by gaining relief from the pressing problems occasioned by the drug epidemic. Several alternate courses can be pursued to achieve this end.

One choice might be the development of specialized drug labs with shortcut techniques for initial identification such as those developed by Cecil Hider. If there is a large enough case load to justify the expenditure, some relief can be gained by modern instrumentation such as the mass spectrophotometer.

Another alternate would be massive reforms in our outdated laws relating to morality and victimless crimes. The 1970 report of the FBI shows that of the total number of arrests made in the United States resulting in almost four million confinements, 48 percent were for crimes where the only victim was the arrested person. And surely we are decades overdue in repealing the Victorian laws relating to the sexual behavior of consenting adults in private.

Most enforcement agencies have special sections devoted to the category of law violations loosely known as vice. Wallowing in the depths of human degradation, the vice squad experience is depressing, sordid, and breeds its own special version of callousness. We are all too aware of one crusading district attorney, noted for clamping the lid on pornographic motion pictures, who always gave guests a private showing of his seized porno collection.

Since the most titillating entertainments tend to be prohibited under one or another of our anachronistic laws inherited from our Puritan ancestors, most of our so-called law-abiding citizens are in fact technical felons, particularly in violating laws regulating sexual behavior.

The terrifying fact is that nearly any one of us could be arrested and charged with a felony offense, if the vice squad in our area chose to use the snooping tools readily available to them. The unbelievable corollary is that the people the vice squads choose to arrest and prosecute end up in mental hospitals or in prisons where the average time served under confinement is twice that of the average murderer!

Until the last few years when a California appellate court's decision overturned the archaic law, it was illegal to enter a motel, hotel, or rooming house with a person of the opposite sex—no matter how innocent the behavior—unless married or closely related. In most other states, many local communities have a rooming house ordinance that prohibits the mere presence of a male and a female in such public lodging unless they enjoy ties of kinship no more distant than uncle and niece or aunt and nephew.

Again and again, thoughtful commissions seeking to remedy major enforcement evils have recommended the elimination of laws relating to victimless crimes, especially those concerned with private behavior between consenting adults. In addition to the ever-present danger that misguided police may actually enforce outmoded laws written during the 1880s, there is an axiom often expressed in cynical circles which says, "Show me a vice squad and I'll show you police corruption." The problem of graft is the major argument for the repeal of vice laws.

The enforcement of laws relating to gambling, prostitution, and even semiprofessional bar-fraternization is the direct route to payoffs and corruption of police and judges. The prime beneficiary from such laws are the Mafia, who cater to human frailty and in the process destroy the effectiveness of the criminal justice system against offenses which cry for attention.

Nevertheless, certain types of behavior, loosely falling into the vice classification, are frowned upon by even the most liberal thinkers.

Gambling seems to be a universal pastime in both its legal and illicit forms. While there is probably little harm in legal gambling for recreation, an enormous evil lies in wait for the compulsive, addicted personality. The gambling folklore says there's a fifty-fifty chance of so-called normal individuals going Nevada when they become residents of the only state to permit nearly all the games of chance. "Going Nevada" destroys any reasonably happy life, since the gambling becomes an end in itself, consuming possessions, friends, families, and careers as the gambling frenzy takes over the lifestyle of its victim.

The penny-ante wagers with the corner bookies and the peripatetic numbers man sow seeds of social destruction because of their direct ties with the underworld and organized crime. No bookmaking can exist without a national wire service. The nickel-and-dime numbers racket brings bread and butter to the lowest levels of the Mafia and provides cream and cake to the upper echelons. And none of this harmless gambling operates without a framework of police and judicial corruption.

An automatic byproduct of the repeal of laws relating to gambling would be to remove baseline income from organized crime.

In still another problem area of the criminal justice complex is the shocking weakness of the prosecution arm of law enforcement. Traditionally, the district attorney's office serves as a training ground for law school graduates. At the expense of the people, the neophyte tangles with the court-hardened defense attorney. All too often, the ends of justice suffer from the prosecutor's ineptness. The average tenure of prosecutors, before entering private practice, is estimated to be less than 2½ years. In other words, about the time the prosecutor may have developed the experience to cope with his responsibilities, he peels off.

Two other pivotal factors affect the success of the criminalistics potential. The more important is the lack of organized research. While the better laboratories around the world mandate a continuing research program, only one United States crime lab, that of Florida, has a position of research director. Contrast that with the Central Research Establishment of Britain, directed by renowned scientist A. S. Curry, which works exclusively on forensic research.

The Stanford Research Institute report commented on the inadequacy of research in criminalistics:

> Full-scale experiments in vehicle collision . . .
> and similar experiments advanced greatly our
> comprehension of the event sequences in the physical
> collisions of automobiles and occupants. . . .
> With the documentation of full-scale experiments
> before, during and after the event, collision
> parameters of vehicle-to-vehicle, vehicle-to-
> occupant, and occupant-to-internal organs became
> more meaningful and reconstruction more
> scientific. . . . Not only are the analytic and
> synthetic aspects of reconstruction inadequately
> explored, but also the incidence, the perceptions,
> and the evaluations of action and nonaction in
> criminal justice administration in relation to
> physical evidence are essentially unexamined.

In the present criminalistic system, knowledge is so fragmented and data storage so limited that it sometimes appears as though each individual crime lab is attempting to invent the wheel on its own. In this regard, the SRI report stated:

In their current disaggregated form, there are
certain questions we cannot ask or answer . . .
despite the fact that there exists a substantial
fund of criminalistic results on physical evidence
pertaining to drugs, it remains disaggregated. . . .
It almost seems incredible that we should have the
scientific and technical possibility of building
a fund of knowledge about crime as it is revealed
in physical evidence and that it remains essentially
untapped.

Considering the advanced state of the computer art, one self-evident answer might be the development of criminalistic data in a form compatible with computer storage and retrieval. The concomitant computer network might be the easiest part of such a program. In California, for example, any law enforcement agency has instant access to the state-wide information system containing the driving and criminal records of the entire state's population, and to another system which provides equally fast intelligence on the status of wanted vehicles. The National Driver Register provides information on all drivers whose driving privilege has been revoked or who have been convicted of drunk-driving laws anywhere in the country.

Once the input system of criminalistics information was designed, the entire discipline could benefit from the intelligence from any parts of the subsystem. A properly conceived and executed method would permit national, even international comparison between any discovered firearm and the firearm evidence which had been collected in the investigation of a crime, wherever each of them had been discovered.

The second vitally needed procedure is some method to insure that men and women of capability and integrity are practicing the art and science of criminalistics.

We've shared some of the relatively infrequent horror stories which a proper system would not permit to occur. Limited self-policing occurs in the movement, with the principal professional associations structured to receive and evaluate complaints about their members. Since no license is required to practice criminalistics, and since the complaint mechanism of the societies is seldom invoked, there is obvious need for improvement. One suggestion made by an eminent authority, is that a criminalistics review board be created within the criminal justice system. Men and women of unquestioned competence and integrity could review complaints about questionable criminalistic practices and make determinations as to their validity. Possibly such a review board could be associated with the supreme court of each state.

Finally, there is the ongoing need to attract competent candidates into the criminalistic field. Certainly the training needs of the entire system call for continuing evaluation, with implementation and assistance where necessary to provide university training up to the demands of the field. While some less qualified institutions have attempted to move into the vacuum created by university abandonment of forensic training, the quality of their product is less than satisfactory. In addition, without adequate field experience, the criminalist is no more qualified to practice his art than the intern physician one of the medical specialties. Agencies such as the Law Enforcement Assistance Administration ought to be concentrating on the availability of adequate university training to meet present and future needs.

Dark as is the present criminalistics picture, there is considerable hope for the future. We are confident the movement would take a giant stride forward if given the legal responsibility and authority for their field parallel to that enjoyed by the medical examiner-coroner in his.

The report of the Stanford Research Institute was initially greeted with shocked silence, even grumbling by the assembled criminalists, who first heard a preview of the coming report. But already the results of such attention to the failures of the field are becoming apparent as intelligent criminalist-administrators seek ways to overcome the weaknesses revealed. The prospect that SRI will follow up with a companion report showing a blueprint for change is encouraging. At this moment there is room for considerable optimism for the role of criminalistics in the future.

Even more important are the monumental stirrings of the youth of today, who will be the leaders of tomorrow. Totally discontent with perpetuation of old mistakes, their energies and hopes already are being channeled in the direction of a better society, a people who will exorcise the social ghosts which are the automatic precursors of a criminally inclined society.

Until that devoutly awaited day, however, we will continue in desperate need for more and better criminalistics.

It is difficult to conceive of a field which offers greater variety and challenge than the application of the broad spectrum of science to the solution of crimes. Added to this is the pure excitement of pitting one's wits on the right side of the cops-and-robbers chase, substituting intellect for brawn. Properly organized and administered, criminalistics provides a career that never grows boring, constantly stimulating the application of a high level of scientific endeavor in the solution of ever-changing puzzles.

Most important, as the unreliability of eyewitness evidence is better understood, the ultimate fairness of the entire criminal justice system will depend almost entirely on the unbiased search for truth which is the hallmark of the detective's detective—the criminalist.

ABO blood typing, 102, 104,
112-13, 244
Absorption-inhibition testing
method, 101, 105
Accidents, traffic
collection of evidence at,
67-68
equipment failure and, 70
murder and, 67
number of people killed every
year in, 76
traffic signals and, 68
Adsorption, definition of, 149
Aerojet General Corporation, 52,
54
Aerospace Corporation, 95
Age dating of paper, 176
Agglutination of blood, 101
Albuquerque, New Mexico, drunk-
driving arrests in, 32
Alcohol, beverage, 31-34
major crimes and, 67
murder and, 80-81
Alcohol Safety Action Program
(ASAP), 32
Ambassador Hotel (Los Angeles),
207-8
American Academy of Forensic
Science, 51, 63, 252
Amicus curiae, 99
Anthropomorphic measurements, 2
Arab-Israeli conflict, 187
Archerd, William Dale, 227
Arsenic poisoning, 6-7, 93, 94
ASAP, *see* Alcohol Safety Action
Program (ASAP)
Associations, forensic, 51-52
Atomic reactors, 50
Atomic theory, 29

AutoAnalyzer, 113-14
Autopsies, clinical diagnoses
and, 225

Balboa, California, 221
Ballistics, 192-217
Barbiturate addiction, 155-56
Beck, Adolph, 4-6
Becke line technique, 79-80
Bell Telephone Laboratories, 124
Bentley, Edgar Eugene, 27
Benzidrine-hydrogen peroxide
procedure, 12, 103
Berkeley, California, 229
Bertillon, Alphonse, 2, 21
Bicycle thefts, 235
Biological precipitan
examination, 15, 101, 104
Black light, 95
Black Panthers
police raid on Chicago
headquarters of, 211-17
sale of black powder to, 190
Blehr, Barbara Warner, 210-11
Blueprints, theft of, 46
Blood alcohols, 22, 23
Blood typing, 102, 104, 112-13,
244
Bloodstains, 7, 12, 18, 55-56
agglutination and, 101, 111
dry, 108, 114
gas chromatograph and, 31
wet, 101-2, 114
Bohr, Niels, 29
Bomb Data Center, National, 187
Bombings, 186-90
Bombs-by-letter method, 187-88
Bookmaking, 259
Boyle, Robert, 29

Drowning, 35-36
Drugs
    illicit laboratories and, 171
    narcotics agents and, 136-42
    Raman spectroscopy and, 49-50
    smuggling of, 121-24
Drunk driving
    highway deaths and, 32-34, 55
    laws against, 18-19, 37
Dyes, fabric, 97
Dynamite, 222-24

Einstein, Albert, 30
Electron capture, 39
Electrons, discovery of, 29
Electrophoresis, 113
Elements, chemical, discovery
    of, 29
Entry, illegal, 47
Escobido decision, 131
Ether, 52-53
Evidence analysis for defendant,
    239-40
Evidence-gathering in large
    cities, 228
Eyewitness identification,
    fallibility of, 4-5, 98,
    115-19

Family fight, 153
Family, murders within, 192
Fargo transmitter, 139-42
FBI, 50, 57, 142
    blood examination at, 101-2,
        103
    Chicago police raid on Black
        Panthers and, 214-15
    establishment of, 1, 13
    fingerprints and, 160, 170
    major crimes and, 228, 238
    soil examination at, 85, 86
    typewriters and, 177-79
Federal Bureau of Narcotics and
    Dangerous Drugs, 157
Fiber, textile, 97
Fingernails, ridge patterns of,
    61

Fingerprinting, 11, 25, 157-71
    burglaries and, 229-30
    history of, 3-4
    on paper, 167-71
Finnigan Corporation, 35, 119
Firearms identification, see
        Ballistics
Florida, crime laboratory in,
    260
Forensic medicine, 7
Forensic Science Group (South
    Africa), 51
Forensics, definition of, 3
Forgery, 167

Gambling, 259
Gas chromatograph (GC), 31-39,
    42-46
    bombs and, 189
    ether and, 52
    See also Pyrolysis gas
        chromatography
Glass, 76-82
    techniques in matching, 78-80
    water and, 147
Glove print, latent, 1, 161
Goddard, Calvin, 8
Gradient density technique, 85
Graft, vice laws and, 259
Grass seed, 58-59
Gravity, center of, definition
    of, 248
Grenz rays, 119-21
Gunpowder, invention of, 186
Guns
    identification numbers of, 23
    limitation of ownership of,
        190-91
    small-caliber, 92
    uniqueness of, 8
Gurgin, Vonnie, 238

Hair, human, 18, 91-97, 246
Hampton, Fred, 211-17
Handwriting, 172-74
Harper, William W., 20, 208-11
Harris, James L., Sr., 165-66

Hastings triple magnifier,
251-52
Helpern, Dr. Milton, 206-7, 245,
247, 250
Hemochromogen test, 103
Henry, Inspector General, 3-4
Henry classification method, 3-4,
159
Heroin addiction, 152-153
Hider, Cecil, 40, 146, 257
Highway Safety Act of 1966, 70
Highway Safety Administration,
National, 77
Hit-and-run cases, 62-63, 240-41
Holzer, Dr. Frank, 101, 105
Homosexuals
as police candidate risks,
134-35
violent crimes between males
and, 24
Honolulu, Hawaii
drunk-driving arrests in,
32-33
evidence-gathering potential
of, 237
Houts, Marshall, 206
Hughes, Howard, 246
Humidity chamber, 169
Hussein, King, 125
Hydrogen flame detector, 38

"I cars," 20
Improvement of criminalistics,
255-57
Index crime categories, 255
Infant mortality, 111-12
Informants, 185
Inks
ballpoint, 176-77
comparison of, 120
Institute of Transportation and
Traffic Engineering (Uni-
versity of California), 72
Insulin poisoning, 227
Instrumentation, cost of, 50
Ions, definition of, 39

Jerome, Thomas Spencer, 5

Jewish Hospital (Brooklyn),
Blood Transfusion Unit of,
111
Jigsaw fit, 55-59, 71, 182, 244
of fabrics, 97
of glass, 78, 82
Jones, Arthur, 197
Jones, Dr. Peter, 95
Jordan, insurrections in (1970),
187
Journals, forensic, 51
Judd, George, 19, 24-28
Juvenile vandalism, bombings
and, 187

Kell factors, 108
Kennedy, President John, 190,
206-7
Kennedy, Senator Robert, 190,
206, 207-11, 239
Kersta, Dr. Lawrence G., 124-27
Kidnapping, 52, 67, 227
King, Dr. Martin Luther, 190
Kinsey, Alfred C., 134
Kirwan, William E., 62-63, 65-66
Klein, Martin, 163-66
Knockout drops, 42-46
Kozelka-Hine method, 39-40

La Bianca and Tate murder cases,
162
Labor disputes, bombings and,
187
Lafarge, Marie, 93
Lakewood, California, 163
Landsteiner, Dr. Karl, 101,
111-12
Lanh, Maj. Zen, 186-87
Laser light, 48-49
Latent glove print, 1, 161
Lattes, Dr. Leone, 101
Lavoisier, Antoine Laurent, 29
Law, elements of violation of,
18
Law Enforcement Assistance
Administration, 114, 116,
187, 217-18, 254, 262
"Lie box," see Polygraph